X

*Narrative Form in
History and Fiction*

Hume
Fielding &
Gibbon

NARRATIVE FORM in HISTORY and FICTION

BY LEO BRAUDY

Leo Braudy is a member of the Department of English and Comparative Literature of Columbia University.

PRINCETON UNIVERSITY PRESS

PRINCETON, NEW JERSEY

1970

*Library of Congress
Catalog Card Number: 69-18052
Standard Book Number: 691-06168-8*

Publication of this book has been aided by a grant from the Whitney Darrow Publication Reserve Fund of Princeton University Press.

*This book has been
composed in Linotype Baskerville.
Printed in the United States of America
by Princeton University Press
Princeton, New Jersey*

FOR MY MOTHER | AND FOR
AND FATHER | SUSAN

Contents

Acknowledgments

ALTHOUGH I was certainly unaware of it at the time, my double interest in the writing of literature and the writing of history began insensibly at Swarthmore College the semester I took a seminar in Shakespeare with Sam Hynes and one in English history after 1789 with Larry Lafore. Dave Cowden, Dan Hoffman, Dwight Culler, and Gene Waith also deserve some blame for creating in large part the preoccupations displayed here. I would also like to thank especially Lee Patterson, Marsh Leicester, Al LaValley, Mike Holahan, and Howard Felperin, and Dave Thorburn for their penetrating remarks about many of the issues I discuss below, and Ron Schaefer for philosophical disentangling at a crucial moment. W. K. Wimsatt, Maynard Mack, J. W. Johnson, Robert Scholes, Mike Holahan, Howard Schless, Steve Arkin, and Ben Nangle made many helpful suggestions about the manuscript itself. Bart Giamatti contributed jocund intangibles.

But my deepest thanks must go to Martin Price, who cajoled and criticized with lucid ferocity. Without the standard of his unremitting clarity, my work would have been much more difficult and much less rewarding.

A Note on the Footnotes and Notes: I have tried to separate my notes into those that expand the argument in the text and those that delve into areas of scholarly interest. At the foot of the page, therefore, I place lettered parallel or contrasting passages from the author being discussed, references to other authors of the period, and the first citation of works frequently mentioned in the text. At the back of the book are numbered references to less frequently cited primary and secondary works, background information, and critical controversies.

*Narrative Form in
History and Fiction*

ONE | Introduction

How well the skilful Gardner drew
Of flow'rs and herbes this Dial new;
Where from above the milder Sun
Does through a fragrant Zodiack run;
And, as it works, th' industrious Bee
Computes its times as well as we.
How could such sweet and wholsome Hours
Be reckon'd but with herbs and flow'rs!
ANDREW MARVELL, "The Garden"

The study of chronology and history seems to be one of the most natural delights of the human mind.
SAMUEL JOHNSON, "Preface" to *Dodsley's Preceptor*

. . . I am not writing a system but a history, and I am not obliged to reconcile every matter to the received notions concerning truth and nature.
HENRY FIELDING, *Tom Jones*

DURING THE EIGHTEENTH CENTURY the novel as we now know it emerged from an indistinct past of romance and fictionalized versions of journals, travel chronicles, and biographies. To achieve this direction and dynamic of its own, it drew continuing sustenance from a growing interest in the writing of history. The continuity of history, both past and present, had become a problem. Both novelists and historians sought to form time, to discover its plot, and to give a compelling and convincing narrative shape to the facts of human life, whether observed directly or through the records and "memorials" of the past. *The History of Tom Jones, A Foundling* has more than a merely verbal similarity to *The History of England from the Invasion of Julius Caesar to the*

Abdication of James the Second, 1688 or *The History of the Decline and Fall of the Roman Empire*. While historians moved away from the Thucydidean study of martial and political events to consider culture, society, and the growth of institutions, novelists began to emphasize that the essence of the novel was the establishment of a specific social milieu and an examination of the relations of individuals and institutions within that society. Both novelists and historians tried to present a plausible world, complete in itself, yet directly relevant to the reader's actual life; both usually asserted that their worlds were based on verifiable facts; and both tended to define the "truth" they sought in the language of general moral precepts.

Paradoxically, the similarities between the novel and history-writing in the eighteenth century had arisen in part from efforts to distinguish further their individual natures. The development of each form shows a tendency to separate itself from the more fanciful forms of narrative through standards of factual authentication, of detail and milieu. In the Middle Ages the line between fiction and history had never been quite clear; Chaucer's *Monk's Tale*, for example, implies a popular view of history in which figures from pagan mythology, the Bible, and actual history are thrown haphazardly together under the rubric of "the fall of princes."[1] The Renaissance Italian historians, especially Guicciardini, began to insist that "true" history was built upon a base of factual and documentary accuracy.[2] But then the early English novelists, like Defoe and his imitators, also seized upon the claim of factual accuracy to distinguish their work from romance.[3]

But the commitment of historians to the factual detail quickly outstripped the commitment of the novelists to what after all was only another literary technique. The spreading influence of source criticism and the appearance of new techniques for collecting relevant data further prepared the way for the "scientific" history of the early nineteenth century.[4] In the course of the eighteenth century the factual world of historical interpretation and the fictive world of the novel gradually achieved more distinct identities.[a]

In this period of transition David Hume wrote his *History of England* and Henry Fielding wrote *Joseph Andrews, Jonathan Wild, Tom Jones,* and *Amelia.* A few years later Edward Gibbon wrote *The Decline and Fall of the Roman Empire.* To put it skeletally: all three writers use a prose narrative to treat problems of the individual in society, problems of the human character in time and history. Each also deals directly with the literary problem of how to present these issues. Hume and Gibbon experiment with narrative form; Fielding speculates on causality and the role of factual detail. Their individual solutions to such problems as verisimilitude, narrative progression, and thematic development have a definite continuity; all involve the establishment and exploitation of an individual narrative voice and point of view. Although I do not actually conclude that Gibbon wrote better history than Hume because he had read the novels of Fielding, such a statement would partially coincide with my interests. I am basically more concerned with juxtapositions than with verifiable influence.[b] To consider novels and histories written at

[a] The view that the essence of history-writing lies in the construction of a narrative has been vigorously advanced in recent years, especially by W. B. Gallie in *Philosophy and the Historical Understanding* (London, 1964). I came upon Gallie's book after the completion of this study and found many of his ideas very suggestive and helpful. The reader interested in pursuing the philosophical issues might also consult Arthur C. Danto, *Analytical Philosophy of History* (Cambridge, England, 1965) and Morton White, *Foundations of Historical Knowledge* (New York, 1965). The views of Gallie, Danto, and White, as well as similar ideas stated by Benedetto Croce, R. G. Collingwood, W. H. Walsh, and William H. Dray, have recently been strenuously criticized by Maurice Mandelbaum in "A Note on History as Narrative," *History and Theory, 6*(1967), pp. 413–19. See also the response by William H. Dray, Richard G. Ely, and Rolf Gruner, "Mandelbaum on History as Narrative: A Discussion," *History and Theory, 8* (1969), pp. 275–94.

[b] The evidence for the direct influence of Hume on Fielding or vice versa is sparse at best. I could not find one mention of Fielding in Hume's work and letters. Fielding's library did contain a copy of the 1748 edition of *Philosophical Essays on Human Understanding*

a historical moment when they shared so many similarities can, I think, refine our approaches to each.

The critical study of history-writing has been too often clouded by questions of "accuracy" and judgment at the expense of an inquiry into narrative form. Novels too fall victim to this kind of closely analytic criticism. Often, for want of distinctive critical vocabulary, terms are transposed and novels are, for example, considered as complexes of images. My own interest is in problems of structure, although I also deal with the ways details fit together and facts are absorbed into the larger narrative form.

This study has, I think, two areas of usefulness: first, it explores to some extent theoretical issues of genre; second, it attempts to describe and interpret certain specific works. On the simplest level, a long work, like the histories and novels I shall treat, develops thematically and stylistically while it is being written. A long prose work may have an ultimate shape, as does a lyric poem, because it is conceived in terms of literary coherence and unity. But its shape is the shape of moving and developing thought, not the shape of instantaneous inspiration. Interpretations of historians like Hume and Gibbon have too often stressed unchanging themes or stylistic devices in order to find a kind of unity. Carl Becker, for example, says that the "new history" of the eighteenth century tried to tell man about himself and others; his view asserts the unity of an invariable theme.[5] J. B. Black remarks that Hume's atomized psychological portraits of historical personages get at no truth about man or history; Black's approach "finds" the unity of a static style.[6] Theme and style are certainly important, and I shall treat them in their place. But I am looking especially for an approach that can include them, a rationale of development, a unity of structure in these eighteenth-century works, a new way Hume, Fielding, and Gibbon have found of

(the *Enquiry*), as item 539. A more extensively documented case can be made for the admiration Gibbon had for both men. These details will be introduced when relevant.

apprehending time and the way man lives within it. The thematic and stylistic approaches of critics like Becker and Black imply and frequently express a belief that eighteenth-century history-writing produced deductively conceived static works, replete with endless illustration. If there is any one assumption in my approach, it is that these works are dynamic. While Hume and Gibbon contemplated the past, they changed their own assumptions about both the nature of the past and the historian's role as the intermediary between past and present.

Description and interpretation of works themselves are therefore more important here than abstract theoretical formulations. A theory about the relevance of history-writing to the novel, or to certain aspects of the novel's development, might be extracted from my remarks; it assuredly forms part of my own assumptions. But even though I will generalize in this area, I will not devote myself to theoretical considerations. Hume, Fielding, and Gibbon have inoculated me well against *l'esprit de système*. I am interested here in particular cases and particular relations. In discussing Hume's *History of England* and Gibbon's *Decline and Fall*, I try principally to discern a logic of narrative progression that can account for the artistic unity of each work. In my view of Fielding all four of his novels are stages in the development of a theory about the relation of the novel to the public history of its own time as well as to the events of the past. In contrast to most critics of Fielding, I argue that *Amelia* occupies an important place in the development of Fielding's interests.

Hume, Fielding, and Gibbon naturally enough explore many common themes: the relation of public and private life, the meaning of the past, the roles of chance and providence, the nature of human character. All three writers also consider in depth a question that binds these themes together: what is the nature of the human intelligence that can perceive these problems of man and time with accuracy and sympathy? The narrators developed by each of the three authors furnish their answers to this question. Appropriately enough, the heroic man of clear perception, both within and outside their works, is a man of literary sensibility, who can mediate the differing claims of public and private life.

One of the main difficulties with a study such as I undertake here is that its limits must be arbitrary. The subject branches out and buds in the most fascinating places, but for lack of space not every ramification can be gathered. The heart of my interest is the interrelation of novels and narrative histories, how several important writers perceived the order of the "great Work of Time" of Marvell's "Horatian Ode," and how they framed their own works. Because of this emphasis I can refer only fleetingly if at all to the great antiquarians who laid the groundwork for the advances in technical historical method in the eighteenth century, men like Camden, Selden, Dugdale, Spelman, and many others. Nor can I speak more than allusively of theorists like Bodin, Heinsius, Vossius, Le Clerc, Blount, Whalley, and the compendious Thomas Hearne, whose *Ductor Historicus* (1705) guided the young Gibbon, and who preserved through republication many of the classic works of seventeenth-century antiquarianism, like Spelman's life of Alfred the Great.[7]

But, although many of these innovating antiquarians and theorists had a much more sophisticated grasp of the techniques of historical study than the writers I treat here, they frequently share similar preconceptions about the use and purpose of history. Despite Bolingbroke's patrician ridicule of the work of the antiquarians and researchers, his emphasis on the use of history as a repository of moral exempla and a handbook for statesmen belongs in a tradition shared by Hearne: ". . . History, a Science of infinite Benefit to Mankind, (for 'tis by the Light it gives the Understanding, that Princes and Generals are enabled to avoid and hinder those evil Consequences that would hurt us all, and to direct the performance of such Actions as tend to our Protection and Defense). . . ."[8]

History for Hearne has many benefits: it makes us "co-eval with the celebrated Heroes of former Times" to excite emulation; it diverts and entertains; it affords instruction to "Persons of all Ages, Degrees, and Faculties" through examples of vice and virtue, good and evil action, and high and dignified events, "not low and groveling" or "trite mean matters"; and it defends religion by demonstrating that the world had a beginning. Many antiquarians must have privately believed their work was an exploration into the unique nature of history. But in their public pronouncements they, like Hearne, followed in the tradition aptly summarized by the title of Richard Brathwaite's handbook *A survey of history: or, A nursery for gentry.*[c] The main purpose of history was to serve as a Thucydidean handbook for the statesmen of posterity, and the frequent Renaissance gloss on this idea emphasized that both statesmanship and history are the proper study of the wellborn: "Thus History appears on all Accounts recommendable to Gentlemen, and the Study of it exceeding useful to them

[c] London, 1638. This is the second and enlarged edition of Brathwaite's *The Schollers Medley* (London, 1614). A more distinguished work of the same period that voices similar ideas is Hobbes's translation of Thucydides (London, 1629). In his Dedication to Sir William Cavendish he commends his patron for the time spent on "that kind of learning which best deserveth the paines and houres of Great Persons, *History* and *Civill Knowledge* . . ." (sig. Av). Hobbes could have recommended Thucydides because he was descended from kings, ". . . but I chuse rather to recommend him for his writings, as having in them profitable instructions for Noblemen, and such as may come to have the mannaging of great and waighty actions" (sig. A2r).

See also J. H. Hexter, "The Education of the Aristocracy in the Renaissance," in *Reappraisals in History* (Evanston, 1961; new edition, New York, 1963), on Renaissance English theories of education: "Something is made of the rights of the aristocrats to office, more of their responsibility through education to prepare themselves for office, and most of their responsibility to turn the education they get to the service of the public weal" (p. 67). For the efforts of George I to establish the study of modern languages and modern history at Oxford and Cambridge in order to prepare men for civil service, see C. H. Firth, *Modern Languages at Oxford, 1724-1929* (London, 1929) and D. A. Winstanley, *Unreformed Cambridge* (Cambridge, England, 1935).

in their Conduct, not in Speculation only, but in Action; in all conditions of Life, but especially in publick Stations" (Hearne, I, 116).

Neither Clarendon nor Bolingbroke, therefore, is an innovator in historical method. But I treat them in brief prelude to my main concerns because their work rests on earlier beliefs even while it contains the possibilities for change. Both Clarendon's main themes and his historical method directly involve the problem of continuity: what is the historical continuity the historian perceives; how does he express this continuity in his form? Raleigh's history could begin with the creation of the world and the Garden of Eden; Clarendon's mentor, Thucydides, thought it appropriate to begin his history in the primitive origins of the Greek people. But the English civil wars marked a great watershed in the English sense of history. Previously assumed continuities like the providential coherence of the mind of God and His plan for man, the immemorial common law and the balanced relation of King and Parliament, and the prelatical establishment of the Anglican Church, were more closely and critically examined through their secondary causes.[9] In literature and the writing of history the search for more workable institutional forms became expressed as the search for new kinds of narrative coherence and continuity. In a similar way Milton presents the postlapsarian universe in Book X of *Paradise Lost* as a place that has to be consciously held together and elaborately worked, whereas before the fall its coherence and order were simple and unquestioned. In some ways one of the greatnesses of Clarendon's *History of the Rebellion* is his recognition that he cannot encompass the historical reality of the civil wars in the old Thucydidean terms. After a nod to Providence and politics has been made, there remains the possibility that the process of writing, the mind moving over historical materials, may discover a new and more vital dynamic.

Bolingbroke's anti-antiquarianism and his invocations of Cicero and Diodorus Siculus reflect the prejudices of many sixteenth- and seventeenth-century writers on history.[10] But his contribution is a new emphasis on the literary qualities of narrative. From Thucydides to Burnet the two main criteria for a historian had been personal acquaintance with the situation and a knowledge of appropriate records and memorials. Bolingbroke affirms that the historian should have firsthand knowledge and participation. But he also implies that these requirements must be supplemented by a very special ability to perceive continuity and to form a coherent literary narrative. Earlier historians may have assumed that a commitment to truth in method and dignity in ideas automatically yielded a coherent narrative. But Bolingbroke implies that the talent for clear and accurate observation is not necessarily related to a talent for structure and form. The great antiquarians of the sixteenth and seventeenth centuries no doubt developed the method and unearthed the details from which an understanding of historical relativism could arise. But it is more notable in the history of thought that the belief that history was a unique study of interest in itself should have been popularized by men like Hume and Gibbon, for whom literary method and a literary sensibility were more important than research.[d]

After this brief consideration of Clarendon and Bolingbroke, I begin my study with Hume. Even though this arrangement represents a slight chronological distortion, Hume in his early practice does represent an older kind of historiography. By aesthetic standards also his solutions are less adequate than those of Fielding and Gibbon. In a sense, Hume and Fielding have similar assumptions and goals. Both believe that their work benefits society by helping to expand individual perception and sympathy. But

d J.G.A. Pocock, *The Ancient Constitution*, argues that the "discovery" of feudalism as a distinct historical period grew out of the researches of antiquarians. But he also points out that it took many years before the insights of Henry Spelman and other writers reached a wider public. For the popularization of ideas of historical relativism, see René Wellek, *The Rise of English Literary History* (Chapel Hill, 1941).

while Hume insists that the past, when transformed into history, can still yield categories for understanding, Fielding turns away from history as the record of public events to establish a history of his own, with all the preoccupations of the older form, but with new materials. Fielding might say that Hume's troubles came from the decision to write history instead of novels.

The consideration of Fielding occupies the largest place in my argument, but he is not the culmination. He is so important because, while readers have often derogatorily called history "fiction," most claims that a novel is a "history" have usually been dismissed as merely whimsical. Since Fielding wrote less obvious historical theory than Hume and Gibbon, it takes more time to understand his assumptions.

Gibbon reflects or even may directly draw upon the insights of Hume and Fielding about the relation of man to time and history.[e] The *Decline and Fall* seems to be a new kind of history, which has absorbed the structural methods of the *History of England* and *Tom Jones* more thoroughly than the themes and historiographical techniques of Montesquieu and Voltaire. All three writers are ultimately sceptical of and hostile to any systematic explanation that claims absolute truth and perpetual relevance. Gibbon's great work is not designed to explain the meaning of history, to establish all the relevant facts, or to discourse on general trends. It is able to do all these things to a greater or lesser extent because of the freedom allowed it by an artistic structure based firmly on the process of creation itself and the controlling unity of Gibbon's voice. Gibbon synthesizes in his work such contrasting benefits as Hume's

[e] I should remark here that I have found it difficult to maintain the tone of probability rather than certainty when I speak of what seem to me to be the views of Hume, Fielding, and Gibbon. Of course I believe that the generalizations I derive from the practice of all three writers are valid, but they are not transcripts of expressed intention. As Gibbon says in another connection, "I owe it to myself and to historic truth, to declare, that some *circumstances* . . . are founded only on conjecture and analogy. The stubbornness of our language has sometimes forced me to deviate from the *conditional* into the indicative mood."

ironic detachment and Fielding's individual but authoritative narrative voice, Hume's emphasis on the body of established law and Fielding's praise of individual vitality, Hume's strict chronology and Fielding's frequently associative flow of events, digressions, and meditations. His achievement is bounded by both his vast admiration for the work of Hume and his firm belief that: "the Romance of Tom Jones, that exquisite picture of human manners will outlive the palace of the Escurial and the Imperial Eagle of the house of Austria."†

Hume, Fielding, and Gibbon are private men contemplating without much pleasure the public world. In their works the strain of optimism runs thin. What remains strong and vigorous, however, is the impression of artistic power that we receive from the worlds they have created. They demonstrate that forms and interpretations can be insubstantial and ephemeral guides to a world necessarily ordered anew by each individual consciousness. Perhaps their final lesson is the need to take on personal responsibility for such a construction. Hume believes history may still be relevant to later action, if used with understanding. Fielding shows a bankrupt public history that is irrelevant to individual problems. Although Gibbon is similar to Hume in many ways, he is a better historian because, perhaps taking his cue from Fielding, he departs from Hume's false ideal of detachment. Through his own control he is better able to articulate the sense of Hume and Fielding that the recognition of time, process, and the role of chance should be a basic part of human consciousness and must be developed fully for a true understanding of the past and the present.

† *Memoirs of My Life*, ed. Georges A. Bonnard (London, 1966), p. 5. Bonnard's is the first scholarly edition since G. B. Hill's and should remain definitive for some time. Dero A. Saunders has edited an excellent reader's edition for Meridian Books (New York, 1961), under the more familiar title of *The Autobiography of Edward Gibbon*. Since Saunders' edition may be more accessible, I have included references to both editions in my text. The present passage is on page 30 in Saunders' edition.

TWO | $Clarendon$ & $Bolingbroke$

I. CLARENDON: THE CONTINUITY OF HISTORY

THE CENTRAL THEMES in Clarendon's *History of the Rebellion*—historical continuity and the validity of the author's personal vision of events—are direct expressions of the accidents of composition. The original *History* was written during Clarendon's first exile, in the Scilly Islands from 1646 to 1648. It covers the events of the wars until March of 1644 and comprises the present books I to VI plus scattered later passages. Then the exiled Court moved to France and the manuscript was laid aside. The Restoration came and Charles II made Clarendon Lord Chancellor. But in 1668, Charles bowed to parliamentary and Court pressure, and Clarendon went into exile once again. Almost twenty years after he had completed the first part of his *History*, Clarendon again began to write, but this time it was a *Life*, an autobiography rather than a history, although told in the same third-person detachment that he had used in the early *History*. In 1671 his son Laurence came to Rouen and brought with him the recently rediscovered manuscript of the *History*. Clarendon then devised the new plan of combining the two works, using the new *Life* for the years after 1644 and writing new sections to fill out the historical narrative. The final work was to be called the *History*.[1] Through the perspective of two exiles twenty years apart, Clarendon sets out to explain, first to the King and selected counsellors and later to a wider audience, what happened during the civil wars, "to inform myself, and some others, what we ought to do, as well as to comfort us in what we have done."[a] His changing sense of what needs to be explained, what kinds of explanation are sufficient, and how these explanations should be presented, while he contemplates "this mass of confusion now before us," controls the frame and order of his history.

The reader, therefore, senses in the *History of the Rebellion* the tension between two modes of composition: the *Life* with its more personal although still detached angle of vision, and the *History* with its broader view and its attempts to make larger and less time-bound sense, whether providential or personal, from the personalities and events of the civil wars. But it is part of Clarendon's historical method and thematic emphasis that he never dwells on this tension. In some very basic way Clarendon does believe the true history of the civil wars to be a history of himself. The ultimate fusion of the early manuscript *History* and the later *Life* into the final work is merely the working out of this belief on the plane of composition. While we read through the *History of the Rebellion*, we may be plagued with questions that Clarendon either ignores or glosses over. But the impulse for the assured flow of his narrative lies in its implicit assertion that all the truly relevant questions are being answered or at least included within the confines of his history. Clarendon's rows of nominative absolutes convey a judicious assortment of preconditions; his frequently almost interminable one-sentence paragraphs imply a firm grasp on factors and relevant details. Clarendon's personal vision shades imperceptibly into a transcendental perspective on events; in the terms of the Thucydidean handbook version of history, his personal ability to deal with the practical politics of a situation leads naturally to an ability to discover timeless maxims of political behavior.[b]

a *The History of the Rebellion and Civil Wars in England*, ed. W. Dunn Macray, 6 vols. (Oxford, 1888), I, i, p. 3. In my citation the capital Roman numeral is Macray's volume and the minuscule Clarendon's book number. Further citations will be included in the text.

b In these early volumes there are many thematic and even verbal similarities between Clarendon's ideas and those in Hobbes's translation of Thucydides. See, for example, Hobbes's remark in "The Life

Clarendon implies that the civil wars are a battle of continuities, and the basic question is whose continuity shall prevail—Parliament's or the King's. It is vital to his argument in the early books that the parliamentary actions that finally decide him to align himself with the King's party should be an aberration in the flow of history. In these early pages he is most upset at the passage of the Perpetual Parliament Bill, "which was to remove the landmarks and to destroy the Foundation of the Kingdom," because this action directly challenges the continuity of the monarchy (I, iii, p. 343). Until 1641 Clarendon's own actions in supporting parliamentary reform are justified because they are in accord with the political and social traditions of England. The forms of English government had existed a long time, if not forever, and because of their continued existence they could be counted on to include the reasonable changes, reconciliations, and rebalancings of parliamentary and kingly power.[2] After 1641, asserts Clarendon, the aim of the King's advisers is to restore the stability that the Long Parliament had disrupted and the continuity that it had unjointed.

These impulses toward the establishment of continuity dictate many of Clarendon's interests throughout the *History of the Rebellion*. He will not seek for causes of the parliamentary agitation in earlier history because he wants to preserve his belief that the Long Parliament is a disruption. Certain "sharp-sighted" ones may see the origin of the conflicts of the civil wars in Elizabethan times, but they are wrong; in fact, the 1630's, he tells us, was a time of unprecedented prosperity and peace.[c] Causes do not accumu-

---

and History of Thucydides" (prefaced to the translation) that Thucydides could have become a great demagogue, but did not, "because in those times it was impossible for any man to give good and profitable counsell for the Common-wealth, and not incurre the displeasure of the People" (sig. 2v). Trevor-Roper remarks that Clarendon considered *Leviathan* Hobbes's rejection of Thucydides and the wisdom of the past ("Clarendon," p. 41).

c Clarendon's argument here may also be an implicit attack against late. Proper action is both pragmatic and precedented. But the Long Parliament has cut itself and the nation loose from precedent and pragmatic politics, and substituted the rage and fanaticism of the moment. Through the statements and plaintive retorts of Charles I, Clarendon wonders why the Parliament no longer holds to one of Pym's remarks in an early speech about the sanctity of law. In one sense, this complaint is merely good debating tactics, to damn your opponent from the mouth of one of his own. But in a more basic way, it also involves the value Clarendon places on continuity. And Clarendon later remarks wistfully on Pym's importance because he had served in earlier parliaments and formed a continuity in himself with an earlier age (III, vii, p. 321).

Clarendon's view of events and causes therefore embodies an interesting paradox: what is both most pragmatic and most embodies the historical point of view is identical with what is most timeless and ubiquitous—whether the legal structure of common law precedent, the verities of political behavior, or the transcendental plan of God's purposes.[3] The paradox is, of course, straight out of Clarendon's great exemplar Thucydides: in the midst of a chaos of secondary causes the historian seeks the uniformities of moral and political truth to bring himself and his reader into a point of view that transcends the present moment. Clarendon toys at the beginning of the *History of the Rebellion* with providential continuity and causation by asserting that "the universal apostasy in the whole nation from their religion and allegiance" caused the civil wars. But his more general concern is with the atemporal continuities of the legal and political structure. At the end of his history, on the verge of the Restoration, Clarendon once again uses the providential language of his first thoughts. But the policy of watchful passivity that he believes is the best for the Court of Charles II in France reinforces his as-

parliamentary views of the Elizabethan Golden Age exemplified in the writings of Tom May. See Trevor-Roper, "Clarendon," p. 37.

sumption that the actions of men will confuse things only further. The national verities of England will naturally reassert themselves through the unplotted actions of General Monk, who "was instrumental in bringing these mighty things to pass, which he had neither wisdom to foresee, nor courage to attempt, nor understanding to contrive" (VI, xvi, p. 164).

The problem of ruptured continuities is therefore resolved by the *History of the Rebellion* itself. Clarendon supplies from his own life and perception a continuity he believes the events of the 1640's and 1650's in England do not innately have. In the conflict between the continuities asserted by King and Parliament the continuity that survives is the continuity of Clarendon's own perspective. It is difficult to call this perspective "historical" in our terms because it is tied to no specific time, no Golden Age of King-Parliament relations. It is instead an immemorial continuity that has always existed and but for the civil wars would have continued to exist. As Charles II's Lord Chancellor after the Restoration, Clarendon tried to bring back the accomplishments of 1641 and obliterate the discontinuities of the Interregnum. But time had not stopped, and the old practical politician could not deal with the new alignments of power. With his exile he began the work of self-justification, and the return of the old manuscript of the *History* presented an opportunity to patch the tear in history and raise his private experience and judgment into timeless truths. The impulse to second-guess that he exhibited in the early books disappears as the main impulse of Clarendon's writing becomes not to say what should have been done or to undo what had been done, but to interpret and thereby include the past into a total vision. He neither seeks nor is interested in long-drawn general causes. "Accidents" in the *History of the Rebellion* are not the result of hidden causes, but the eruptions of unexplainable nature into the narrative, usually in the form of weather, sickness, or death. Clarendon believes that the combination of his detached narrative voice and his continuously privileged experience is enough to hold together all events and accidents and personages. In the later books his previously England-wide vision narrows to the restricted scope of the English Court in its French exile. Instead of being at the center of great events, Clarendon now acts amid the backstairs intrigues for Charles II's favor. But the impression we receive from the narrative is still that the author has placed us at the center of things. He is there, the King is there, and so, in some fundamental sense, history is there too. The Commonwealth government is an aberration. Here is the true continuity.

The elevation of personal perception into historical truth suits Clarendon's understanding of the forces at issue in the civil wars. He attempts to mediate the separate claims of the older system of personal feudal relation to the king and the newer system of civil loyalty to the head of the government. Personal loyalty and public loyalty should be the same, and he chastises the Archbishop of York during the Strafford case for his "unprelatical, ignominious" arguments to Charles I "that his public conscience as a king might not only dispense with, but oblige him to do, that which was against his private conscience as a man . . ." (I, iii, p. 338). The ideal public man easily combines these two obligations, and Clarendon uses his detached historical voice to indicate the kind of reconciliation necessary. Charles I is the head of an enlarged feudal family; his execution is "unparalleled murder and parricide" (IV, xi, p. 492). But he is also the contemporary embodiment of political and social tradition, and therefore the details of his execution may be too purely personal to dwell upon, even while its symbolic importance is paramount. The great fault of the men of the civil wars period is their excessive dependence on the personal aspect of things and their subsequent neglect of what is timeless. While Clarendon translates his personal perspective into the realm of political, ethical, and religious truth, he habitually reduces the political, ethical, and religious principles of others into the immediate meanness of personal motive. He disdains equally the Cavalier empha-

sis on the private chivalric self and the parliamentary protestations of conscience. Clarendon doubts the belief of
Charles I that Parliament would never execute him because
his death would mean that Parliament was dissolved
(III, viii, pp. 502–03). But Parliament, Clarendon knew,
was equal to the opposition of continuities when the problem of the trial of the King arose: "So that they must make
a new form to warrant their proceedings. And a new form
they did erect, never before heard of" (IV, xi, p. 473).

In the same way, he speaks caustically of parliamentary
pleas for tolerance and treats phrases like "freedom of conscience" as a "barbarous dialect," mere rhetoric, not so fit
for political discourse as his own language of timeless precedent. His identification of private and public loyalties
frequently blinds him to the real conflict between obligations to institutions and obligations to individual conscience and principle that many men of his time felt. His beliefs as both politician and historian rest on the necessary
compatibility of such loyalties.

Clarendon's privileged historical perspective is the foundation for his general pronouncements. He believes that
there is no disparity between his private views and the
public truth because he accepts without question the belief
that the historian is appropriately a public man dealing
with public materials. The many remarks about the King's
"evil counsellors," made both by Clarendon and Parliament,
reinforce the idea that Clarendon and by extension his
History of the Rebellion are the good counsellors Charles
I, and later Charles II, needs to carry on the proper management of public affairs. The overwhelming array of documents he includes—in their dual role as the materials of
public history and the (frequent) product of Clarendon's
own pen—fuses the detached historian and the involved
participant into an image of historical continuity.[4] In the
later books, his own vision has become even more closely
identified with "history." He can drop the normal chronology of his narrative to follow the career of Montrose
until his execution (V, xii, p. 115). His emphasis on his own

interests can even make him short with what one might call his historian's responsibility to deal with important events: ". . . now to finish this business of Pontefract. . . ."d The later books also display a greater effort to make political and psychological generalizations and to support them with the parallel authority of the historians of the past. Clarendon in *The History of the Rebellion* is both actor and historian. When he appears on the scene, he is treated like another character: "Mr. Hyde" or "the chancellor of the exchequer." Behind this mask of Thucydidean detachment Clarendon's personal prejudices may be dictating his choice and emphasis. But he can do this because he believes there is no contradiction between the roles of the politician and the historian. His vision holds them together. Perhaps his only rival may be Cromwell, who came from "a private and obscure birth" to hold together tradition and change in a way Clarendon was never able quite to achieve in the world of action. But Clarendon believes he has gone beyond Cromwell and therefore he can afford to be magnanimous toward him. By encompassing both royal and parliamentary ideas of continuity within his *History of the Rebellion,* Clarendon has defined, preserved, and thereby mastered the continuity of time.

II. BOLINGBROKE: THE PURPOSE OF HISTORY

A prime topic for essayists in the first half of the eighteenth century was the lack of good English history. Most English historians who had attempted to write more than an antiquarian history served partisan interests, Whig or Tory. They interpreted the events and personalities of the past in relation to contemporary controversy. Clarendon's

d This phrase is not included in Macray, nor is it among his variants. It may be found in Bulkeley Bandinel's 1826 edition (VI, xi, p. 123). This kind of magisterial and peremptory tone exists elsewhere in Clarendon's *History of the Rebellion.* See, for example, his refusal to go into too much detail about the battle of Marston Moor: ". . . as I can take no pleasure in the draught of it, so posterity would receive little pleasure or benefit from the most particular relation of it" (Macray, III, viii, p. 375) .

History of the Rebellion was not exempt from such attacks, since it was finally published with a preface (1702) and two dedications to Queen Anne (1703 and 1704) by Laurence Hyde, Earl of Rochester and Clarendon's second son, that firmly placed it on the side of the Tories. Voltaire pointed out that the only English history not distorted by party prejudice was by a Frenchman, Rapin-Thoyras. In the seventeenth century Bacon, Raleigh, and others had made similar complaints about "the unworthiness of the history of England in the main continuance thereof."[5] When Hume was in the middle of writing the first volume of his history of the Stuart reign, he wrote to John Clephane: "You know that there is no post of honour in the English Parnassus more vacant than that of History. Style, judgement, impartiality, care—everything is wanting to our historians; and even Rapin, during this latter period [the seventeenth century], is extremely deficient."[6] Over one hundred works of history had appeared between 1700 and 1754, the publication date of Hume's first volume. But most of these were either specialized studies of biblical and ecclesiastical history or bare chronologies.[7]

After Hume had begun his *History of England*, Tobias Smollett was commissioned by a group of London booksellers to write a rival work; it was completed in 1758, before Hume's own work was done (1762).[8] Oliver Goldsmith was soon to follow suit (1764). Theory quickly moved to keep pace with practice. Between the composition (1735) and the publication (1752) of Bolingbroke's *Letters on the Study and Use of History* there were three new works on historiography; by 1800 twelve more had appeared.[9]

Bolingbroke's reflections come, therefore, midway through a period of rising interest in the methods of writing history. His theoretical preoccupations afford a convenient prelude to the problems considered more practically by Hume and Fielding.[10] Written in the form of a series of letters to Henry Hyde, Clarendon's great-grandson, the *Letters on History* attempt to transcend the controversies of national history by two methods: a concentration on foreign affairs and a search for useful generalization. Drawing on his philosophical scorn of party divisions and his desire to emulate the great models of Thucydides, Livy, and Tacitus, Bolingbroke produces a theory of history that ignores mere partisan argument and tries to provide precepts for general behavior. In place of the false partialities of the ecclesiastical and party-historians he proposes a history that can yield generalizations about man in society, a history from which the reader can extract a "general system of ethics and politics."[e] Unlike the party-historians, who used precedent to validate and justify the present, Bolingbroke seeks to generalize the past and apply it to the future.

But even though he frequently asserts that the study of history should make "better men and better citizens," Bolingbroke's real purposes are not so general. He builds instead upon the common belief that historical knowledge is personally desirable for a gentleman because he may be called upon to do public service for his country.[11] Bolingbroke accordingly makes himself the paradigmatic reader of history—the statesman-philosopher. The history he outlines should supply the gentleman-politician with knowledge that is immediately transferable to the problems of running the state. The reading of history must necessarily be a benefit to the public man.

Public life in general—the disinterested service of the state—should in theory be a corrective for the meanness and self-seeking of private life. But in Bolingbroke's experience of the factions of his time, this adjustment was not occurring. Instead, private selfishness was poisoning public life. In the later letters Bolingbroke speaks often of the "particular motives of private men" that conflict with the good of the state (p. 320). He says that Marlborough is one example of a good private man who through merit has reached a position of both personal power and state serv-

[e] Henry St. John Bolingbroke, *Letters on the Study and Use of History*, A New Edition Corrected (London, 1770), p. 53. Further citations will be included in the text.

ice (p. 299). But such a figure is rare in Bolingbroke's view of society. He takes a more pessimistic view than Clarendon of the compatibility of private and public interests. When men are out for personal gain, the state suffers, and the presence of many such men have brought England to her present position: "Few know, and scarce any respect, the British constitution: that of the church has been long since derided; that of the State as long neglected; and both have been left at the mercy of the men in power, whoever these men were" (p. 388).

When respect for political institutions deteriorates, there is an analogous degeneration in the rest of society: ". . . arts and sciences are scarce alive; luxury has been increased but not refined; corruption has been established, and is avowed" (p. 388).

The study of history is to be the specific for these ills of the state. Through contemplation of the great characters of history and examination of the causes of events, a young gentleman could learn the appropriate functions and duties of a public position. History teaches us how to understand our public roles. Bolingbroke remarks that, since there are so many histories and life is so short, we ought "to confine ourselves almost entirely in our study of history, to such histories as have an immediate relation to our professions, or to our rank and situation in the society to which we belong" (p. 140). In his famous phrase, ". . . history is philosophy teaching by example" (p. 14). History presents to future statesmen "images of virtue and vice" (p. 28) that can help them better understand the world around them. History increases the capacity for clear perception by furnishing abstract structures and categories by which to shape the immediate stuff of experience.

In accord with this emphasis on the instrumental purpose of reading history, Bolingbroke implies that it is more important that the examples of history be relevant than that they be true. If the primary role of history is to furnish precepts for the conscientious reader, then "what really happened" becomes irrelevant. In Letters VII and VIII Bolingbroke sketches how history should be written. In his example he requires that the historians focus on the way Louis XIV manipulated everything in the first thirty years of his reign toward the object of supreme power in Europe. Such an interpretation might seem to attribute too much to the power of men to mold events. But Bolingbroke, even if he does not believe that such an assumption is strictly true (a hard point to judge), believes that it is true in terms of the necessities of his theory of history; that is, it is useful for the reader to believe it and allow for it in his own future decisions. The distortions of party-historians turn out to be bad, not because they are untrue, but because they are useless. They salve men's feelings and provide ammunition for pamphleteering, but they cannot be used as guides to future action because they distort in the service of their own partisan present. Bolingbroke's precepts look to the future. Behind his attack on the historicity of the Bible, for example, lies a recognition that a history dealing in portents and miracles, like one that interprets everything in terms of the party alignments of the present, is no longer relevant to the business of running nations. Utility is the criterion of historical truth. History furnishes generalizations that are both immediately and continually applicable to action.

Because of his instrumental view of historical truth, Bolingbroke has an ambiguous attitude toward research and factual accuracy. Using the language of Cicero, he violently attacks the annalists and chronologers who make history into a *"nuntia vetustatis"* rather than a *"magistra vitae"* (p. 123): "I had rather take the DARIUS whom ALEXANDER conquered, for the son of HYSTAPES, and make as many anachronisms as a Jewish chronologer, than sacrifice half my life to collect all the learned lumber that fills the heads of an antiquary" (p. 9).

On the evidence of such statements D. G. James convicts Bolingbroke of ignoring, if not sabotaging, the great age of English antiquarian scholarship, which flourished between 1660 and 1730.[12] But Bolingbroke's attack upon antiquarianism is not so indiscriminate. Accuracy can aid utility because it validates the record of prior human experience. Bolingbroke primarily dislikes the grubbing for what he considered to be "immaterial" facts. Public records and "authentic memorials" are "the sole foundation of true history" (p. 64); but collecting folktales and speculating about origins and customs can have no application to action in the present or the future.[f] In "A Letter occasioned by one of Archbishop Tillotson's Sermons" Bolingbroke declares that "authentic history" should be written only by a contemporary observer or one who has access to contemporary observations. Such a history could be judged only by those who took part in the same action and knew the author; in addition the account must be corroborated by "those who had no common interest of country, or religion, or of profession, to disguise or falsify the truth."[13]

The idea of a retrospective and critical historian, separating fact from fiction, seems far from Bolingbroke's contemporary observer. Indeed, because of Bolingbroke's emphasis on "the study and use of history," the figure of the historian appears only dimly in his theory. Bolingbroke's historian does not didactically present historical characters, facts, and causes. Instead he gives "the end of a clue" or a "guide" to "that truth which the example before us establishes or illustrates" (p. 138). It is obvious that there must be a historian who arranges his materials to achieve such effects. But Bolingbroke concentrates instead on the attention and insight actively supplied by the reader. The lesson should be absorbed into a total understanding rather than be swallowed by rote. The reader should at least partially believe, therefore, that his own acumen has helped to define the special truth involved. After all, with this knowl-

[f] On the basis of this distinction Bolingbroke could assert that "naked facts, without the causes that produced them and the circumstances that accompanied them" are insufficient, while at the same time he deplored the lack of historians *and* antiquarians in England (pp. 135, 179).

edge the prospective statesman must make decisions creatively, not mechanically. Bolingbroke emphasizes, therefore, that the examples of history must not be used rigidly but elastically, as approaches rather than formulaic solutions. Despite Bolingbroke's disclaimers, however, the selection of historical materials is always dictated by the purposes of example. The past has no coherence of its own, except in the political and ethical generalizations displayed by the writer or extracted by the reader (a choice that depends on Bolingbroke's epistemological mood). The study of history—the written record of the past—serves as a corrective for the world of disparate facts and impressions facing the reader every day. The generalizations derived from history then become a grammar of experience. Bolingbroke frequently uses the metaphor of literature to express the process: "History is the ancient author; experience is the modern language" (p. 55). We should use the examples of history, he says, in the same way that Boileau counsels us to imitate rather than translate another language (p. 49). Through these metaphors Bolingbroke implies that the coherence of history, the exemplary relation of past and present, exists within a literary sensibility: the best possible user of language is a man with literary training. History may be more effective than poetry in teaching the statesman because it draws upon a vast repository of codified political experience.[14] Yet the desire for structure that one brings to history is not appreciably different from that suited to contemplate literature:

> Examine [a] period of history as you would examine a tragedy or a comedy; that is, take first the idea or a general notion of the whole, and after that examine every act and every scene apart. Consider them in themselves, and consider them relatively to one another (pp. 187–88).

The only superiority history has over fiction of any type, the quality that gives its examples their persuasive power, is the reader's knowledge that it really happened.

This under-theme of literary coherence shakily holds together Bolingbroke's ideas about the past, present, and
future. His attitude toward the past ultimately rests on its
relevance to the acts of an individual. And the exemplary
theory of history, however subtle it may be, when pressed
always reveals a past that is only a discontinuous collection of discrete incidents, with perhaps their immediate
contexts. The coherence of exemplary history is at best a
function of the mind that generalizes from it and thereby
becomes the container for all its examples. Since examples
are relevant only to immediate situations of like kind, there
arises no need to postulate or seek either a development
or flow in events. The past is a grab-bag of unrelated parts.

Bolingbroke does seem to recognize this problem, but he
does not deal with it. All the force of his *Letters on History*
finally rests in the assumption that the study of history co-
ordinates for the reader what would otherwise be the
chaos of experience. The past, like the present, is a welter of
discrete facts and impressions that must be ordered by the
mind. But the past is not history. Written history resembles fiction because it is purer and more accessible to the
understanding than are the immediacies of life, whether past
or present. In contemporary history, the reader can be at
his ease, detached, contemplating a completed whole, rather
than the rush of fragments he contemplates in his own life.
The partiality of party-historians results from an excess
of zeal (pp. 102–03), but true history shows us men and
events "through a medium less partial at least than that of
experience . . ." (p. 32). History and experience are the
great teachers. But by itself experience is usually confusing.
The events we see in life "appear to us very often original,
unprepared, single, and unrelative. . . . [They] are called accidents, and looked upon as the effects of chance . . ." (p. 34).
The examples of history present us with clear and simple
categories for understanding. History itself calms us by its
pattern and coherence. It "shews us causes as in fact they
were laid, with their immediate effects: and it enables us to

guess at future events" (p. 41). In a world of confusion, history makes sense.[15]

But even Bolingbroke's generalizations about ethics and politics do not have the necessary amount of pattern and coherence. Searching for an even less subjective ordering, he falls back on the previously scorned chronologies.[g] When he writes "A Sketch of the State and History of Europe" in Letters VII-VIII, he sticks to a tedious chronology and a finical delineation of "epocha." He presents no more than a superficial diplomatic history of Europe from the end of the fifteenth century to the present, with particular attention to the period from 1659 on. Paragraph after paragraph appears on the provisions of various military treaties, which are announced only to be abrogated in various sections of ensuing paragraphs. Not a breath of vitality enlivens the whole performance. Bolingbroke demarcates eras in history by the treaties that are signed at either end; Letter VII, for example, examines 1659 to 1688, the period between the Pyrenean Treaty and the Treaty of Ryswick. He asserts that private rather than public interests are at work in diplomatic history, but never analyzes them except to allude cryptically to the machinations of Louis XIV. Such history is reliance upon "public monuments" with a vengeance. All it can possibly teach the statesman-reader is how to write good treaties, and even that topic is dealt with only by implication. The one personal anecdote that Bolingbroke includes, the one glimpse beyond a purely external pattern, he declares "too trivial for history," but fit for a letter (p. 335).

With Bolingbroke's *Letters on History* the unspoken certainties that enabled Clarendon to assert continuity amid the chaos of the civil wars have vanished. The attenuated

[g] Compare Locke, *Some Thoughts Concerning Education*, pp. 331–32: ". . . without Geography or *Chronology*, I say, History will be very ill retained, and very little useful; but be only a jumble of Matters of Fact, confusedly heaped together without Order or Instruction."

practice that issues from Bolingbroke's theory can perhaps be best explained if we assume he had some feeling for the dark side of his ideas, the chaos of past, present, and future that the study of history might stave off. He imposes a chronological and documentary coherence to shield himself from the possible problems of complex interpretation. His detached and superficial historical sketch implies that the generalizations he seeks may be equally simple and reductive. By directing his remarks so specifically to a person who may be in a position to write or sign treaties, he chooses not to speculate about the more ambiguous problems of human behavior, leaving for someone else "the course of accidents, and a multitude of irregular and contingent circumstances" (p. 189).[16]

THREE | *Hume:*
THE STRUCTURE OF THE PAST

I. INTRODUCTION

Could I even surmount these obstacles [of past great historians], I should shrink with terror from the modern history of England, where every character is a problem, and every reader a friend or enemy, where a writer is supposed to hoist a flag of party, and is devoted to damnation by the adverse faction.

> Gibbon, *Memoirs of My Life*

. . . the study of history [is] difficult to reconcile with the traditional empiricist theory of knowledge.

> E. H. Carr, *What is History?*

BOLINGBROKE SOUGHT to remedy the abuses of partisan history-writing by concentrating on the general political and ethical truths potential statesmen could discover through the study of the past. Yet his approach merely emphasized a different kind of teleology: the partisan historians directed their histories toward contemporary controversy; Bolingbroke similarly concentrated on the "purposes" to which the lessons of history could be applied—the present relevance of past examples. He does not discuss retrospective history or the philosophic historian because his idea of the past allowed it no structure or continuity of its own. The best "historians" were contemporary observers.

Clarendon found continuity in his own life and the easy commerce between his private and his public duty. Bolingbroke obviated the problem by concentrating on exempla and easily detaching them from their place in the past. Hume makes the problem of coherence the center of his attempt to write history.[a] He immediately grasps the need to define the role of the historian and his relation to the materials that the past offers. Bolingbroke's scattered comparisons between the literary man and the interpreter of history become a guiding principle of Hume's practice. But while Bolingbroke's literary analogies emphasized the act of "translating" past events into present practice, Hume's refer to the more inclusive issues of style, theme, and structure. Going beyond Bolingbroke, he considers the writing of history to be first of all a literary problem. His experimentations with literary method finally lead him to researches into the unique nature of the past. But when he begins his *History of England,* he says that the motive that most animated him to write was the desire for "literary fame."[1] Style was at least as important a concern as matter: "The more I advance in my undertaking, the more I am convinced that the History of England has never yet been written, not only for style, which is notorious to all the world, but also for matter; such is the ignorance and partiality of all our historians."[2]

In his early writings Hume's emphasis on the structural interrelation of history and fiction is close in form to Bolingbroke's. He says in *An Enquiry Concerning Human Understanding*: "The PELOPONNESIAN war is a proper subject for history, the siege of ATHENS for an epic poem, and the death of ALCIBIADES for a tragedy."[3] Hume here cares little about the criterion of verifiable facts that would make a distinction between fiction that deals with a historical subject and history itself. The principles of coherence in both draw upon similar literary methods: "The unity of action . . . which is to be found in biography or history, differs from that of epic poetry, not in kind, but in degree."[4] Without a design any literary pro-

[a] Since I am not concerned directly with textual problems, I have used the most readily accessible edition of Hume's *History,* in my case, a six-volume 1856 edition printed in Boston. References to this edition will be included in the text. I cite chapter as well as volume and page numbers because of the many editions extant.

duction "would be like the ravings of a madman" (p. 294). And historical "design," like literary design, depends first of all on a continuity of time and a contiguity of space: "All events, which happen in [a] portion of space, and period of time, are comprehended in this design, tho' in other respects different and unconnected. They have still a species of unity, amidst all their diversity" (p. 294).

The historian refines this abstract "species of unity" by discovering lines of cause, tracing them from their origins to their "most remote consequences." The better his penetration of causes and "the more unbroken the chain is," the better the historian, for the study of causes is not only "the most satisfactory" part of reading history, but also "the most instructive; since it is by this knowledge alone, we are enabled to control events, and govern futurity" (p. 294). Such an optimism about the control that knowledge can give over events befits the philosophical *Enquiry*. Here Hume is also optimistic about dispelling the claim that chance rules history. He denies chance an operative role and calls it only "our ignorance of the real cause of any event ... " (p. 315). The coherence of this more Bolingbrokian approach to history lies not in history's special nature, but in the control of the historian, who traces causes and discerns the general principles of human nature. By the end of his *History*, however, Hume feels satisfied if historical knowledge has succeeded in "humanizing the temper and softening the heart" (II, xxii, p. 466). Although he does not want to personalize the historian, history has become a study which is valuable in itself for its ability to extend sympathies and perceptions beyond the immediate.

Hume gradually discovers in the course of writing his *History* that history is a problem with unique terms, rather than a mere adjunct to moral philosophy or political science. As the volumes flow on and Hume moves backward in his search for the shape of English history, he tries out themes, experiments with style, and investigates new possibilities for narrative structure. He gradually will become more and more disenchanted with some of the structural techniques he has imported either from past historio-graphical practice or from his own philosophical precepts. But Hume begins to write history within a tradition that defines public event and public personality to be the basic elements of history. His first discussions of character are, therefore, overstated in both the exactness of their formulation and his claim for their causal relevance. J. B. Black criticizes Hume's use of the character sketch by saying that it explains too much, that it "atomizes" character and makes historical figures into reductive "types" rather than recognizable individuals: "He will not allow for any irrational element that breaks up the chain of causation; every character he meets in history must be reduced to type."[5]

R. G. Collingwood supports this appraisal with a more inclusive condemnation. He believes that Hume's "substantialist" conception of character is "really quite inconsistent with his philosophical principles." He also charges that Hume, although he did not believe in the possibility of achieving absolute truth when he considered history theoretically, did so when he finally came to write history.[6] Such a wholesale condemnation obscures the development of Hume's view of character in his *History*. Hume may believe in the centrality of human character to the understanding of history, but he also appreciates how the "character" as a device of literary organization can be more binding than liberating. Hume's most obvious uneasiness in the *History* appears when he must follow previous historiographers in narrative techniques like the literary "character." However it changed in expression, Hume's interest in the role of character in events does persist throughout his *History*. His practice becomes the realization of Bolingbroke's injunction that "Man is the subject of every history; and to know him well, we must see him and consider him, as history alone can present him to us, in every age, in every country; in every state, in life and in death."[7]

But Hume becomes more and more disenchanted with the claim that the balanced psychological portrait of the public man is as much a historical explanation as a literary technique. Not only is the public "character" deficient, but the public man becomes deficient also. Hume asserts finally the greater moral and historical significance of the private man, who stands in detached contemplation of public life.[b]

The movement of Hume's *History* in fact often results from a tension between the demands of sympathetic character analysis and those of detached narrative. As the uniformity of human character "in all ages, and in almost all countries,"[8] becomes a topic insufficient to support a six-volume history, so the received tradition of public narrative is found similarly wanting. Hume introduces stately denunciations of the dull repetitions of military battles, martyrdoms, and revolutions that spot histories. History has become a problem for Hume. He can experiment with different types of narrative. In the early volumes he is uncomfortable when he finds it necessary to break the narrative flow; he continually apologizes for digressions. As he says in the Tudor volumes, he wishes to avoid "as much as possible the style of dissertation in the body of his History" (IV, Note CCC, p. 568). This discomfort does not vanish by the medieval volumes, but by then Hume has found new strength in the form of chronological narrative.

Because of Hume's emphasis on chronological structure, events often seem isolated within his history, connected only by the meditative, unhurried flow of Hume's narration and the consecutive pages. The method seems almost doggedly anti-dramatic, as if Hume were attempting, for all his em-

b Hume often mentions, though ruefully, the commitment of history to examine only public life. In the suppressed Preface to the 1756 edition of the second Stuart volume he writes that ". . . the beneficent Influence of Religion is not to be sought in History: That Principle is always the more genuine, the less figure it makes in those Annals of Wars, & Politics, Intrigues, & Revolutions, Quarrels & Convulsions, which it is the business of an Historian to record and transmit to Posterity." Quoted by Ernest C. Mossner, *The Life of David Hume* (Austin, 1954), p. 306. Given in full by John Hill Burton, *Life and Correspondence of David Hume*, 2 vols. (Edinburgh, 1846), II, pp. 11–13.

phasis on style, to develop a rhetoric of truth, which does not dazzle by effects and arrangement, but presents his facts and generalizations only through the clearest medium possible. His narrative voice, except for a few one-sentence outbursts, mainly in the Stuart volumes, is careful and measured. No search for inevitable causal chains disturbs the serenity of his detachment. In place of concentration on a few main themes, Hume concentrates on the chronological flow of events and the power of his narrative voice as the contemplator of history *en philosophe*. In his balanced sentences and juxtaposed contraries we sense no irrepressible movement except the flow of time.

Hume's concern with the literary and philosophical problems of narrative structure expands his concept of cause in history. As Hume goes further into the *History*, he emphasizes more and more that causes, especially both causes in character and in the development of society, can never necessarily imply their effects. He continually points out plausible effects that never materialize and unlooked-for ones that do. His tone is impartial and moderate, and the standard of his *History* is the need to avoid extremes. Both his method and his observations counsel moderation and balance by insisting on the gradual but insistent accretions of time. He corrects the work of past historians and emends his own in order to balance possible prejudice. It is notorious that he said more of his revisions favored the Tories than the Whigs.[9] But this was less a concession to party than, as he also said, an effort to be above party and to rid himself of the "plaguy whig prejudices" with which he began the work. As Gibbon writes, "Mr. Hume told me that in correcting his history he always laboured to reduce superlatives and soften positives."[10]

Both Hume's expansive view of cause and his effort at narrative detachment are in great part reactions to the work of the party-historians whom he detested. Whether Whig or Tory, they partook of what Herbert Butterfield has called "the whig interpretation of history": studying the past "with direct and perpetual reference to the present," mistaking an imposition of interpretation as an actual line of cause, over-dramatizing the agency of "friends" or "enemies" at the expense of complex process, and generally assuming a "false continuity" in events that can justify whatever contemporary position the "Whig" historian is defending.[11] Like the Whig historians, Hume is often interested in passing moral verdicts on past action, but not such verdicts as were defined by contemporary controversy. He is the historian above party, and in the medieval volumes he continually ridicules both sides of the eighteenth-century political arguments that drew upon equally biased interpretations of early English history.[c] Such arguments were born in the era of the civil wars, when each side used historical examples to justify its own position. Hume believed that the time had come when these events could be viewed with detachment. He was too sanguine; he was attacked by almost everyone.[d] But gradually the impulses behind Hume's impartiality, detachment, balance, and praise of moderation become the mainspring of his *History*. In the Stuart volumes he makes firm and usually unqualified adjudications of rights and wrongs. In the later volumes, as his sense of the complexity of the accumulating causes of history becomes more refined, Hume's desire to make ethical judgments grows weaker. The urge to judge individual action becomes secondary to his effort to understand that essential part of history that is expressed in the unimpeded flow of time.

[c] The most important of these arguments concerned the "gothic" history of the English parliament. Hume argues that early parliaments had little or no power; but he does not therefore conclude that the present power of parliament was unprecedented. To the Gothicists and their rivals, history was *"fundamentum doctrinae."* But Hume did not believe that history could authenticate when reason was lacking. See Kliger, *The Goths in England*, p. 253.

[d] He alludes to many instances in his letters, some humorous, some bitter. A typical example of the former is in a late letter to Benjamin Franklin: "I expected, in entering my literary course, that all the Christians, all the Whigs, and all the Tories should be my Enemies: But it is hard, that all the English, Irish, and Welsh should be also against me. The Scotch, likewise, cannot be much my Friends, as no man is a Prophet in his own Country" (Klibansky and Mossner, *New Letters*, p. 194).

Even though general themes like the growth of law and the relation between the ruler and the constitution become stronger methods of organization in the medieval volumes, the *History* never really coheres thematically. There are no overall movements and few short summaries of what Hume was "shown." Hume experiments with different kinds of coherence. But, perhaps perversely, he rests with the coherence of space and time he recommended in the *Enquiry* and in the hard-won detachment of his own narrative voice. Hume's focus is upon specific situations and what caused them, rather than great historical movements. His examination of causes is more proximate than long range. Even the Stuart volumes, with their apparent theme of progress of liberty in England as the result of the interaction of kingly prerogative and parliamentary privilege, deal with larger themes only sporadically.

As Hume more firmly demonstrates our inability to move from historical causes to their effects, he also emphasizes the problematic relation of the historical past to future action. Hume in his *History*, like Voltaire, often takes the opportunity to exhibit human foolishness and cruelty. But it also gradually emerges into a recognition of the complexity of circumstances and the confusion of motives, an appreciation scarcely to be found in Voltaire or Bolingbroke.[12] Hume's sections on economic and cultural history exhibit his efforts to translate a feeling for the immediate context of action into an appreciation for the special quality of a historical era.[e] Throughout the *History* there is a growing realization of the inadequacy and perhaps the irrelevancy of the didactic role of history envisioned by Bolingbroke. Hume includes very few references to contemporary society beyond remarks about political controversialists who wrongly draw

e While Hume wrote, Thomas Warton published *Observations on the Faerie Queene of Spenser* (1754), Richard Hurd *Letters on Chivalry and Romance* (1762), and Thomas Percy was collecting materials for the *Reliques of Ancient English Poetry* (1765). For a discussion of these stirrings of historical relativism, see Wellek, *The Rise of English Literary History*, and W. K. Wimsatt and Cleanth Brooks, *A Short History of Literary Criticism* (New York, 1957), pp. 522–51.

upon history for their arguments. Hume has become more at ease with the variety of history and begins to evolve more flexible forms to deal with his material.

In the Stuart volumes, Hume has as yet made no real break with past historians. Despite his emphasis on cultural and economic history, he still writes the history of great figures engaged in military and political events. Successive volumes show him, however, more and more dissatisfied with these methods of organization. Finally, by the medieval volumes, the process of writing itself has uncovered a new rationale and new methods for the contemplation of history. Through his problems in centering history on great personages, Hume has learned to appreciate the need in the study of history to emphasize the gradual growth and continuity of law, rather than the eruptions and idiosyncrasies of personality. He associates the evils of system with the evils of political bias, and attempts to make his own narrative voice stand in place of specifically formulated moral and political standards. In short, he abandons the systematic treatment of history in much the same way that he abandoned the systematic treatment of philosophy.[13] In his commitment to the narrative of history and the exploration of his own stance as historian, he points toward a method that might encompass both structure and chance, established institutions and human innovations. In the process of writing history and testing literary methods for its presentation, he comes to discover something of its unique nature.

II. THE STUART VOLUMES: CHARACTER VERSUS NARRATIVE

Hume is attracted to great figures in history because he believes at first that a scrutiny of them can be a species of causal explanation. As he says in "Of The Rise of Progress of the Arts and Sciences": "Had HARRY IV, Cardinal RICHELIEU, and LOUIS XIV, been SPANIARDS; and PHILIP II, III, and IV, and CHARLES II, been FRENCHMEN, the history of these two nations had been intirely reversed."[14]

But only in the Stuart volumes does Hume seem to treat the "character" as an accurate transcript of human personality and a sufficient explanation for human action. He finds in practice that the use of the "character" often conflicts with his commitment to the chronological flow of history and the measured detachment of his narrative voice. When a "character" appears in the later volumes, we sense keenly the gap between the seemingly complete explanation it offers and the vagaries of action for which it must account. Finally, in the medieval volumes, the character sketch loses its primacy as a tool for understanding history; it becomes instead an attempt to appreciate the individual nature of a historical figure. The individual need not finally be a "hero" to attract Hume's attention, for Hume is no longer interested in the causal potency claimed for such descriptions; he uses them instead for the insight into the variety of human character they can give.

Hume's first uses of the character sketch seem to draw upon earlier methods of history-writing. Joseph Hall and John Earle brought together the Theophrastan character, which represented the stereotype through a picture of an individual, and the English homiletic tradition, which delighted in the human representation of vices and virtues.[15] From such sources David Nichol Smith traces the character sketch to its prominent role in the historical works of seventeenth-century England.[16] Although the "character" had traditionally exemplified universal moral types, Nichol Smith points out that it was used primarily in history-writing to vary and thereby improve historical narrative. It became a device to extend the range of history beyond the chronologies and annals which were the common productions of the medieval period. The presence of detailed human figures could dramatize and shape what might otherwise be a plodding or disjointed narrative. The moral content of the "character" could concomitantly function as a bridge between the older typological histories and the new emphasis on the actions of great men.

But aesthetic devices easily develop into philosophical statements, especially if they, like the "character," come from a tradition in which moral value is important. What in one author may be a literary method introduced to vary the texture of the narrative may in another become an epistemological statement about the materials of truth itself. The extensive citation of contemporary prophecy can lead into or reflect a belief in the providential interpretation of history. The reliance upon oration and the character sketch as dramatic devices are similarly related to a belief that the figure of the hero, the public man, is centrally important to the structure of history.[f] To understand history you must understand character. Clarendon's *History of the Rebellion,* with its many portraits of the principals in the civil wars, set much of the tone for the eighteenth-century use of the "character." Some critics have charged that Clarendon used the character sketch so extensively because his main purpose was not to understand history but to exonerate the actions of himself and his friends.[17] But Clarendon's emphasis on character actually continues his interest in the relation between personal code and public action: the personal loyalties of Englishmen to their king should have prevented their rebellion. Clarendon notes that one of the main indications of the chaos of the period is the inability of men to keep their word. Personal consistency and integrity is a trait to be honored in Royalist and Parliamentarian alike, for in a world of institutional chaos, personal oaths and personal loyalty represent the only kind of ethical and historical continuity that survives. If such loyalty is preserved, it can be the means to institutional regeneration.

The way men react to their times embodies some important historical truth about those times. Clarendon says in his

---

[f] D. T. Starnes points out the precedent in classical historians for the use of oration, prophecy, and character sketch by Renaissance and later historians. See "Purpose in the Writing of History," *MP*, 20 (1923), p. 298. Hume uses the first and third; perhaps the second is replaced by his narrative voice.

opening paragraphs that in his history there would be no more talk of individuals "than as the mention of their virtues and vices is essential to the work in hand." Yet a few paragraphs later these virtues and vices seem the most operative of all causes in public life:

> . . . the pride of this man, and the popularity of that; the levity of one, and the morosity of another; the excess of the court in the greatest want, and the parsimony and retention of the country in the greatest plenty; the spirit of craft and subtlety in some, and the rude and unpolished integrity of others, too much despising craft or art, like so many atoms contributing jointly to this mass of confusion now before us (I, i, p. 4) .

Men change allegiances because of insults or slights, imagined or true. The greatest events are caused by the sense of what Clarendon calls "disobligation" in one man or the chance family relationships of another. The emphasis on the character sketch involves less self-serving apologetics than it does Clarendon's belief in the directly operative role of individuals in public affairs and his feeling that the most important problem during the period of the civil wars was the attempt made by public figures like himself to integrate individual conscience and public service.[g] For Clarendon individual interest should ideally and actually be directly translatable into public good. He dwells upon the individual defections from King or Parliament because such men have not been able to accomplish the transition from private to public interest with his ideal facility. If history is to have a didactic as well as an apologetic function, it must

[g] For a suggestive treatment of Clarendon and the group of parliamentary royalists for which he was the spokesman, see Irene Coltman, *Private Men and Public Causes* (London, 1962) . Trevor-Roper calls Clarendon's emphasis on character the mark of a practical as opposed to an academic historian: "Where the cloistered ideologue tends to see the cause of revolution in the workings of Providence, or the Dialectic, the politician tends to see it in the somnolence of a minister during a vital meeting or the delay, or re-drafting, of an important message" ("Clarendon," p. 35) .

furnish examples of both good and bad political behavior. The best of the good examples in Clarendon's history is his own combination of the privileged participant and the detached historian. In the dual literary history of the "character," these examples embody both pragmatic political precept and abstract moral injunction. While narrative emphasizes the continuity that the historian has achieved, character sketches indicate the values he wishes to enshrine.

Although Clarendon's "characters" may exemplify his belief that niggling personal causes impel the great events of history, they nevertheless fail to "explain" either the great events or even the individual actions. Clarendon senses the unbridgeable gap between the character sketch of an individual and the actions of his life. Individual quirks may influence events, but they do not imply the conscious exercise of will. In some of his most frequent metaphors Clarendon recounts the way men become locked into the chain of their own votes, or lost in the labyrinth of their actions. After a commission or a council meets to deliberate some great issue, Clarendon will present sketches of the commissioners or councillors. But the reader emerges from these sketches no more enlightened than before. To observe the avarice of a certain duke implies no ability to predict where that avarice might lead him. Character is a nonce continuity, an eddy in the rush of narrative, an attempt to make momentary sense of otherwise arbitrary causes. In the early books of *The History of the Rebellion* it is at best only a flat summation, and characters are readily summoned forth, in the manner of the *Iliad*, at the point of death. In the later books, Clarendon seems to have decided that his own survival, after the long rush of history, is all the continuity he needs, contemplating time and deciding what is relevant to his story. Characters therefore appear when they have made a figure in his narrative, rather than when they die. Instead of supplying causal links, they convey tone and atmosphere. In the tradition of earlier histories, they become isolated "images of virtue . . . to transmit to posterity." The most extensive "character" in the early volumes is that of his friend Falkland, who died too early, and whose entire life as retold by Clarendon shows how sublimely unfit he was for the times in which he lived. But in the later books the celebration of Falkland's anachronistic grandeur has given way to Clarendon's grudging admiration for Cromwell, the man for the times, whose character must be expressed in paradoxes and whose actions encompass what is contradictory.

Hume's own use of the "character" has something of the flavor of Clarendon's ambiguous practice. But at first he places more weight on its pretensions to causal explanation. The character sketch may be the proper way to structure the events of history beyond a merely annalistic presentation, and an emphasis on great figures may help to explain the dynamic of history. In 1755 Hume had written to Adam Smith about the account of the 1641 Irish Rebellion in the *History*:

> Your Objection to the Irish Massacre is just; but falls not on the Execution but the Subject. Had I been to describe the Massacre of Paris, I should not have fallen into that Fault: But in the Irish Massacre no single eminent Man fell, or by a remarkable Death.[18]

For most of the Stuart volumes Hume seems to believe that moral action is the center of history, and history, therefore, is best understood as a complex of consciously and unconsciously willed events, all ultimately effected by distinct personalities. Because character is so important, it must be closely scrutinized. When the scrutiny becomes refined by the methods of abstract moral philosophy, greater causal force is ascribed to the individual. The private qualities of a king can characterize his whole reign. In this way Hume invokes the "indolence" of James I, the "haste" of Charles I, and the "lenity" of Charles II. The great figures of history are the key to causal explanation.

Hume does appear to be aware of the problems of this chosen method. When he presents a "character" in the Stuart volumes, it is difficult to escape the impression that he implies a causal certainty in order to try out the emphasis on character as a historical method, to see if it serves well to explain the causal chains that he believes it is the historian's duty to analyze. After all, the very nature of monarchical government makes one emphasize the influence of the monarch's character and, by extension, the characters of his followers or opponents. When the character of a public man is assessed, a relation between the individual and public events is necessarily implied. An understanding of the motives for individual behavior might plausibly afford a start for the understanding of political problems: "The movements of great states are often directed by as slender springs as those of individuals" (V, lx, p. 427). In the language of sixteenth-century political theory, for example, the analysis of the character of the king's mortal body private could shed light upon the nature of his immortal body politic.[19] In order to explore the possibilities of this relation, Hume may in the Stuart volumes imply a greater coherence and consistency in individual character than he has previously asserted in his philosophy or will later accept in the *History* itself.[h]

Character as a key to understanding events is therefore greatly emphasized in these early volumes. For example, the character of the first Duke of Buckingham ("Headlong in his passions, and incapable equally of prudence and of dissimulation; sincere from violence rather than candor; expensive from profusion more than generosity. . . .") is closely

---

[h] This implied "consistency" becomes an issue even in Hume's consideration of minor figures. He thinks it peculiar, for example, that there was no indication in the early lives of the Gunpowder Plotters that they were capable of such a deed (IV, xlvi, p. 405). He is surprised by Bacon's anti-Catholic prejudice in the Somerset trial (IV, xlvii, p. 437) and by Milton's pamphleteering for the Puritans. Hume seems to believe at this point that all men of genius must necessarily possess a tolerant detachment equal to his own. He says about Milton: "It is . . . remarkable, that the greatest genius by far that shone out in England during this period, was deeply engaged with these fanatics, and even prostituted his pen in theological controversy, in factious disputes, and in justifying the most violent measures of the party" (V, lxii, p. 529).

followed by events in which his role and his actions can be explained with reference to his character (IV, xlix, pp. 475–82). Such a juxtaposition can serve the function of irony: Buckingham schemes and tries to control, but Hume's analysis of his character and subsequent events shows how Buckingham himself is controlled by his passions and predilections. But obvious distortions often result. The emphasis upon the individual nature of Buckingham overvalues the importance of his rivalry with Richelieu for the favor of the French queen in causing the brief England-France segment of the Thirty Years' War (V, 1, p. 28). Such an interpretation accords with the belief in the role of the individual will in foreign affairs that Hume asserted in "Of the Rise and Progress of the Arts and Sciences."[1] But it is also a clear distortion of what actually occurred.

Some of Hume's assertions of the causal links between character and action are more illuminating and scant other factors less. For example, here is his analysis of an action by the Duke of Montrose: "Some of his retainers having told him of a prophecy, that 'to him and him alone it was reserved to restore the king's authority in all his dominions,' he lent a willing ear to suggestions which, however ill grounded or improbable, were so conformable to his own daring character" (V, lx, p. 403). As this quotation indicates, the idea of character and the literary device of the "character" offer a method of ordering, at least momentarily, the irrational motivations that make men act as they do. Where action is often the result of impulse, such a means of ordering is one possible way to achieve understanding. When men believe character is a prime historical cause, the study of character may become crucial to the later historian, even if his own ideas about history are quite different.

[1] In that essay Hume remarks that "the foreign and violent" affairs of a state "are commonly produced by single persons, and are more influenced by whim, folly or caprice, than by general passions and interests" (*Essays*, p. 71). See the comments on this passage by Godfrey Davies in "Hume's History of the Reign of James I," *Elizabethan and Jacobean Studies presented to Frank Percy Wilson* (Oxford, 1959), pp. 243–44.

Hume's experiment with the causal relevance of character in history does seem in part also to be an effort to vary the dull progression of chronological narrative. Like Bolingbroke and Fielding, he has many harsh things to say about "mere chronologers." His own early use of chronological narrative is often flat and perfunctory. Early in the first volume of the *History* is a typical statement: "Next year [1608] presents us with nothing memorable . . ." (IV, xlvi, p. 411). He apologizes at many points for not following a strictly chronological progression, and he tends to use pure chronological connectives like "while," "now," "then," and "after." Although Hume may use their method, his argument with the chronologers, like Bolingbroke's, revolves around questions of relevance.[j] He bases his criticism on their refusal, as he saw it, to weight any fact in their accumulations. Only by complete inclusiveness do they sometimes turn up something of value.[k]

Although Hume's attack against "mere chronologers" reflects the beliefs of most of the "philosophical historians," it obviously conflicts with his own philosophical ideas about causality. If causality, as he said, is a mere euphemism for temporal sequence, the clearest order that a historian could assert is the strictly chronological. As the Stuart volumes go on, Hume begins to distrust the "character" as an appropriate and accurate causal nexus. Late in his *History* Hume characterizes history as a "collection of facts which are multiplying without end" and must be generalized in some way (II, xii, p. 1). His feeling for the vexed operation of cause has made him suspicious of the supposed

---

j For an expression of the common idea that Hume "disregarded accuracy" in his methods of composition, see Robin Winks, "Hume and Gibbon: A View from a Vantage," *Dalhousie Review*, *41* (1961), pp. 496–504. Hume is defended by John V. Price in *The Ironic Hume* (Austin, 1965), pp. 99. For a good example of Hume pursuing a fine point, see his discussion of the authenticity of the letter from Mary, Queen of Scots to Bothwell (IV, Note L, pp. 532–35).

k "The painful and laborious collector above cited [John Strype, author of *Ecclesiastical Memorials*], who never omits the most trivial matter, is the only person that has thought this memorable letter worthy of being transmitted to posterity" (III, xxxv, p. 379).

clarity that the "character" seemed to afford. Its balanced clauses and minute distinctions give the literary appearance of a cool and complete analysis of all possible factors. But uncertainties soon appear when character is juxtaposed with action.

The socio-cultural appendix, like the character sketch, is another means devised by Hume to vary the purely chronological organization of history. While the "character" was an older form, the "transactions," as Hume usually calls them, are an innovation, and prove to be a more viable way of opening up the chronologies of "eventish" history. In his first concluding summary of non-political and non-military history—the Appendix to the Reign of James I— Humes states flaty that he must pause to consider "government, manners, finances, arms, trade, learning. Where a just notion is not formed of these particulars, history can be little instructive, and often will not be intelligible" (IV, p. 496).[1]

The appendices have been criticized because of Hume's "inability" to integrate them more firmly into the narrative.[20] But in the course of the *History*, these sections change too. In the Stuart volumes they are composed primarily of the materials that the great actors worked upon. Later, as Hume de-emphasizes the direct causal relevance of individual character, these sections achieve a coherence of their own; even though the appendices remain undramatic and unclearly organized, they still encompass the special details of an age. In the Stuart appendices there are bare lists of the names of government officials, without any analysis of function, as if to show that the continuity of the government

[1] When William Robertson wrote to ask for suggestions about a history of the age of Leo X, Hume cautioned: "But how can you acquire Knowledge of the great Works of Sculpture, Architecture, Painting, by which the Age was chiefly distinguished? Are you versd in all the Anecdotes of the Italian Literature?" (Klibansky and Mossner, *New Letters*, p. 46). To consider the age of Charles V also required legal training: "A competent Knowledge, at least, is required of the State and the Constitution of the Empire, of the several Kingdoms of Spain, of Italy, of the Low Countries; which it would be the work of half a Life to acquire" (*New Letters*, p. 48).

was in the procession of individuals in office. In later "transactions" such lists disappear as Hume concerns himself with the functions of offices, not individuals.

The movement of the "transactions," the accumulation of fact and detail, is closer to the spirit of chronology than is the character sketch. Hume turns away from the character sketch as a literary method and a historical truth because he feels the importance in history of the accumulations of time, the force of "mere chronology." In the medieval volumes he emphasizes the continuity of historical narrative at the expense of the outstanding historical character. His own voice supplies the coherence that history demands. As the rush of narrative moves by the reader, it is no longer important to emphasize specific figures. Shadowy personages, like a certain Edric, drift in and out of a one-hundred-and-fifty-page account of fifty years of medieval history. Hume has begun to understand chronology as an essential part of history rather than something that is aesthetically inconvenient and must be gotten over through the dramatics of character sketches.

But in the Stuart volumes this view is still emerging. Hume later will withdraw his narrative voice to allow the slow accretions of time to shape history. For the moment, however, we sense only his uneasiness with a heavy reliance on the power of character in history. In the Stuart volumes he is also uneasy with chronological organization because it is undirected and reveals no truth. Hume's standard of coherence is instead the "mixed" government that he repeatedly asserts is the "peculiar genius" of England. He believes that in his own time the mixture of power in English government is as perfect as it could be, a precise limitation of authority, yet without strict lines of demarcation between groups.[m] Whatever in the seventeenth century con-

---

[m] "Perhaps the English is the first mixed government where the authority of every part has been very accurately defined; and yet there still remains many very important questions between the two houses, that, by common consent, are buried in a discreet silence" (V, Note K, p. 544).

tributed toward that mixed form he applauds; whatever threatened to upset the balance he deplores. Although he never asserts it, Hume implies that the movement toward a "mixed" government may be an entelechy in history itself, rather than a form imposed to make events more understandable. At best Hume decides that most of his major actors have "mixed" characters, just like the government he so praises.[n] Only the distortions of factions have made them caricatures of good and evil. A simple view of causality might enjoy such oversimplification. But Hume's characters, unlike the balanced and mixed state, are often confused in their motives and interests. Once again, his philosophy undermines his method.

Hume is of course aware that he is trying to balance almost opposing views of history:

> With regard to politics and the character of princes and great men, I think I am very moderate. My views of *things* are more comfortable to Whig principles; my representations of *persons* to Tory prejudices. Nothing can so much prove that men commonly regard more persons than things, as to find that I am commonly numbered among the Tories.[21]

The Tory view of history concentrated upon personalities, while the Whig emphasized the teleological growth of abstract principles, like liberty.[22] Both parties arose in the civil wars as parties of principle. But, as they developed, each began to caricature its own point of view; the Whigs searched out the principle of liberty on every page of English history, while the Tories believed all precedent rested in the actions of past monarchs. Hume hopes that his narrative detachment can balance these two views, but his attempt to show how individual action was directly responsi-

[n] For a similar statement of the analogy between a mixed government and a balance of humours, see "The Character of a Trimmer" in *The Complete Works of George Savile, Marquess of Halifax*, ed. Walter Raleigh (Oxford, 1912), p. 103: ". . . our Laws are Trimmers, between the Excess of Unbounded Power, and the Extravagance of Liberty not enough restrained."

ble for the growth of laws and institutions increasingly conflicts with some of his basic philosophical ideas. To postulate that individual action is the most important kind of
cause can solve many problems of historical reconstruction
and explanation. Even though history supposedly concerns
itself with general causes, we must examine the individual to see the often irrational and idiosyncratic motives
which caused them to act and thereby contribute to general
causes. But what then is more important: the general cause
or the causative individual? Which comes first? Is the character sketch merely a stab at the ultimately unsystematiza-
ble, an attempt to give the impression of grappling with a
complex system of causes by labelling it "Charles I"? Are
the psychological observations in the "character" circular,
supposedly drawn from events, then reimposed to interpret events? In order to observe these tensions at closer
range in the Stuart volumes of Hume's *History*, let us examine closely his treatment of Oliver Cromwell.

ON THE LEVEL of direct assertion, Hume's portrait of Cromwell appears irremediably inconsistent: he says on one page
what he denies a few pages later. The specific tension in
Hume's interpretation is between agency and context, between causative character and the exigencies of circumstance, between Cromwell the long-range plotter and
Cromwell the opportunist. Hume implies two contrasting
interpretations of Cromwell's ability to act that are reminiscent of the distinction between strategy and tactics in
military history: one emphasizes Cromwell's total planning
of his life; the other explains how he took advantage of
existing situations. Behind these two views of Cromwell's
actions are two views of Cromwell's character, one that
emphasizes hypocrisy and fanaticism and the other, balance
and control.
　The first view dramatically reflects Hume's general estimate of the fanaticism of the times. In one of the few specific presagings that appear in the *History* Hume first presents Cromwell as a young M. P. complaining about a

preacher of Popery: "It is amusing to observe the first words of this fanatical hypocrite correspond so exactly to his character" (V, li, p. 58). But when Hume begins to focus more extensively upon Cromwell, there is a hint that character may not necessarily be a perfect or inclusive guide to action: ". . . the strokes of his character are as open and strongly marked, as the schemes of his conduct were, during the time, dark and impenetrable" (V, lxi, p. 289).

Hume implies here that if people had clearly seen Cromwell's character, they would have been able to understand and even foretell his devious plans. Accordingly, he continues to depict Cromwell as an "artful and audacious conspirator" who deviously plots so he can "secretly pave the way for his future greatness" (V, lix, pp. 335, 336). Without documentation, for example, Hume asserts that Fairfax, while head of the Army, was completely subservient to the wishes of the second-in-command Cromwell. Although this conclusion draws on prevalent myths about Fairfax's character, it seems primarily derived from Hume's estimate of Cromwell's character and then adduced to support it; there is no analysis of Fairfax's own interests. While it is true that Fairfax was generally unpolitical, that does not necessarily imply Cromwell's complete control over him.º This side of Hume's interpretation of Cromwell parallels the general view of Julius Caesar held by the Augustans and most fully expressed in Conyers Middleton's *Life of Cicero* (1741).[23] Middleton assesses separate actions in terms of what he decides is the "grand purpose" of Caesar's life, giving consistent purpose to what may have actually been nonce decisions. Hume in this mood metaphorically

---

º Modern historians tend to believe that Fairfax and Cromwell generally agreed, whereas Hume would make Fairfax almost a crypto-Royalist who had however been overwhelmed by Cromwell's personality. For the fruitless later efforts of the Royalist leaders to penetrate "the wall of evasive neutrality surrounding Fairfax" in retirement at Nun Appleton, see David Underdown, *Royalist Conspiracy in England, 1649–1660* (New Haven, 1960). Hume tries further to imply Cromwell's complete control of events by asserting his direct agency in Cornet Joyce's seizure of the King (V, lix, p. 335).

emphasizes the series of visors before Cromwell's face, always a new one ready after the old is discovered (V, lix, p. 337).

But the strain of allowing such total manipulation to one man begins to show. Cromwell's consummately devious "character" reveals itself as an overly dramatic way of avoiding real analysis of the specific situations. Perhaps Hume recognizes that Cromwell's "irresistible" control is out of place in a history that purports to furnish materials for a philosophy of government. Elsewhere Hume says that forms of government are more important than administrators; if administration determined the nature of government, there would be no political disputes, only gossip about individuals:ᵖ "But, tho' a friend to *Moderation* I cannot forbear condemning this sentiment, and should be sorry to think, that human affairs admit of no greater stability, than what they receive from the casual humors and characters of particular men."

Hume had attacked the party historians for their purely teleological reading of history. Yet his presentation of Cromwell's character, following historiographical tradition, is exemplary, static, and determined by teleological considerations. Can he introduce a feeling for the vexed operations of process into his view of character as he had into his view of causality?

Hume begins to limit the Machiavellian interpretation of Cromwell's character by a greater attention to the context of his actions. Instead of totally foretelling and controlling action from the outside, Cromwell in this view takes advantage of situations through his understanding and adaptability:

Where delay was requisite, he could employ the most

ᵖ Compare Pope, *An Essay on Man*, III, ll. 303–04) : "For Forms of Government let fools contest;/ Whate'er is best administer'd is best. . . ." Pope later remarked that he did not mean that no form of government is preferable to any other, but that the best form, if corruptly administered, can be the most dangerous. See *The Poems of Alexander Pope*, ed. John Butt (New Haven, 1963) , pp. 534–35.

indefatigable patience; where celerity was necessary, he
flew to a decision. And thus by uniting in his person the
most opposite talents, he was enabled to combine the most
contrary interests in a subserviency to his secret
purposes (V, lix, p. 337).

"Secret purposes" still exist, but the outside world is now
more recalcitrant. Instead of completely manipulating Fairfax, Cromwell must argue and plead with him to lead an
army against the Scots (V, lx, pp. 410–11). Cromwell's
"new" character remains in his times, instead of standing
outside them. He is "suited to the age in which he lives"
(V, lx, p. 388), and it is "accident and intrigue" together
that made him the Cambridge member of the Long Parliament (V, lxi, p. 436).q These new judgments of Cromwell
also bring Hume to a new attack on past historians. His
sense of the process of change in context that characterizes
the actions of Cromwell leads him to question restrictive
"definitions" of Cromwell's character, even though they
are similar to those he had held himself. "Most historians"
have said that Cromwell was never sincere and in all his actions "thought of nothing but the establishment of his own
unlimited authority": "This opinion, so much warranted
by the boundless ambition and profound dissimulation of
his character, meets with ready belief; though it is more
agreeable to the narrowness of human views, and the darkness of futurity, to suppose that this daring usurper was
guided by events, and did not yet foresee, with any assur-
ance, that unparalleled greatness which he afterwards
attained" (V, lix, p. 347).

Despite such remarks, however, Hume's assessment does
not show a clear progression from Cromwell controlling to
Cromwell reacting. He tries to keep both interpretations

q Compare Hume's final remarks about Charles I: "Unhappily, his fate
threw him into a period, when the precedents of many former reigns
savored strongly of arbitrary power, and the genius of the people ran
violently toward liberty" (V, lix, pp. 379–80). This contrast is similar
to that implied by Clarendon in his characters of Falkland and Cromwell. See above, p. 44.

in solution, but just as often they separate. Hume refers almost epithetically to "the uncontrollable fury of [Cromwell's] zeal" (V, lxi, p. 437), even while he continues to emphasize Cromwell's measure and control. He shows Cromwell trying out different methods of rule and says that he had "no deliberate plan" except experiment in calling the Parliament which he later dismissed (V, lxi, p. 444). Yet he goes on to stigmatize the checks and balances that Cromwell instituted between power groups as "probably nothing but covers to his ambition . . ." (V, lxi, p. 448).

All these mismatching judgments seem to derive from Hume's unsureness about the "consistency" of Cromwell's character. At this point in his *History* Hume is so committed, either through his authorities, his philosophy, or a mixture, to the total influence of fanaticism on character that he dismisses as "inconsistent" what does not "fit." Unlike Clarendon, he is at this point not ready to deal with the way Cromwell's character integrates contrarieties. He mentions, for example, a few instances of Cromwell's love for practical jokes, in contrast to his normal dignity: "That vein of frolic and pleasantry which made a part, however inconsistent, of Cromwell's character, was apt sometimes to betray him into other inconsistencies, and to discover itself even where religion might seem to be a little concerned" (V, lxi, p. 470).[r] The anecdote that follows hardly seems "inconsistent" except to one who looks for the unity of mathematical logic in a biographical sketch. The belief that character is an important and ascertainable cause in history has bred an insistence upon a simplistic integration of traits. Hume avoids dealing with real contraries and qualifications of character. Although he is a little more com-

---

[r] Compare Pope, *Moral Essay I*, ll. 146–47: "What made (say Montagne, or more sage Charron!) /Otho a warrior, Cromwell a buffoon?" Gibbon is more magnanimous in his similar remarks on Constantine: "He delighted in the social intercourse of familiar conversation; and, though he might sometimes indulge his disposition to raillery with less reserve than was required by the severe dignity of his station, the courtesy and liberality of his manners gained the hearts of all who approached him" (Bury ed., II, xviii, p. 215).

fortable with the simple and balanced contrast between public dignity and private joking, it is still an "inconsistency."[8]

But the most relevant point to be made about Hume's method from this example is that he included it. Feeling uneasy about sketching Cromwell and his activities as philosophical demonstrations of "truths" about human nature and political power, Hume introduces what he thinks might be relevant to a total view of Cromwell, however "inconsistent" it might seem. Cromwell is a "singular personage" (V, lxi, p. 470), parts of whose character could motivate either panegyric or invective (V, lxi, p. 486). Hume, in his *History*, has, however, undertaken to keep his distance from "all Party & Dependance, from all Satyre and Panegric."[24] Hume never resolves the paradoxical elements of "penetration" and "absurdity" that he finds in Cromwell's character, and he remains puzzled by the mixture of fanaticism and ambition with a regard for justice and humanity (V, lxi, p. 489). But he places these disparate elements side by side in his *History*. Character can explain and be explained only so much. Hume has quickly reached the point beyond which it is inadequate. Human character in the Stuart volumes is usually a mixture rather than a reconciliation of psychological traits. The character of Cromwell marks a growing tension between the isolated and static character sketch and the contextual and changing character. So long as Cromwell or any other figure is considered as a psychological type, it is possible to make exaggerated claims for his power to control and to cause. Once the context of contemporary details and circumstances is

---

[8] W. B. Gallie offers another formulation of this problem: ". . . it is worth noticing . . . that an individual's capacity to conceive of his life as a fulfillment of a particular destiny (which means, virtually, a role in a particular story) may be a necessary condition of his being able to exploit the opportunities which the situations facing him have to offer" (*Philosophy and the Historical Understanding*, p. 116).

brought in, the belief in the totally causative individual can no longer be so absolute.[t]

But there remains an irresolvable opposition between the history that concentrates on heroes and that, like Hume's, which supports the virtues of essentially non-dramatic narrative. The bold character with his egregious heroic traits disrupts what Hume decides is the best and most normal pattern of historical movement—the order of chronology and the stable calmness of his own narrative detachment.[u] Hume's uneasiness about the heroic figure reflects his growing feeling that causes in history grow by slow accretion, rather than by violent, self-dramatizing acts. The traditional heroes of history are too flamboyant and too self-centered to contribute to the public good.[v] They disrupt the state as they disrupt the calm movement of time. Hume seems also to identify the self-dramatizing individual in history with the self-dramatizing historian. He attacks the idea of the totally controlling hero because such a conception disregards the calm detachment of his own inclusive vision. Understanding can achieve a greater control than action.

[t] One might compare the typical satirical view, exemplified in Pope's "characters," which sees at once the power of the character at close range and its place in a larger plan of which it is totally unaware: " 'Tis but by parts we follow good or ill, / For, Vice or Virtue, Self directs it still; / Each individual seeks a sev'ral goal; / But HEAV'N'S great view is One, and that the Whole: / That counter-works each folly and caprice; / That disappoints th'effect of ev'ry vice . . ." (An Essay on Man, II, ll. 235–40). It might be argued that Hume's work brings into history an appreciation for complex character previously developed only by imaginative writers. See, for example, the relation between his view of Shaftesbury and Dryden's in Absalom and Achitophel, below, p. 62.

[u] "The unhappy prepossession which men commonly entertain in favor of ambition, courage, enterprise, and other warlike virtues, engages generous natures, who always love fame, in such pursuits as destroy their own peace, and that of the rest of mankind" (IV, xlvii, p. 425).

[v] Compare Letwin, The Pursuit of Certainty, on Hume's stand against "heroism" in politics (pp. 96–97) and his dislike for Chatham, the "man with a mission" (p. 107). Compare also Bolingbroke's remark that the interests of particular men work against the interests of the public, above, p. 23.

Hume's preliminary stress on the character of the heroic individual had seemed to solve the causal problem he posed in the *Enquiry*:

> . . . upon the whole, there appears not, thro' all nature, any one instance of connexion, which is conceivable by us. All events seem entirely loose and separate. One event follows another; but we can never observe any tye betwixt them. They seem *conjoined*, but never *connected*.[25]

Human personality was both the key to immediate causes and a means of unifying the undifferentiated congeries of circumstance and event that is the past:

> Would you know the sentiments, inclinations, and course of life of the GREEKS and ROMANS? Study well the temper and actions of the FRENCH and ENGLISH. You cannot be much mistaken in transferring to the former *most* of the observations, which you have made with regard to the latter. Mankind are so much the same, in all times and places, that history informs us of nothing new or strange in this particular. Its chief use is only to discover the constant and universal principles of human nature, by shewing men in all varieties of circumstances and situations, and furnishing us with materials, from which we may form our observations, and become acquainted with the regular springs of human action and behavior. These records of wars, intrigues, factions, and revolutions, are so many collections of experiments, by which the politician or moral philosopher fixes the principles of his science; in the same manner as the physician or natural philosopher, becomes acquainted with the nature of plants, minerals, and other external objects, by the experiments, which he forms concerning them.[26]

Hume's "static" character sketches had been an effort to explain retrospectively the vagaries of individual personality through the discovery of uniformities and types. But this effort loses much of its urgency when Hume begins to believe that character is not the only or even a major cause in history. The great men of history, the kind of men Hume finally admires in the Stuart volumes, are the men of moderation—Bishop William Juxon, Admiral Blake, General Monk—who possessed "disinterested zeal" and contributed to the smooth running of a state too often disrupted by a profusion of drama, gestures, and striking personalities. Hume praises those who contribute to stability rather than excess.[w] Their moderation mirrors his own narrative detachment, his own attempt to balance judgments. They rose above the party squabbles of their own times as he hopes to transcend those of his. The idea of a past filled with notable events and exemplary individuals gives way to a past defined by movement, process, and the tangled accumulation of causes. Hume's commitment to chronological narrative has begun to override his first emphasis on the operative power of human character. He becomes more interested in the way individuals can be metaphors for their times, and in the relation between the individual and his age.

The two most important manifestations of Hume's growing emphasis on context in the Stuart volumes are the appeals to "necessity" to explain action and "sincerity" to exonerate character. Both words indicate an effort to appreciate deeper levels of motivation, where what might on the surface seem more calculation and self-interest are shown to be the result of genuine beliefs, whether rationally or irrationally based. The recourse to "necessity" appears only sparsely in the Stuart volumes. Perhaps the most outstanding examples are, as might be expected, in the explanations for Cromwell's assumption of the Protectorship:

> Had Cromwell been guilty of no crime but this temporary usurpation, the plea of necessity and public good, which

[w] For a similar Augustan attitude toward heroism, see Martin Price, *Swift's Rhetorical Art* (New Haven, 1953), pp. 103–104: ". . . there is a heroic ideal implied throughout [Swift's] works. It is a heroism of moderation." ". . . the heroes of moderation are singular only in their resistance to tyranny, whether of a man or a faction."

he alleged, might be allowed, in every view, a reasonable excuse for his conduct (V, lxi, p. 446).

His subsequent usurpation was the effect of necessity, as well as of ambition; nor is it easy to see how the various factions could at that time have been restrained, without a mixture of military and arbitrary authority (V, lxi, p. 489).[x]

For a moment at least Cromwell has become one of Hume's heroes of moderation, seeking to quiet rather than raise faction and dissension. A similar mutation takes place in Hume's account of the relation between the motives and the actions of the religious "fanatics" of the time. He at first calls them "hypocrites" because he believes their religious protestations often veil private interest. But again there occurs a gradual movement from deploring and dismissal to an understanding of sincerely held beliefs.[y] Even though Hume never really succeeds in fully appreciating the impulses of a deeply religious faith, he comes to see that it is not all "hypocrisy": "The murder of the king, the most atrocious of all [Cromwell's] actions, was to him covered under a mighty cloud of republican and fanatical illusions; and it is not impossible, but he might believe it, as many others did, the most meritorious action that he could perform" (V, lxi, p. 489).

Hume's method in the Stuart volumes, by its air of balance and completeness, has often implied that virtues and

---

[x] Hume here harkens back to one of his old ideals through a different route. In a passage cancelled from the original Stuart volume of 1754 he remarks that a consideration of "the philosophy of government" will tend to quiet party disputes about personality because it shows "that those events, which they impute to their adversaries as the deepest crimes, were the natural, if not the necessary result of the situation, in which the nation was placed, during any period." Quoted by Mossner, "Was Hume a Tory Historian?" p. 234. Historical relativism has paradoxically taken the place of generalized precept.

[y] This view naturally goes counter to those who believe Hume remained intolerant of religionists and could never understand the motivations of the Puritan party. A similar development of understanding can be observed in Gibbon, who has of course received similar criticism. See below, pp. 247–48.

vices can really be pinpointed and arranged. The thematic introduction of necessity and sincerity shows that the balance may not be so clear. In Hume's note on the character of Hampden, he is clearly aware of the presence of the same kind of "inconsistencies" he found in the character of Cromwell. But he also clearly admits now that his versions of character are more often literary construction than complete and final assessments: "But whether, in the pursuit of this violent enterprise, he was actuated by private ambition or by honest prejudices, derived from the former exorbitant powers of royalty, it belongs not to an historian of this age, scarcely even to an intimate friend, positively to determine" (V, lxi, p. 247). Hume remarks that some readers have construed this note to mean an approval of Hampden's actions and a disapproval of his intentions. But the truth, he says, is that ". . . as they were derived from good motives, only pushed to an extreme, there is room left to believe that the intentions of that patriot, as well as many of his party, were laudable" (V, Note M, p. 545).

But, continues Hume, the actions of the King himself can also be justified from necessity and "a natural desire of defending that prerogative which was transmitted to him from his ancestors." Sincerity does not totally rule out judgment by the historian, for extreme measures can still be deplored: "The worst of it is that there was a great tang of enthusiasm in the conduct of the parliamentary leaders, which, though it might render their conduct sincere, will not much enhance their character with posterity" (V, Note M, p. 545).

The criteria of sincerity and necessity do imply that the past has a uniqueness that history should be able to take into account. The voice of absolute judgment has dropped back. Extenuation appears, and the historian has to admit he hesitates before actually going into the mind of a historical personage.

In the course of the Stuart volumes character has therefore become less and less an appropriate answer to the problems of history, in great part because Hume has come to believe individuals create the problems in history. In the first part of the Stuart volumes Hume could make an almost strictly causal relation between character and general history:

> From the mixed character, indeed, of Charles [I], arose in part the misfortunes in which England was at this time involved. His political errors, or rather weaknesses, had raised him inveterate enemies: his eminent moral virtues had procured him zealous partisans, and between the hatred of the one, and the affections of the other, was the nation agitated with the most violent convulsions (V, lx, pp. 224–25).

But the force of that qualifying "in part" becomes stronger and stronger. The comment on Hampden comes only a few pages later. By the time Hume considers the reign of Charles II, he is no longer prepared to couch his ideas in such strict terms. While considering Shaftesbury, he invokes previous methods of literary and psychological balance in the estimate of character, but then focuses on their inadequacies—the actual gap between motives and actions, between character and its external expression:

> It is remarkable, that this man, whose principles and conduct were in all other respects so exceptionable, proved an excellent chancellor; and that all his decrees, while he possessed that high office, were equally remarkable for justness and for integrity: so difficult is it to find in history a character either wholly bad or perfectly good; though the prejudices of party make writers run easily into the extreme both of panegyric and satire (VI, lxix, p. 262).[z]

The character of Charles II presents similar problems: "If we survey the character of Charles II, in the different lights which it will admit of, it will appear various, and give rise

[z] Dryden of course recognizes the "consistency" of the character of Shaftesbury in *Absalom and Achitophel*. See footnote t, above.

to different and even opposite sentiments" (VI, lxix, p. 281).
Such ambiguity increases our feeling for the human complexity of a historical character, but its presence severely
qualifies our ability to assign character an important causal
role. Accordingly, Hume's frequent reference to Charles
II's "lenity" to characterize his reign has little of the controlling power of his previous use of James I's "indolence"
or Charles I's "haste."[a] Literary effects have been taken
from the analytic realm and restored to the impressionistic
and metaphoric. Since human character need not stand as a
total cause, it can be appreciated for its variety. The urge
to see man the same, "in all times and places," fades away.
Hume appreciates both the anecdotal Plutarch and a more
serious Plutarch, who emphasizes the vexed relation of vices
and virtues in a single person, and their uncertain relation
to his actions.[b]

Although "necessity" and "sincerity" may first be attempts to break from the straitjacket of the "character,"
they also foreshadow Hume's later concentration on two
new thematic preoccupations: the submersion of individual
interest in community good and the reassertion of private

[a] Hume's first glimpse of Charles II similarily provides impression
rather than analysis: "He possessed a vigorous constitution, a fine
shape, a manly figure, a graceful air; and though his features were
harsh, yet was his countenance in the main lively and engaging" (VI,
lxiii, p. 1). Compare Halifax's "A Character of King Charles II" in
Raleigh, *Works of Halifax*, pp. 187–208. Halifax includes no physical
description at all. Compare also Hume's description of Henry V, one
of the few others in his *History*: "The exterior figure of this great
prince, as well as his deportment, was engaging. His stature was somewhat above the middle size; his countenance beautiful; his limbs gen-
teel and slender, but full of vigor; and he excelled in all warlike and
manly exercises" (II, xix, p. 370). Also in this vein are the descriptions
of Joseph Andrews and Fanny Goodwill. See discussion below, pp.
102–03.
[b] Hume still enjoyed the frivolous side of biography and could write
to Robertson: "Were you to write the Life of Henry the 4th of France
after [the model of Plutarch], you might pillage all the pretty Stories
in Sully, & speak more of his Mistresses than of his Battles" (Klibansky and Mossner, *New Letters*, p. 49; written April 1759). But despite
what he may enjoy in reading history, Hume has seen the inadequacies
of this method for understanding the past.

values in public life. As we have seen, the argument from necessity is closely related to an argument from social utility. The zeal Hume desires is a zeal for community good. In "That Politics May be Reduced to a Science" he says that in a free state the people must, "with the utmost ZEAL," maintain ". . . those forms and institutions by which liberty is secured, the public good consulted, and the avarice or ambition of particular men restrained and punished."[27] A merely private virtue like friendship, if it is without regard for community or public spirit, is completely useless. Hume concludes that " . . . perhaps the surest way of producing moderation in every party is to increase our zeal for the public." Zeal for public good contributes to a smoothly running state; it also contributes to a smoothly flowing narrative. There may be a place for the public man in such theories, but not for the kind of public men Hume observes in the Stuart volumes. He concentrates instead on the abuses that private individuals inflict upon public affairs. Despite the many indications that Hume is experimenting with more complex ideas of human character, he still allows too much weight to the individual will, although it is now a disrupter of the proper order of things rather than the source of truth about the movements of history.

Both individual interest and religious fervor could be equally inimical to the orderly growth of the state. In later volumes Hume is better able to accept the whims of individuals as only one of the many causal streams in the flow of history. But in the Stuart volumes, except for the declining emphasis on the causal power of character, there is no clear indication as yet where Hume will go. The mere fact that he decides to consider the Tudor period next indicates that the attribution of causal power to individuals is less than an adequate solution. There may be something in chronology itself that secretes meaning and relevance beyond detached exempla and "characters."

Hume's stylistic principles of moderation and balance are an attempt to provide a coherence for history. At first he uses the device of contraries: the juxtaposition of opposing arguments, the balancing of opposing character traits, the arraying of unweighted and sometimes contradictory causes. When, in the Stuart volumes, Hume attempts a resolution of the contraries, it is often oversimplified. But in later volumes, as he works out different implications of the principles of moderation and balance, he becomes more and more comfortable with what he had previously called "inconsistency." In the Stuart volumes he works with a received tradition of historiography. He is committed to rethinking the materials of history, but without a specific program. He is against the party historians and their assertion that history has a plot, with heroes and villains, that necessarily leads up to the controversies of the present. But he experiments with their dramatic method and concentrates on the great disruptive personalities and their supposed ability to effect and control. In the process of writing Hume comes, however, to rest value in principles that are opposed to the heroic and character-oriented conception of history. His problem is to define his own voice, and thereby to ascertain how a historian chooses and arranges the materials of history for best effect. What he values in his own approach to history becomes translated into what he values in history. In all the rush of the Stuart volumes, the historical and stylistic value that emerges is stability. Hume's estimate of Richard Cromwell gives a hint of how the historian and literary stylist may best deal with this value: "His social virtues, more valuable than the greatest capacity, met with a recompense more precious than noisy fame, and more suitable—contentment and tranquillity" (V, lxii, p. 494).

But before the value of such virtues can be firmly asserted, a continuing frame for them must be found. The Tudor volumes find this frame in the slowly accumulating body of laws.

III. THE REIGN OF THE TUDORS AND THE CONTINUITY OF LAW

As I have tried to indicate above, Hume's thoughts about history do not develop systematically. His major beliefs about human nature and politics were probably substantially the same at the beginning of the *History* as at the end. But his emphasis does change. He continually redefines the relation between his philosophical beliefs and the appropriate way of presenting historical materials to an audience; and he further strengthens the role of his narrative detachment. When he first begins to write the *History,* Hume perceives a distinction between his general beliefs and his literary method. In a letter dated September 1, 1754, he answers charges of religious libertinism in the first volume: " . . . I cannot tell, but you will see little or no occasion for any such imputation in this work, I composed it *ad populum,* as well as *ad clerum,* and thought, that scepticism was not in its place in an historical production."[28]

Hume's early emphasis on the extraordinary in personality and event severely limited any effort to achieve generalizations of human nature and politics. The Stuart volumes show the tension between these two approaches. Almost as if it were a remedy for the caprices of personality canvassed so diligently in the Stuart volumes, Hume introduces in the Tudor volumes a closer consideration of the slowly building structure of institutions and law.

Hume's political ideal is the state of laws, not of men. Law is the repository of the great generalizations and the great ideals for human behavior: "So great is the force of laws, and of particular forms of government, and so little dependence have they on the humors and tempers of men, that consequences almost as general and certain may be deduced from them, on most occasions, as any which the mathematical sciences afford us."[29]

Laws have the power not only to control, but potentially also to shape and improve a society, if they truly become guides for behavior:

The ages of the greatest public spirit are not always the most eminent for private virtue. Good laws may beget order and moderation in the government, where the manners and customs have instilled little humanity or justice into the tempers of men.[c]

Law corrects both the vagaries of the individual character and the traditions of antisocial irrationality. The history of the Stuarts showed how individual passions could overthrow and remake a society in which men no longer understood the guiding role of law. The emphasis on characters in literary structure reflected Hume's feeling for the way the rupture in society was a conflict between personality and law. Hume's famous critique of the inner orientation of the Puritans continues this antithesis. If history is to be truly didactic, it must concentrate on what is most important rather than what is most interesting or entertaining, on the accretions of day-to-day struggle rather than the violent gestures, on the undramatic plodding of legislation rather than the dramatic characters. The historian of the Tudor volumes emphasizes the business of making and appreciating law; the medieval volumes attempt to place man within the framework of law and time.

Hume's defense of the power of precedent is one reflection of the importance he rests in a legal system. Respect for precedent insures public peace and orderly, intelligible development. The lists of public officials in the Stuart volumes foreshadow Hume's concern in the Tudor volumes with the daily content of government. Near the end of the Stuart volumes Hume had commented on the distortions of faction that culminated in the Popish plot: " . . . however singular these events may appear, there is really nothing altogether new in any period of modern history . . . " (VI, lxxxi, p. 365). This is a strange statement for a historian to make, especially one who goes on to write four more

[c] *Essays*, p. 16. Laws can also be a key to manners for the historian. See I, Appendix I, p. 161 for an example of Hume's deduction of facts about social status among the Saxons by comparing laws and "the nature of things."

volumes of history. But Hume implies in the Tudor volumes that the "real" theme of history is the workings of law in each period. The history of human character in all ages and places is a history of discrete events and actions. Generalizations about character imply only a psychological coherence. But a study of the growth of law in government and its effects in society can discover a more purely historical coherence. In addition, such a study illustrates that stability can be achieved only when men support the system of law. The lesson of the Tudor volumes is that law is the most essential part of the modern state and should therefore be the part of history that should receive the most study and analysis.

Under the arching unity of law Hume more freely experiments with variety. The Tudor volumes form a transition to the medieval volumes in concerns and themes. The old themes are present, although transmuted; the new ones appear more and more frequently. General remarks about character, law, custom, religion, and philosophy of history are few. Yet these volumes are as long as the others. Hume in these middle volumes seems to be mounting an array of events and incidents, proclamations, treaties, and statutes to supply by mere bulk the gap of causation left by the change in attitude toward character. Digressions would make his own voice too apparent and he therefore emphasizes that he stays with a strictly narrative presentation, despite slight deviations (III, xxviii, p. 112; IV, xxxix, p. 113; IV, xl, p. 119). Before, great figures erupted, while the narrative flowed around them; now the historical personages are more subdued, and the flow of incident carries the force.

Toward the beginning of the Tudor volumes Hume comments on the "certainty" possible in this first period of "modern history" because of the abundance of material that the historian can select, adorn, and relate to the present (III, xxvi, p. 77). But this abundance yields a certainty of detail rather than interpretation. What happened receives more emphasis than who or what made it happen. The complications of cause and the concatenation of events receive more attention than they did in the Stuart volumes, where much space was devoted to such excursions into character as Charles II's adventures while in hiding. Hume rules out, for example, the degeneracy of Roman Catholicism as the sole cause of the Reformation: "A concurrence of incidents must have contributed to forward that great revolution" (III, xxix, p. 130). The causality of character is replaced in the Tudor volumes by a feeling for many possible contributing causes. Toward the end of these volumes Hume remarks on the "peculiar causes" in the situation and character of Henry VII that served to augment the authority of the crown. But he never specifies what they are. "The manners of the age," that is, the tendency of aristocratic luxury to diminish financial and thus political power, appears as a "general cause." But then the problem is glossed over: " . . . the further progress of the same causes begat a new plan of liberty, founded on the privileges of the commons" (IV, Appendix III, p. 374).

This flat statement indicates the general uneasiness with which Hume considers the Tudor era. His new emphasis on undramatic stability and everyday continuity has not quite allayed his older commitment to public history—the history of great events, political acts, and military maneuvers. He complains that the government of Elizabeth is so "peaceable and uniform" that it affords "few materials for history." Because of the "small part" Elizabeth took in foreign affairs, " . . . there scarcely passed any occurrence which requires a particular detail" (IV, xl, p. 72). Yet in this same volume Hume can cast doubt on the relevance, interest, and even importance of the public event. Trivial incidents, he says, can show the "manners of the age." These incidents "are often more instructive, as well as entertaining, than the great transactions of war and negotiations, which are nearly similar in all periods and all countries of the world" (IV, xxxvii, p. 41).[d] In his early theoretical

[d] In the medieval volumes Hume remarks that the really important aspects of a historical era, like the development of executive power,

statements Hume frequently mentioned the uniform human nature independent of time and country. Yet here he shows an almost exuberant desire to search for variety in the materials of the past and to discover the uniqueness of a historical period. It is the events of public life, the grand gestures of war and politics, that have become blandly uniform.

WHEN HUME DOES DEAL with historical personages, he shows a greater awareness of the complexities within their individual characters, and between their characters and events. His methods vary. Martin Luther appears as a neat balance of traits, while Henry VIII's "character" is more confused. Hume fits each for a special purpose.[30] The more formulaic portrait of Luther indicates, I think, how far Hume has come from the delicate balances of vices and virtues he attempted in the Stuart volumes. He is interested in Luther as an agent of the complex causes that brought about the Reformation rather than as an individual personality with ultimate causal power. Like Cromwell, Luther is, in Sidney Hook's phrase, an eventful man.[31] Hume recounts the abuses practiced in Roman Catholicism at the time, ending with the transfer of indulgence power from the Franciscans to the Dominicans. Then he turns to Luther: "All these circumstances might have given offence, but would have been attended with no event of any importance, had there not arisen a man qualified to take advantage of the incident" (III, xxix, p. 132). The rhythms of history are expressed through human actors, but not determined by them. As Hume remarks in another connection, "Fortune alone, without the concurrence of prudence and valor, never reared up of a sudden so great a power as that which centered in the emperor Charles [V]" (III, xxviii, p. 120).

can never be ascertained so much from great events or even public records ". . . as by small incidents in history, by particular customs, and sometimes by the reason and nature of things" (I, Appendix I, p. 165).

The simplicity of the "character" of Luther enables us to see transparently the movement of general causes in history. The character of Henry VIII, as if to afford an instructive contrast, prevents that king from appreciating and using the historical situation in which he finds himself. His very complexity thwarts appropriate action in the contention between Charles V and Francis I:

> Henry possessed the felicity of being able, both by the native force of his kingdom and its situation, to hold the balance between those two powers. . . . But this prince was in his character heedless, inconsiderate, capricious, impolitic; guided by his passions or his favorite; vain, imperious, haughty; sometimes actuated by friendship for foreign powers, oftener by resentment, seldom by his true interest. And thus, though he exulted in that superiority which his situation in Europe gave him, he never employed it to his own essential and durable advantage, or to that of his kingdom (III, xxviii, p. 121).

Cromwell also had a complex personality, but it was under his control. Henry's complication appears to be the result of fragmentation rather than real complexity. For that reason it is a useless tool for understanding the movement of the past. Instead, a sense of historical process must be used to understand his character: "It is so difficult to give a just summary of this prince's qualities: he was so different from himself in different parts of this reign, that as is well remarked by Lord Herbert, his history is his best character and description" (III, xxxiii, p. 308).

Hume does essay a character of Henry, but it quickly dissolves:

> A catalogue of his vices would comprehend many of the worst qualities incident to human nature: violence, cruelty, profusion, rapacity, injustice, obstinacy, arrogance, bigotry, presumption, caprice: but neither was he subject to all these vices in the most extreme degree, nor was he, at intervals, altogether destitute of virtues;

he was sincere, open, gallant, liberal, and capable of at least a temporary friendship and attachment (III, xxxiii, p. 309).

For the Hume of the Tudor volumes such observations are no longer related to either general causes or specific circumstances. He therefore concludes his summary of Henry's reign by concentrating on his actions and policies.

The "characters" of both Luther and Henry VIII are simplistic in different ways, one by its reductive motivation, the other by its unweighted inclusiveness. But both indicate something of what Hume believes is important or true in history. In their own ways both "characters" make the general forces that swirl around them clearer, unaffected by the intrinsic complexities of an actual personality. Both also indicate Hume's loss of interest in the causative role of character in history. Toward the end of the Tudor volumes he winds up a long consideration of Elizabeth's character only to obviate the relevance of such study. He no longer considers the analysis of private tempers and traits to be an important tool of the historian: " . . . the true method of estimating her merit, is to lay aside all these considerations, and consider her merely as a rational being placed in authority, and intrusted with the government of mankind. We may find it difficult to reconcile our fancy to her as a wife or a mistress; but her qualities as a sovereign, though with some considerable exceptions, are the object of undisputed applause and approbation" (IV, xliv, p. 343). Hume has as much trouble with the character of Elizabeth as he did with that of Cromwell. He cannot, for example, quite disentangle the threads of policy and personal emotion in Elizabeth's treatment of Mary, Queen of Scots. His sense of the relation of public and private life remains uncertain, and instead of including both possibilities, he irresolutely shifts back and forth.[32] But this uncertainty has a rationale: the impulse in the historian to pin down the elements of character in a historical personage is no longer very pressing.

HUME'S INTEREST in Elizabeth's relations with Mary as queen and cousin indicate a growing interest in the relation between the public and private sides of personality. Private morality and justice begin to appear where Hume before saw only private interests and prejudice. Once again his interest in law brings about a new realization. Hume's previous view of law tended to concentrate on its use for the nation. Now he also recognizes that the gradual growth of law absorbs private whim and furnishes a medium for private virtue. Law embodies the best in individual thought and action much as Hume's narrative voice impartially moves over and assembles the materials of history. Like Hume the historian, law mutes the idiosyncrasies of heroes and dramatizes the virtues of more private men. While the Stuart volumes displayed the historian as a moral and political philosopher, the Tudor volumes redefine him as a lawyer and student of the history of law. Whereas previously Hume might pause to approve the apt observers of character, like Abraham Cowley on Cromwell, he now praises the lawyer-historians: "Let me remark, in passing, as a singularity, how much English history has been beholden to four great men who have possessed the highest dignity in the law, More, Bacon, Clarendon, and Whitlocke" (III, Note A, p. 450).

Such an observation only affirms Hume's emerging practice. In the Stuart volumes there was some concern with specific laws while the King and the parliamentary leaders each asserted their own interpretation in the struggles of the moment. The progress of history was measured in personalities, battles, and occasional documents—bills, letters, proclamations, and set speeches. In the "peace" of the Tudor volumes Hume experiments with the literary possibilities of the calm of continuity. His practice still has the weakness of a method in embryo: "The following were the principal laws enacted this session" (IV, xl, p. 141). But such an awkwardness now has a point. Like the awkwardness of strict chronology, it reveals a growing feeling for the principle of inclusiveness in law, a body of codified acts and principles that preserves a continuity through the discrete moments of history. From this long and neutral view of developed law, previous judgments of individuals by universal moral and psychological standards appear to be inadequate estimates made in a historical vacuum.[e] History should be more than a moral and political casebook of the past. Hume includes the possibility of both views, for example, when he considers the conflict between Catholics and Protestants in Scotland at the beginning of Elizabeth's reign: " . . . whoever considers merely the transactions resulting from it, will be inclined to throw the blame equally on both parties; whoever enlarges his view, and reflects on the situations, will remark the necessary progress of human affairs, and the operation of those principles which are inherent in human nature" (IV, xxxviii, p. 16). This kind of detachment is more valuable than that of the Stuart volumes, where historical personages are judged by rigid standards unrelated to their historical situations.

To underline the need for such an expanded view of the past Hume refers more frequently in the Tudor volumes to his ideal readers, the "men of sense" and "men of moderation," who can view the events of history with detachment and sympathy.[33] The gradual development of law is their guide through the multiplicity and confusion of recorded history, a confusion perhaps increased by Hume's own early emphasis on character. In speaking of the actions of Mary, Queen of Scots, Hume counsels us to consider

e Machiavelli appealed to the lawyers and professors of jurisprudence to bring order to the study of history. But paradoxically enough they had little historical sense. See Gilmore, "The Lessons of History," p. 92: "Machiavelli was pleading for both "history" and "system" but the very jurisconsults who most completely realized the ideal of a systematic body of knowledge, applicable to the present, were the least historical. . . . [They] were much more interested in the achievement of a system of rules than they were in the achievement of any historical understanding of the growth of law or even of the existence of different periods in the history of institutions." Pocock, in *The Ancient Constitution*, p. 89, remarks that Scotsmen in the seventeenth century excelled the English in historical understanding because they had a greater experience with different systems of law.

her faults "as the result of an inexplicable, though not uncommon inconstancy in the human mind, of the frailty of our nature, of the violence of passion, and of the influence which situations, and sometimes momentary incidents, have on persons whose principles are not thoroughly confirmed by experience and reflection" (IV, xlii, p. 244).

Once we realize these things about human personality, despite the assertion that they may be present in all times and places, we are not helped much in our understanding of what is unique about history. Such chaotic motives cannot do much to change or initiate historical processes. Law regulates the multiplicity of human impulses and provides a frame for disparate motives and beliefs, a frame which creates a society. It can function similarly in the writing of history.

IV. THE MEDIEVAL PERIOD: CHARACTER AND CONTEXT

The "character" as a literary method and character as a concept for understanding history drop out completely in the medieval volumes of Hume's *History*. Hume may still believe that "character" controls and appropriately explains individual action. But it only confuses matters in historical narrative. A full account of the elements of a person's mind does not easily yield a causal analysis of the situation in which that mind is at work. Character as explanation has changed into character as merely another factor in history: " . . . the aspiring genius of Edward [III], which had so far transported him beyond the bounds of discretion, proved at last sufficient to reinstate him in his former authority, and finally to render his reign the most triumphant that is to be met with in the English story . . ." (II, xv, p. 209). Character exists in time and is subject to time's motion; what happens in history is at once more ascertainable and more important than who made it happen. The characters Hume pays most attention to in the medieval volumes are the great female figures like Joan of Arc and Margaret of Anjou, and they are celebrated not for their power but for their inherent interest.^f

It is appropriate that the final demise of the "character" occurs in Hume's medieval volumes. The great figures of the Stuart period could conceivably foster the idea that characters should be the historian's primary concern. But the dearth of important medieval figures opens the way for more general considerations. In the face of their actual insignificance Hume ironically emphasizes that the great fault of medieval man is his absolute reliance on the claims of the individual. The essence of medieval man for Hume is his doggedly personal and individual approach to everything, an approach which by definition precludes peaceful community interest. Accordingly, medieval man also blames individuals for everything: " . . . men, instead of regretting the manner of their age, and the form of their constitution, which required the most steady and most skilful hand to conduct them, imputed all errors to the person who had the misfortune to be intrusted with the reins of empire" (II, xiv, p. 169). This kind of explanation exactly parallels Hume's own early overstress on the great figure. Moved by a developing idea of the importance of the continuity of law, Hume comes to a period that completely disdained law and indeed all general causes but the transcendental. Hume immediately makes an analogy to the history-writing of the period. Such views of the purely personal basis of causality can of course be explained in a medieval writer by a lack of perspective. But they are unacceptable in a historian of the present: " . . . it is a shameful delusion in modern historians, to imagine that all the ancient princes who were unfortunate in their government, were also tyrannical in their conduct; and that the seditions of the people

---

f There is a possible counter-example in which Hume uses his sense of individual character to decide a historical crux. He asserts that "the most probable account" of the death of Prince Arthur includes the direct personal action of King John. The only basis for this belief seems to be Hume's negative judgment of John's character, although why this would preclude John's *indirect* responsibility is unclear (I, xi, pp. 400–01).

always proceeded from some invasion of their privileges by the monarch" (II, xiv, p. 169).

Because the medieval constitution depended so much on the personal character of the ruler, says Hume, England was then "necessarily in many of its parts . . . a government of will, not of laws" (II, xiv, p. 169).[g] Yet behind the egocentric values of the medieval world is the slow accretion of law that can replace these values. Hume compares the actions of Edward II and Richard II: "There cannot be a more remarkable contrast between the fortunes of two princes: it were happy for society, did this contrast always depend on the justice or injustice of the measures which men embrace; and not rather on the different degrees of prudence with which those measures are supported" (II, xvii, p. 318).

Hume's ideal is the state that can absorb the uncertainties of personality, in which "the government, by the force of its laws and institutions alone, without any extraordinary capacity in the sovereign, [can] maintain itself in order and tranquillity" (III, xxv, p. 20). The anarchy of the medieval period refines his idea of the elements of such a state.

The individual naturally cannot be dispensed with entirely in the running of a state or the writing of history. Hume therefore must re-examine character to find features that support stability rather than disrupt it. In the medieval volumes it is increasingly apparent that these good features

g This was the same idiom in which Stuart "tyranny" was condemned by its critics. "All that men read of mixed government in the classical masters and their Renaissance exponents told them that in mixed politics the monarchial element was subject to greater limitations than royalists could admit." The proponents of mixed government, what Hobbes called "mixarchy," wished specifically to limit the ruler's ability to promulgate arbitrary laws. See Zera S. Fink, *The Classical Republicans* (Evanston, 1945), p. 24. For Hume's association of mixed government and mixed character, see above, p. 50. Compare Michael's remarks in *Paradise Lost*, XII, ll. 86–95: "Reason in man obscur'd, or not obey'd, / Immediately inordinate desires / And upstart Passions catch the Government / From Reason, and to servitude reduce / Man till then free. Therefore since hee permits / Within himself unworthy Powers to reign / Over free Reason, God in Judgment just / Subjects him from without to violent Lords. . . ."

are found in the proper integration and weighting of the private and public parts of the personality, the adjudication of individual conscience and public good. Previous remarks about public and private character in the *History*, like those on Richard Cromwell, usually implied that the private part of the personality either weakened or was irrelevant to public concerns. The public and the private virtues tended to be separate. Hume remarks of Edward VI that "His virtues were better calculated for private than public life . . ." (III, xxxv, p. 375). In the Tudor volumes Francis I seemed to possess, as much as any public man can, the quintessence of private virtue. But his character is inferior to that of Charles V:

> . . . Francis, open, frank, liberal, munificent, carrying these virtues to an excess which prejudiced his affairs; Charles, political, close, artful, frugal; better qualified to obtain success in war and negotiations, especially the latter. The one the most amiable man; the other the greater monarch (III, xxviii, p. 120).

Hume writes that the emulation between the two monarchs "kept their whole age in movement," but it symbolizes far better the uneasy conceptual truce between private and public claims in the Tudor volumes. The medieval volumes attempt to reconcile these claims.[h]

The most recognizable hero in the medieval volumes, a person who "may with advantage be set in opposition to that of any monarch, or citizen, which the annals of any age, or any nation, can present to us," is Alfred the Great (I, ii, p. 69). In an age that envied physical prowess and spoke familiarly of its rulers in terms of their physical features (I, iii, p. 121), Alfred exemplifies the best side of an emphasis

---

[h] For other examples of Hume's consideration of the relation between public and private life, see his criticism of Parliament's use of a private letter from Charles I to Henrietta Maria as evidence for treason (V, lviii, p. 312); his remarks that Henry VIII's problems with his wives were due to the fact that kings could not choose wives "like private persons" (III, xxxii, p. 260); and Elizabeth's possible deficiencies as a wife or mistress (IV, xliv, p. 343 and see above, p. 72).

on the individual, exhibiting those qualities that are easily absorbed into the furtherance of the public good: "His civil and his military virtues are almost equally the objects of our admiration; excepting only that the former, being more rare among princes, as well as more useful, seem chiefly to challenge our applause" (I, ii, p. 70). The cloistered virtue of Richard Cromwell is no longer a worthwhile value. Private virtue should inform, not retreat from, public life.[34]

With this new approach, *raison d'état*, the former standard of exonerating "necessity," is also no longer adequate. Speaking of Edward I's reduction of Scotland to the authority of England, Hume remarks: " . . . though the equity of this latter enterprise may reasonably be questioned . . . those who give great indulgence to reasons of state in the measures of princes, will not be apt to regard this part of his conduct with much severity" (II, xiii, p. 136). Hume was one of "those" in his earlier volumes, but he has changed. He has finally achieved a balance both of point of view and value. He can criticize the operations of private passions in a sovereign or a statesman (II, xxii, p. 478) and attack a form of government that makes public crimes of private affairs (II, xiv, pp. 147, 157). At the same time he also contends that private virtue can rectify corrupt public affairs, and on almost the final page of the *History* criticizes the English people for not rising against Richard III: "Were men disposed to pardon these violations of public right, the sense of private and domestic duty, which is not to be effaced in the most barbarous times, must have begotten an abhorrence against him . . . " (II, xxiii, p. 498).

The establishment of the Magna Charta marks a turning point for Hume, not because it is the clear source of the "ancient English liberties," for he details its many abrogations and revisions, but because it indicates the transition from a country composed of individuals and factions to a civil society: "Acts of violence and iniquity in the crown, which before were only deemed injurious to individuals, and were hazardous chiefly in proportion to the number, power, and dignity of the persons affected by them, were now regarded, in some degree, as public injuries, and as infringements of a charter calculated for general security" (I, Appendix II, p. 474).

Law and established behavior are general frames for the unplanned and capricious individual actions that are so often injurious to civil society. They also provide a channel for the good motivations and impulses of individuals, which otherwise may be lost in the rush of public drama. Law is the great balancer between individual and public interest, between the immediate and the long-range: "If subjects would enjoy liberty, and kings security, the laws must be executed" (II, note K, p. 521). The proper attitude for the sovereign to assume is a mixture of the best private virtues with a respect for law. The trouble with the medieval world, says Hume again, was that the most the people could expect from the king was the part-private, part-public virtue of justice, while "the formalities of law, which are often as material as the essentials themselves . . . were sacrificed without scruple to the least interest or convenience" (II, xix, p. 354).[1]

Hume's interest in law and his movement away from great figures closely parallel his refusal to applaud grandiose public actions. Early in his letters he had written that a prospective historian should study the acts of government and the strategy of battle.[35] Accordingly, the Stuart volumes regaled the reader with minute descriptions of every move-

---

[1] Hume does not give all precedent unqualified approval. Precedent without legal basis also needs pragmatic justification in "necessity" and social utility. Here are his comments on the question of female descent in the French royal line: "The principle of excluding females was of old an established opinion in France, and had acquired equal authority with the most express and positive law: it was supported by ancient precedents: it was confirmed by recent instances, solemnly and deliberately decided: and what placed it still farther beyond controversy, if Edward [III] was disposed to question its validity, he thereby cut off his own pretensions . . ." (II, xv, p. 193). Hume here employs the principle of pragmatism with an ironic deflation worthy of Gibbon.

ment of the Parliamentary and Royalist armies.ʲ But in the medieval volumes, Hume does not value military narrative so highly: "Were we to relate all the military events transmitted to us by contemporary and authentic historians, it would be easy to swell our accounts of this reign [of Stephen] into a large volume; but those incidents, so little memorable in themselves, and so confused both in time and place, could afford neither instruction nor entertainment to the reader" (I, vii, p. 278).

Chivalry, which, for Hume, symbolizes the worst aspects of the medieval emphasis on individual whim, receives as much abuse as military narrative.³⁶ Hume debunks the heroics of Richard I and praises instead Charles V of France, for being the first monarch in Europe to make it a practice never to appear at the front of his army: "The events of his reign, compared with those of the preceding, are a proof how little reason kingdoms have to value themselves on their victories, or to be humbled by their defeats; which in reality ought to be ascribed chiefly to the good or bad conduct of their rulers, and are of little moment towards determining national character and manners" (II, xvi, p. 255). Since law can correct the whims of individuals and translate individual virtue into public policy, the kind of individuality Hume approves is that which, like Alfred's, can be expressed as civic virtue.³⁷

HUME'S VIEW OF HISTORY in the medieval volumes emphasizes its flow and its multitude of material, the sheer multiplicity of facts and incidents and personages. He increasingly enforces the reality of his history by an accumulation of minute but relevant facts. In his letters he said that the concise style of the ancient historians had no place for

---

ʲ Irene Coltman suggests that Clarendon's view of the actual importance of Prince Rupert is warped by his overvaluation of Rupert's military success (*Private Men and Public Causes*, pp. 169–75). Hume seems to have fallen into the same error. Myron Gilmore, Felix Gilbert, and others have spoken of the way the humanist historians adopted the classical emphasis on military strategy and battle detail.

"minute, uninteresting facts," and his own practice emphasizes their interest rather than their minuteness. His manipulation of the facts of history is part of an effort
to plumb its uniqueness. Hume is less harsh upon the antiquarians than is Bolingbroke because he believes that facts
should be ascertained, even if they can show only the practice of the times, rather than who was right (II, xvi, p. 271).[k]
Yet, for all his emphasis upon the "material fact," Hume
includes in his narrative many facts that seem immaterial
or at least unintegrated. In his effort to include more and
more of the data of the past, his philosophical belief in the
lack of necessary connection between causes and effects (as
it is argued in the *Enquiry*) becomes more important.
He extends his idea of cause into his history, affirming
the constant conjunction of time, and at the same time the
possibility that many different and often contrary effects
may come from the same cause. Such a belief might seem
inimical to the purposes of a historian, but Hume absorbs
it in his philosophy of history. Instead of depending on
generalizations for coherence, he emphasizes his own perspective. Hume's detached narrative voice unites the disparate facts of history in much the same way that law absorbs individual vices and virtues into a uniform growth.
The vexed relation of cause and effect points to another
kind of continuity. As Hume remarks in the first Tudor
volume, "There is no abuse so great in civil society, as not
to be attended with a variety of beneficial consequences . . . "
(III, xxxv, p. 354). Such judgments occur more frequently
in the medieval volumes.[1] The continuity of civil society is
the main criterion of value. Even religion may be praised

---

[k] Even though Hume is conventionally thought to be uninterested
in accurate documentation, he can criticize Froissart for "his want
of exactness in material facts" (II, xvii, p. 300). Hume delves minutely into records to prove a point about the hostility between Richard
III and Buckingham (II, xxiii, p. 497).

[1] See Hume's comments on the invention of artillery (II, xv, p. 225)
and the good effects from the bad title of the Lancastrians (II, xix,
p. 373).

for the unity and stability that it can afford; even superstition can hold communities together (II, xii, p. 12).

Hume's definition of the proper role of the historian is therefore expressed primarily through his emphasis upon continuity and coherence. Emphasis on character militates against these principles; emphasis on law alone is too abstract; emphasis on the interaction between character and law allows the greatest latitude for analysis and interest. Causality is most apparent in immediate contexts, and it is here that Hume makes his most general comments. Faced with the party historian who writes apologetics or polemics, Hume attempts to replace him with the philosophical historian, who contemplates with a minimum of abstract language and a maximum of detachment the characters and events of the past.[m]

As the *History* moves on, however, Hume seems to feel that the general causes of the philosophical historian have a degree of imposition in them not unlike the formulations of the party historians. He increases his detachment even further in order to delve into the true nature of history, mediating the facts and materials as little as possible. Voltaire, in his review of the French translation of the *History* (*La Gazette Littéraire*, 2 mai 1764), characterizes Hume's detachment as being much like his own: " . . . dans le nouvel historien on découvre un esprit supérieur à sa matière, qui parle des faiblesses, des erreurs, et des barbaries, comme un médecin parle des maladies épidémiques."[38]

But this is not the quality of Hume's detachment. Instead of contemplating the record of irrationality and cruelty, he seeks the materials of continuity and the growth of community interest. The historian, according to Hume, is concerned with the issues of the past in their own con-

---

[m] See the concluding remark to Note CCC in IV, p. 568: "This note was in the first editions a part of the text; but the author omitted it, in order to avoid as much as possible the style of dissertation in the body of his History. The passage, however, contains views so important, that he thought it might be admitted as a note." This statement was inserted in Hume's first revision of the Stuart volumes, 1756.

text, rather than as material for philosophical generalization. Above all, Hume attempts to convey a sense of the problematic about the past, an impression opposed to the pat judgments of "history."

Hume's awareness of the need to redefine the role of the historian appears most strongly in the medieval volumes when he openly attempts to adjudicate the disputes of past historians. He is now a historian among other historians. He says he is not affected by nationalistic prejudices and sorts out the rights and wrongs of disputes between English and Welsh historians on the reasons for the Saxon invasion (I, i, p. 16), between English and Norman historians on the motives for the revolt of the barons against the Norman rule (I, iv, p. 185), and between English and French historians over the abrogation of the truce at Vannes (II, x, p. 217).[n] He frequently criticizes the "monkish historians," who distort the causes of history through their constant subordination of civil to ecclesiastical affairs. Their histories, he says, are filled with characters without actions, abstractly called good or bad as they conform to the purposes of Providence: "The history of that period abounds in names, but is extremely barren of events; or the events are related so much without circumstances and causes, that the most profound or most eloquent writer must despair of rendering them either instructive or entertaining to the reader" (I, i, p. 22). These historians do not explain events by the characters and actions of men but by divine intervention. Providential explanation for Hume is a retreat into an all-embracing system based on self-interest, whenever the historian faces problems of fact which he cannot solve. He remarks about trial by ordeal: "When any controversy about a fact became too intricate for those ignorant judges to unravel, they had recourse to what they

[n] Perhaps Hume himself is not as free from nationalistic bias as he would like to think. He cannot understand why William the Conqueror left to revisit Normandy after only three months in England (I, iv, pp. 185–86). Hume does not consider that William may have thought that being king of England was somewhat less important than ruling Normandy.

called the judgment of God, that is, to fortune" (I, Appendix I, p. 172).

The party historians place a similar construction upon history. And, in these final volumes, Hume might finally accept a criticism by Addison that would have been relevant to Hume's practice in the Stuart volumes: "It is a Fault very justly found in Histories composed by Politicians, that they leave nothing to Chance or Humour, but are still for deriving every Action from some Plot and Contrivance, for drawing up a perpetual Scheme of Causes and Events, and preserving a constant Correspondence between the Camp and the Council-Table."[39]

Hume replaces the obsessive desire to connect and to generalize with his sense of the slowly accumulating movement of history. The historian is an appropriate guide through much of this material, but he should connect it only "in some tolerable measure" (I, i, p. 22). Hume's model of the operation of chance and fortune in history involves not the odd event that upsets systematic plans, but the multiplicity of circumstances that can never be fully analyzed or even encompassed. Hume's *History* purported at its outset to be a repository of political and moral philosophy. But in Hume's final state of mind the precepts for direct action that can be drawn from his work are few indeed. Historical problems are all circumstantial. Hume must qualify and adapt his original general statements to fit them for specific situations. The medieval volumes of the *History* give new force to Hume's remark in the *Essays* about the difficulty of getting a complete account of circumstances into words: "All questions concerning the proper medium between any two extremes are very difficult to be decided; both because it is difficult to find *words* proper to fix this medium, and because the good and ill, in such cases, run so gradually into each other, as even to render our *sentiments* doubtful and uncertain."[40]

If anything practical can finally be extracted from the reading of Hume's *History*, it is a method of action and a number of testable maxims, with a constantly repeated injunction to be prepared for any contingency as we live among the vexed causal relations of life. Hume never completely praises private virtue, for that would be ludicrous in a work called *The History of England*. But his repeated qualification of the importance of the great figures of history finally yields an attitude toward the scope of human action. The seeds of this attitude are in the character of Cromwell, who always knew how to take advantage of the present moment. But that conception grants too much to heroic opportunism to be really useful. Fortune—the many causes and circumstances of history—can dominate men if they are not careful.[41] With perception and good will, however, Fortune may be understood and even manipulated, for it is a neutral force of history, not a malevolent qualifier of man's ability to act (I, iii, p. 135). In order for his action to be most effective, man must make it coincide with the developing forces of history, which Hume optimistically hopes will always coincide with the good of the community. Leicester's establishment of the first real parliament in London only brought about a little sooner something which "the general state of things" had already prepared (II, xii, p. 54).

Hume's final statement in the *History* further strengthens this idea of the haphazard combination of individual action and circumstances that produces in time a complex body of tradition and institutions. He concludes after almost four thousand pages that knowing history is "useful" and "curious." It is useful because it helps us to find out how "our" present constitution developed and how it has become "the most perfect and most accurate system of liberty that was ever found compatible with government"—Hume's final bow to history's relation to the present. But his last words return to history itself. History is curious, he says, because it reveals the "disfigured originals of the most finished and most noble institutions," and meanwhile instructs us "in the great mixture of accident, which commonly concurs with a small ingredient of wisdom and foresight, in erecting the complicated fabric of the most perfect government" (II, xxiii, p. 514).

Unlike Bolingbroke, Hume has attempted to find ways of understanding the past that make us less apprehensive about its "accidents" and more involved in its variety.

THROUGH THE APPLICATION of a semi-systematic analysis I have tried to analyze a work that ultimately seems to eschew any systematic organization. Certain principles may be dramatized by Hume's detached narrative voice, but they are only partial expressions of its central value as an inclusive point of view. To assert that the chronological narrative itself supplies a sufficient structure for the past does not resolve the fact that materials must first be chosen. But Hume adopts methods of organization, which I have noted, only to drop most of them when he becomes more comfortable with and more philosophically committed to an accretive chronological structure that answers only to the inarticulate logic of organic nature. This structure often appears mindless and undirected, controlled only by "the general state of things" that has called it into being. Hume remarks on the growth of Leicester's parliament: ". . . it is otherwise inconceivable, that a plant, set by so inauspicious a hand, could have attained to so vigorous a growth, and have flourished in the midst of such tempests and confusions" (II, xii, p. 54).

The methods that have been dropped concentrate on the "tempests and confusions." Those that have remained emphasize the continuity of things. The lists of officials may have vanished, but the genealogies of succession are with us to the end. The question that remains in an assessment of the coherence of Hume's *History* is whether the narrative voice works. Does it control as well as contain?

I must confess that I believe Hume's narrative method to be a failure. He makes time itself provide the cohesion and continuity, as if the conjunctions of chronology told all. True, he seeks for causes, adjudicates questions of fact, assesses personalities, and tries to maintain a tone of measured detachment. But, perhaps in reaction to the pervasive points of view that he deplored in other historians, he does not speak enough in his own voice. He sacrifices more complete and possibly more interesting coherences because he appears to believe that a recognizable point of view automatically means bias and distortion, and a total interpretation of history must necessarily be either Whig or Tory.[42] History, he implies, needs a form instead of an interpretation. Like the "ideal observer" in his ethics, therefore, Hume's voice remains cool and remote, and his humor is Olympian irony. His appreciation for the fullness of history seems to grow with his increasing withdrawal from it, until he can make comments like that upon the Turkish rule of the Levant: "Jerusalem, by its situation, became one of their most early conquests; and the Christians had the mortification to see the holy sepulchre, and the other places consecrated by the presence of their religious founder, fallen into the possession of infidels" (I, v, p. 226).

But the onward push of narrative is too insistent, and finally Hume's method is too undiscriminating to keep us from being frequently bored. The feeling that we can sense Hume's own boredom, in the writing of military description, for example, makes the situation even worse. His greater emphasis upon the adjudication of past historians in the medieval volumes shows that he felt this deficiency also. Hume's greatness is in his attempt to establish the past as a unique problem that needs exploration. Instead of imposing his own interpretations upon it, he increasingly presents it in its own whirl of uncertainty and lack of connection. The medieval "transactions" are as fragmented and unrelated as were the Stuart: " . . . we are here collecting some detached incidents, which show the genius of the age, and which could not so well enter into the body of our history . . . " (I, ix, p. 363). Hume has said something like this so often that one is inclined to believe that this must be the way such materials should be presented. The tone of his remark is less apologetic than assertive. But while such devices can be justified, they cannot be made pleasing. Hume's basic literary desire in writing his *History* becomes a determined anti-literary effort to ferret out and remove any aesthetic device that could possibly be an impediment to the understanding. The anti-dramatic character of the paragraphs that conclude his chapters increases as the *History* goes on, until even the last sentences often appear to be peculiar *non sequiturs*. Despite a minimal coherence, the appendices are like huge compendia, which threaten to split apart at the slightest unbalancing of their loads of disparate elements. The measured narrative voice, which Hume hopes can control these disjointed materials with a minimum of distortion, finally fails to hold them together. His dissociation from partisan interpretation becomes a revocation of aesthetic and historical responsibility.

Hume does convey a sense of the uniqueness of history, the contingency of the facts, people, and events that produced the present. But the didactic implications of his detached narrator are in conflict with his presentation of contingency and chance. One holds out the possibility of lasting generalizations, while the other points to the perpetual presence of qualification and exception. Hume resolves this problem for himself by insisting that his formulations are not absolute. In "Of Civil Liberty" he keeps the door open for change: "'Tis not fully known, what degrees of refinement, either in virtue or vice, human nature is susceptible of; nor what may be expected of mankind from any great revolution in their education, customs, or principles."[43]

The role of Hume's historian is to generalize and present the past as truly and as relevantly as he can, without a claim to being final. But I do not think that Hume's dual attitude is realized in the structure of his *History*. There is a palpable gap between the seeming finality of the measured voice and the bursting potentiality of the historical material it relates to us.

Hume tries to follow two paths at once. He writes with a species of didactic intention in a mode whose purposes had always been didactically directed toward the present. Yet he also hastens with his work the anti-didactic trend of appreciating the past for its own sake. He believes finally that any important historical knowledge is always retrospective and wedded to context; its application to future behavior is vexed and uncertain. Hume's prescriptiveness gets less and less apparent as his *History* moves on. He continues to make general statements, but we are more mindful of the frequency with which he uses "in great measure," "on most occasions," and "almost with certainty." Hume's *History*, then, does clearly reflect the antisystematic trend that can be followed in his philosophy. He experiments with certainty and then becomes comfortable with uncertainty. For Bolingbroke's history of discrete exemplary incidents, he has tried to substitute a history of development, in which events, facts, and persons may be considered in their own contexts rather than with complete and necessary reference to the present. Yet Hume's optimism often appears more philosophical than actual. His final remarks on the role of chance in the establishment of institutions can be a prelude to a pessimism about the ability of an individual to do anything that counts against the accretions of time, when institutions turn out to be corrupt. His faith in the possibilities of impartiality grows weaker as his claims of impartiality grow more shrill, and his belief in the benevolent effects of development becomes less certain. About five months before his death, he writes to Gibbon about the possible negative reception to chapters fifteen and sixteen of the *Decline and Fall*:

> . . . in every other respect your Work is calculated to be popular. But, among many other marks of Decline, the Prevalence of Superstition in England, prognosticates the Fall of Philosophy and Decay of Taste; and though no body be more capable than you to revive them, you will probably find a Struggle in your first Advances.[44]

FOUR | *Fielding:*

PUBLIC HISTORY AND INDIVIDUAL PERCEPTION

I. INTRODUCTION

But apt the Mind or Fancy is to rove
Uncheckt, and of her roving is no end;
Till warn'd, or by experience taught, she learn
That not to know at large of things remote
From use, obscure and subtle, but to know
That which before us lies in daily life,
Is the prime Wisdom; what is more, is fume,
Or emptiness, or fond impertinence,
And renders us in things that most concern
Unpractic'd, unprepar'd, and still to seek.
    MILTON, *Paradise Lost*, VIII, 188–97

I was chiefly disgusted with modern history.
    SWIFT, *Gulliver's Travels*

HUME ACCEPTS THE FRAME of past historiography when he begins to write; Fielding rebels against it. Hume finally judges public history according to the two standards of private virtue and social utility. He believes that his measured detachment can make the lessons of history more transparently available. Fielding denies this point of view on two counts. First, he believes that public history is bankrupt as a source for moral value or even informative analogies. He attacks the idea that we should read history to learn about either human nature or political systems. Basing his fictional world on the virtues and experiences of private life, Fielding then emphasizes a vital interplay between the narrator and the materials he presents to the reader. For Hume's impartial narrator and inclusion of all the loose ends of reality, Fielding substitutes the obviously partial narrator who openly manipulates and controls an obviously constructed story.[a] Both writers frequently use the analogy of the historian and the judge. But Hume's judge makes decisions between right and wrong and establishes legal precedent, while Fielding's judge works in the courts of equity, upholding the importance of specific situation and the individual nature of the case before him.[b] Fielding deals with the same problems that preoccupied Hume: the use of detail, the operative role of the individual (the Great Man), the patterns of causality, and the nature of the narrative voice. But he denies public history any validity at all. In *Joseph Andrews*, for example, the public moral imperatives—obedience to institutional forms or social customs—are comic because they collide so obviously with and are qualified so often by the individual reality. Fielding does not write the history of ordinary people merely as an analogy to the history of the great and notable. Private history is a corrective to the biases and faulty generalizations about human nature that are secreted within the interstices of any public history bent consciously or unconsciously on proving a particular thesis. The "new" history of Montesquieu, Voltaire, and Hume tried to liberate man from what Robert Hanning in another context has called "the tyranny of an

a Fielding knew much of Hume's work, although the *History of England* did not begin appearing until after Fielding's death. As I mentioned earlier, I could find no reference to Fielding in any of Hume's works or letters. An explorable possibility may be their common relation to the publisher Andrew Millar. See Austin Dobson, "Fielding and Andrew Millar," *The Library*, 3rd ser., 7 (1916), pp. 177–90.

b Compare G. Kitson Clark's analysis of the validity of the legal analogy: "It is the object of an historian to get as near to the truth about people and events in the past as he can. That is, however, not the primary object of a law court; its object must be to come to a decision, a decision which must as far as possible correspond with the realities of the case, but also a decision which must be fitted into those categories which the general framework of the law supplies, and on which action can be taken. Problematical conclusions, or conclusions which are irrelevant to the restricted purposes of the law, are of no use" (*The Critical Historian* [New York, 1967], p. 15).

eschatological-exegetical history." Fielding in his turn attempts to liberate men from the public history that dealt in deductive political and social exempla, subsuming the individual in its search for generalization.

Fielding's ideas for the possibilities of his "new species of writing" arise therefore from a background of past historiographical practice. If the catalogue of his library is any testimony, he had done wide reading in all the varieties of history that were written in his time.[1] In addition to the Greek and Roman historians, it also included modern historians like Rapin-Thoyras, de Retz, Echard, Whitelocke, and Clarendon. It was especially strong in books dealing with the English seventeenth century and the period of the civil wars. Throughout his writings, the many allusions to past and contemporary historians indicate that he was familiar with most of their works.[2] But Fielding's references to history in his novels have usually been explained to be his way of speaking about his interest in the minute details of physical reality and social relations. Both these formulations apply well enough to parts of Fielding's practice. His early use of the word "historian" owes much to a theory of fiction that would administer the purge of facts to the excesses of romance. *Joseph Andrews* puts romancing novelists and partisan historians in the same category, while "we biographers" pay proper attention to fact and detail (III, i).[3] The sense of social reality that we receive in Fielding is certainly also very palpable. If this is the usage of "historian" Fielding has in mind, it is quite new, and Fielding could stand with Hume, Montesquieu, and Voltaire as one of the first to believe that the role of the historian necessitated a commitment to the chronicling of customs and classes.[4]

But Fielding is redefining the nature of the historian even beyond these two categories. Although his own position is like that of the historian, his medium is fiction instead of history. Fiction can accomplish ends that history cannot; fiction concerns itself with problems that history should explore but does not. The factual or social definition of

Fielding's usage of "historian" implies a passive author, who calmly records facts and chronicles social details, however incisively. Fielding's approach to history in both theory and practice, however, is much more active. His large library of historical literature exhibits his interests in history as a mode of knowledge, a method of creating and expressing a world, not a collection of facts or character types. Neither the social world nor the empirical method emerges unscathed. "We biographers" may have the appropriate kind of understanding in *Joseph Andrews*, but the novel also severely criticizes a view of actuality built on factual detail alone.[5]

Fielding believes that the study and writing of history raised many of the same problems that should concern the novelist. But public history too often perpetuated falsely unified views that scanted the actual variety of the world. The private history displayed in fiction stands in opposition to public history. Through the importation of themes and methods from history and biography, Fielding seeks to renovate in the reader of his fiction a sense of actuality that had been debased by the categories and assumptions of romancers, moralizers, party historians, and "mere" chronologers—in short, anyone who screened life through literary and epistemological forms that were fixed, arbitrary, and absolute.[6] *Joseph Andrews* and *Jonathan Wild* are epistemological and aesthetic manifestoes, in which Fielding, faced by the problems of an embryonic literary mode, explores in minute detail its claims to approximate reality. He imports the categories for such examination from history, an already established "realistic" form. He asks what is the nature of that literary presentation of actuality that most compels the reader's assent. History becomes the skeleton of method and ideal that lies beneath the surface of Fielding's novels. By the time of *Tom Jones* and *Amelia,* once the inquiry is past, he has begun to formulate his own categories.

All of Fielding's novels, then, are basically exercises in the reinvigoration of perceptions that have been dulled by the overheated fantasies of the romance writers and "romancing historians." Although Fielding's concerns are also the preoccupations of history-writing—facts, institutions, Providence, causality, and human will—he does not deductively impose static conceptions of historical pattern. Each novel focuses on different aspects of the literary presentation of real life, and each alters and rearranges the insights of the previous one. I may err in my emphasis when I find the origin of Fielding's concerns in the problems of history-writing, but this is a corrective. To see Fielding, as is currently popular, in terms of "moral" aims implies a peculiarly static writer, whose novels are primarily designed to illustrate ethical abstractions.[7] A more attractive and, I believe, more accurate view of Fielding involves a concentration on the problems I have sketched above. In these we may observe his search for the literary embodiment of the materials of real life that would at once assert their truth and significance. By this study also we might hope to discern the nature of a novel-writing career at the end of which Fielding could write:

> I am far from supposing that Homer, Hesiod, and the other ancient poets and mythologists, had any settled design to pervert and confuse the records of antiquity; but it is certain they have effected it; and for my part I must confess I should have honoured and loved Homer more had he written a true history of his own times in humble prose, than all those noble poems that have so justly collected the praise of all ages; for, though I read these with more admiration and astonishment, I still read Herodotus, Thucydides, and Xenophon with more amusement and more satisfaction.[8]

II. *Joseph Andrews*: THE RELEVANCE OF FACTS

In *Joseph Andrews* Fielding examines what many writers and historians had considered a necessary method in the presentation of actuality: the accumulation of facts. He does not deny the importance of facts; they are, for example, useful tools for puncturing the fantastic. But he does seem to imply that the accumulation of irrelevant facts is a useless process that actually weakens the realistic illusion and distracts the reader from more important matters. Because Fielding believes that observations tend to be faulty, he qualifies the theory of dramatic irony that finds truth when motives and actions are compared. At one point in *Joseph Andrews*, for example, the narrator "exonerates" a constable from the charge of being bribed to let Joseph's attackers go: "But, notwithstanding these and many other such allegations, I am sufficiently convinced of his innocence; having been positively assured of it by those who received their information from his own mouth; which, in the opinion of some moderns, is the best and indeed only evidence."c

Fielding also objects strongly to the assumed connection between factual or "objective" presentation and moral truth. If a biographer believes that facts solely or primarily define reality, then every fact is in some way relevant, if only to strengthen the atmosphere of truth. Fielding attacks the implication that there is a necessary relation between the claim that an "editor" reports facts and the claim that his moral vision is similarly clear.[9] One of Fielding's literary goals in *Joseph Andrews* involves the rehabilitation of facts as an important technique in the authentication of a world, whether fictional or historical. To accomplish this he also shows how the sanction of facts can be misused and distorted. *Joseph Andrews* is an experiment in writing about life without deductive pattern, an experiment in using facts properly to convey a plausible world.

In Fielding's eyes Lucian and Hogarth represent the best possible use of facts, most scrupulous, most accurate, most relevant, most indicative of an inner and larger reality. Fielding's admiration for Hogarth is well known.[10] Throughout his career Fielding also admired the work of Lucian and says in *Covent-Garden Journal* #52 (June 30, 1752) that he had formed his style on Lucian's model.[11] Fielding

---

c *Joseph Andrews* and *Shamela*, ed. Martin C. Battestin (Boston, 1961), I, xvi, p. 59. Further citations will be included in the text.

refers to Lucian and Hogarth as standards to criticize two classes of less expert manipulators of factual and physical detail: the antiquarians who collect volumes of unrelated facts and the physiognomists who depend on the testimony of physical facts for an immediate and unqualified insight into human character.

Lucian's monologue "How to Write History" attacks the distortions worked by both party historians and romancing historians. The first distort facts; the second dispense with them. Like Fielding, Lucian believes that the proper use of facts can explode their false and biased patterns of explanation. But for Lucian, as for Fielding, facts are not a value in themselves.[12] An unadorned, undiscriminating collection of facts is at best a repository for a "true" historian to draw upon.[d] Pure facts, existing discretely, do not define a reality at all. The historian instead uses them to evoke a reality. After he has defined the facts of a situation, he arranges them with "beauty, expression, figure and rhythm."[13] Like a sculptor he is given materials and must shape them.

The analogy to the sculptor does not imply manipulation or change. Lucian does not discuss the imposition of pattern on facts, for he seems to feel either that facts dictate a pattern of their own (like Michelangelo's stone blocks) or that any fair and judicious mind will extract the same causalities and patterns from them. He compares the mind of the historian to a mirror: "clear, gleaming-bright, accurately centered, displaying the shape of things just as he receives them, free from distortion, false colouring, and misrepresentation."[14] Lengthy descriptions point too much

---

[d] Speaking of one of the chroniclers of the incessant Roman wars in Armenia, Lucian writes: "Another of them has compiled a bare record of the events and set it down on paper, completely prosaic and ordinary, such as a soldier or artisan or pedlar following the army might have put together as a diary of daily events. However, this amateur was not so bad—it was obvious at the beginning what he was, and his work has cleared the ground for some future historian of taste and ability" (Lucian, *Works*, VI, trans. K. Kilburn [London, 1959], pp. 25–27).

to the historian himself. He should be interested in un-adorned truth, and Lucian frequently uses similes of dress and cosmetics to show his distaste for the over-rhetorical historian. Like Hume and Fielding, Lucian makes frequent analogies between the role of the historian and that of a judge.[e] He believes, no doubt following Aristotle, that the intrusion of the historian or the poet in his own person only detracts from the illusion of recreated history. The chronicler is indiscriminate in his collections of facts. The historian administers the test of relevance and truth and then integrates the facts into the pattern that they all must necessarily fit.[15]

Lucian's position is finally much like Hume's. He believes that the detachment of the historian, his view from above, is a necessary part of the truth of his work.[f] Fielding obviously parts company with Lucian over the question of identifying truth with "objectivity" and impersonality. But he also uses the factual method to criticize the various kinds of false historians. Like Lucian and Hume, he attacks party historians, panegyrists, and the purveyors of the fantastic. But Lucian ceases to be a guide when Fielding begins to present his own standards for excellence in a historian. A detached contemplation of facts can help to find truth, but it is not an ideal in itself. It is finally too superficial, too public, to be an accurate standard of judgment. In this mood Fielding asks instead whether historians have given an accurate and convincing picture of human character. He calls most modern historians "topographers or chorographers" because often it is only their facts, actually only their geographic facts, that have even the semblance of truth.

e The biased historian is "like a bad judge who sells his verdict to curry favour or gratify hatred"; the good historian is "an impartial judge, well disposed to all men up to the point of not giving one side more than its due" ("How to Write History," pp. 53, 57). Might this be a common source for the judicial analogies of both Hume and Fielding? See above, p. 92.

f Lucian compares the historian's perspective to that of Zeus, considering both sides of a battle from above ("How to Write History," p. 61).

When they deal with the complex facts surrounding the actions and characters of men, their interpretations can be completely contradictory:

> . . . of which there needs no other proof than those eternal contradictions occurring between two topographers who undertake the history of the same country: for instance, between my Lord Clarendon and Mr. Whitlock, between Mr. Echard and Rapin, and many others; where, facts being set forth in a different light, every reader believes as he pleases; and, indeed, the more judicious and suspicious very justly esteem the whole as no other than a romance, in which the writer hath indulged a happy and fertile invention (III, vii, p. 157).

Only the scene is right. Because they have been forced into a biased pattern, usually through political prejudice, most facts beyond the geographic no longer have the absolute value granted them by Lucian.

> But though these widely differ in the narrative of facts; some ascribing victory to the one, and others to the other party; some representing the same man as a rogue, to whom others give a great and honest character; yet all agree in the scene where the fact is supposed to have happened, and where the person, who is both a rogue and an honest man, lived (III, i, p. 157).

Although the age and the country may be wrong, Fielding claims that his own use of facts will correspond to a truth about human nature. He is concerned with the accurate portrayal of character, not the circumstantial establishment of an actual scene. The way to truths about the characters of men is not necessarily through the use of empirical and verifiable detail: "Is there in the world such a sceptic as to disbelieve the madness of Cardenio, the perfidy of Ferdinand, the impertinent curiosity of Anselmo, the weakness of Camilla, the irresolute friendship of Lothario?" (III, i, pp. 257–58).

In order to mock biographers who use facts as an end in themselves, Fielding often assumes the pose of a scrupulous researcher, gathering information from the principal characters. The fumbling antiquary of the second chapter of *Joseph Andrews* represents the biographer who searches for facts indiscriminately. In the effort to give Joseph a suitable set of ancestors, conjectures are made about tombstone inscriptions; obscure and irrelevant learning is extensively displayed. Fielding caricatures the indiscriminate accumulation of "circumstance, which, though mentioned in conformity to the exact rules of biography, is not greatly material" (I, ii, p. 15).[g] Fielding's antiquarian biographer casts about in the past, putting together fragments of relevancy and irrelevancy.[16] Such a procedure might not be culpable if it stopped at the level of neutral information. But this antiquarian proceeds to derive from his mishmash of "facts" false causal assumptions about the nature of heredity. Because so much effort has been expended on the collection of these details, they must "explain" something. The antiquarian has come to his work with the assumption that one's ancestors are responsible for one's own "honor"; the man himself is irrelevant. Assumptions precede the collection of facts; facts substantiate the assumptions. Antiquarian facts are not the liberating influence they can be when conceived as a scrupulous method. Instead they are binding and limiting. All of Fielding's novels deal with the repressive results of the unthinking acceptance of simplistic theories of heredity. In *Joseph Andrews* he especially ridicules the practice of the antiquarian biographer because it represents a clear case of the false reliance on the accumulation of fact elevated into an absolute (and limiting) truth.

As Lucian's injunctions indicate the best use of facts to seek a truth about the past through the description of situation and event, Hogarth's practice implies a possible way

---

[g] This caricature continues the criticism of Richardson, who, in the previous chapter, was described as "an historian who borrows his lights, as the common method is, from authentic papers and records" (I, i, p. 14) .

to use the facts of human appearance to discover truths about individual character. In the Preface to *Joseph Andrews* Fielding distinguishes between Burlesque, which purveys facts without a framework, and the Ridiculous, which describes only those observable features which have internal relevance:

> He who should call the ingenious Hogarth a burlesque painter, would in my opinion do him very little honour; for sure it is much easier, much less the subject of admiration, to paint a man with a nose, or any other feature, of a preposterous size, or to expose him in some absurd or monstrous attitude, than to express the affections of men on canvas. It hath been thought a vast commendation of a painter, to say his figures *seem to breathe*; but surely it is a much greater and nobler applause, *that they appear to think* (pp. 9–10).

But Fielding, in his efforts to define the peculiar nature and role of the novel, is again very sensitive to the abuses of Hogarth's method by men of less genius.[h] Hogarth's details, whether personal or situational, are always related to larger moral and especially literary effects. But individuals who base estimates of character in daily life on mere physical features deal in the same kind of superficial reality that preoccupied the fact-grubbing biographers. *Joseph Andrews* is the most Hogarthian of Fielding's novels because it is so concerned with the abuses to which Hogarth's method is liable.[17] In "An Essay of the Knowledge of the Characters of Men," printed in the *Miscellanies* and written after 1735, Fielding points out that most people who think they can judge by countenance are easily taken in by exaggeration and sham: ". . . the true symptoms being finer, and less glaring, make no impression on our physiognomist; while the grosser appearances of affectation are sure to attract his eye, and deceive his judgment."[18]

[h] Harrison has nothing in his house "that may not be absolutely necessary, except books, and the prints of Mr. Hogarth, whom he calls a moral satirist" (*Amelia*, III, xii, p. 149).

The standard of observed action, despite its own problems, Fielding considers to be much more accurate. In fact, in his efforts to define fiction as a special way of understanding the world, Fielding seems to imply that the insights of painting are by their nature almost opposed to those yielded by the novel. The tension between scene and presentation, often complexly expressed in the novel, can be at best expressed only simply in painting. *Joseph Andrews* keeps the special claims of the painter's view of life close to the surface because Fielding is entranced with its possibilities, even while he is aware of its deficiencies.[19]

The critical scrutiny of physiognomy begun in the "Essay on Characters" is clearly intensified in *Joseph Andrews*, where physiognomics is criticized both as a science and a literary technique. Many physiognomic descriptions at first seem to coincide with actual character. Mrs. Towwouse rails at those who have brought the naked Joseph to her inn: "And indeed, if Mrs. Tow-wouse had given no utterance to the sweetness of her temper, nature had taken such pains in her countenance, that Hogarth himself never gave more expression to a picture" (I, xiv, p. 54). But it is nevertheless difficult to derive from her face how she will act. The narrator must intervene to explain that she is later cordial to Joseph, not because she had had a change of heart, but because she has noticed Joseph's white skin and his acquaintance with Parson Adams, whom she deems a gentleman. She herself acts from appearances. But the narrator implies the existence of a complexity of motivations that physiognomy cannot appreciate. Fielding is basically more interested in the way people interpret facts than in the individual facts themselves. Joseph and Fanny, who bear most of the brunt of the misinterpretations in the novel, do not have individualized physical descriptions. In some particulars they seem interchangeable:

> His hair was of a nut-brown color, and was displayed in wanton ringlets down his neck. His forehead was high, his eyes dark, and as full of sweetness as of fire. His nose

a little inclined to the Roman. His teeth white and even. His lips full, red, and soft (I, viii, pp. 30–31).

Her hair was of a chestnut brown, and nature had been extremely lavish to her of it, which she had cut, and on Sundays used to curl down to her neck in the modern fashion. Her forehead was high, her eyebrows arched, and rather full than otherwise. Her eyes black and sparkling; her nose just inclining to the Roman; her lips red and moist, and her underlip, according to the opinion of the ladies, too pouting. Her teeth were white, but not exactly even (II, xii, p. 129).

The problems of physiognomy and description imply the problems of presentation and interpretation. In light of the falsifications of physiognomy, how might we criticize the historian or the novelist or the individual whose main claim to our trust is that he is a reporter, an editor, or a collector of facts?

Fielding's attitude toward physiognomics can refine our understanding of Abraham Adams, "who ne'er saw farther into people than they desired to let him" (II, x, p. 122), and who, of all the characters in *Joseph Andrews*, has the most complete and most philosophic commitment to physiognomic explanation. His innocent belief in appearance is a critical commonplace. Yet it is not often remarked that he elevates this belief, in the form of physiognomics, into an elaborate and total philosophic system. Far from being an optimistic *naïf*, he fashions his own vision into general precepts by which he proceeds to judge the world. When later actions upset the assumptions he has derived from countenances, he questions the actions, rather than his own interpretations.[i]

Toward the center of *Joseph Andrews* occur several scenes in which Fielding explores the inadequacies of Adams'

---

[i] I here emphasize Fielding's criticisms of Adams' view of the world because the critical stress is usually in the other direction. For a good account of Adams as innocent hero, "Fielding's errant Christian knight," see Martin Battestin's introduction to his edition of *Joseph Andrews* and *Shamela*.

view of the world. At an inn Adams, Joseph, and Fanny meet a gentleman who, after a long discussion of charity, commends Adams for having "the true principles of a Christian divine" and promises him a benefice, horses, money, and a lodging at his home for several days.[j] When none of these gifts materialize, Adams does not wonder if he has been gulled. He had called the gentleman "a Christian of the true primitive kind" and can believe only that the gentleman's servants have somehow thwarted his generosity:

> Was ever anything so unlucky as this poor gentleman? I protest I am more sorry on his account than my own. You see, Joseph, how this good-natured man is treated by his servants; one locks up his linen, another physics his horses; and, I suppose, by his being at this house last night, the butler has locked up his cellar. Bless us! how good-nature is used in this world! (II, xvi, p. 148).

Joseph draws upon his experience as a London servant and says that perhaps the gentleman is at fault; the host comments that this man had done similar things before. Adams is finally convinced. But he has lingering doubts, which appear in subsequent discussions of physiognomy.

Because Adams believes that his first judgment was based on immutably true grounds, he argues that "promising" is only an aberration in a basically good character. The proof of this goodness is in the gentleman's face:

> Nay, if he could but once see the meanness of this detestable vice; would he but once reflect that he is one of the most scandalous as well as pernicious liars; sure he must despise himself to so intolerable degree, that it would be impossible for him to continue a moment in such a course. And, to confess the truth, notwithstanding the baseness of this character, which he hath too well deserved, he hath in his countenance sufficient symptoms of that *bona indoles*, that sweetness of disposition,

[j] In the "Essay on Characters" Fielding identifies this type of person as "the Promiser" (Henley, XXV, p. 293) .

which furnishes out a good Christian (II, xvii, pp. 153–54).

Most of the innkeepers in *Joseph Andrews* are too quick to judge from externals and would agree with this estimate, but Adams' companion is different. He has traveled widely and believes that nothing about a man can be learned from his countenance except physical facts about that countenance: "Symptoms in his countenance, quotha! I would look there, perhaps, to see whether a man had the smallpox, but for nothing else." Adams says that he has travelled more in books than the innkeeper has on land and sea.[k] The only knowledge of value is gained from books and that is where he got his ideas on physiognomy: "From them I learn what I just asserted now, that nature generally imprints such a portraiture of the mind in the countenance, that a skilful physiognomist will rarely be deceived."

Adams then tells the story of Socrates and the physiognomist, which, although it purports to show that a good physiognomist is usually right, actually turns back upon itself. What matter is it that Socrates had admitted that he is as naturally inclined to vice as the physiognomist said? Socrates also points out that philosophy has changed his natural inclinations; thus he implies the irrelevancy of physiognomic explanation to an immediately valid picture of an individual.[20]

Adams relies totally on physiognomy, and appearances in general, because he believes he has a deductive system—the authority of the ancients and the precepts of Christianity—into which the facts of existence automatically fit.[1] His phi-

---

[k] Fielding slyly casts doubt on Adams' pretensions to "travel" by having him misplace the Levant geographically because he has relied solely on its etymological derivation.

[1] Adams is not above using a Biblical text for his own purposes in what he believes to be a good cause. He assumes, for example, that Joseph and Fanny want to marry before the banns have been posted three times because Joseph is overcome with carnal desires. (Actually, Joseph wants to avoid further interference by Lady Booby.) Adams therefore scolds Joseph with a "suitable" quotation from the

losophy has little sense of immediate context. The world fulfills the forms established by books; change and time are not a factor. The views of the ancients are equally applicable to their time and his own; often there seems to be little difference. The host fruitlessly asserts the importance of knowledge gathered from observation, while Adams upholds ancient authority. Each overstates, and each is unmoved.

> "Friend," cries Adams, "if a man should sail round the world, and anchor in every harbour of it, without learning, he would return home as ignorant as he went out." "Lord help you!" answered the host; "there was my boatswain, poor fellow! he could scarce either write or read, and yet he would navigate a ship with any master of a man-of-war; and a pretty knowledge of trade he had too." "Trade," answered Adams, "as Aristotle proves in his first chapter of Politics, is below a philosopher, and unnatural as it is managed now" (II, xvii, p. 255).[m]

The innkeeper can understand this slur only in a contemporary context as a support of Walpole's attacks against tradesmen: "The host looked steadfastly at Adams, and after a minute's silence asked him, 'if he was one of the writers of the *Gazetteers*? for I have heard,' says he, 'they are writ by parsons.' " Adams remains as blissfully ignorant of contemporary politics as he had been of contemporary social

---

Bible: "The text will be, child, Matthew the 5th, and part of the 28th verse, 'Whosoever looketh on a woman, so as to lust after her.' The latter part I shall omit, as foreign to my purpose" (IV, viii, p. 264). The actual text continues: "hath committed adultery with her already in his heart." This "adaptation" by Adams must have been important to Fielding's presentation of his character, for it was added in the second edition. Martin Battestin notes the inappropriateness of the text for Adams' purposes, but considers it a case of "Fielding having some fun here at Adams' expense" (Notes to *Joseph Andrews*, p. 363). Perhaps more interesting is the distance Fielding has come from the simpler satire of a character like Parson Tickletext in *Shamela*.

[m] The phrase "he could scarce either write or read, and yet" was added by Fielding in a later edition.

trends in his misunderstanding of the meaning of "coquette":

> "*Gazetteers!*" answered Adams, "what is that?" "It is a dirty newspaper," replied the host, "which hath been given away all over the nation for these many years, to abuse trade and honest men, which I would not suffer to lie on my table, though it had been offered me for nothing." "Not I truly," said Adams; "I never write anything but sermons. . . ."

Adams' ignorance might, in fact, be characterized as the lack of a sense of history.

This fairly harmless obtuseness can, however, have a more serious effect, for Adams' innocence is peculiarly dogmatic. It is not so much a lack of knowledge about the world as it is a wilful adherence to only one way of gaining that knowledge. Facts are for Adams only specific instances of already established truths. He tells Joseph that "knowledge of men is only to be learnt from books" (II, xvi, p. 150). But Joseph's experience as a London servant clearly gives him much more insight into the behavior of the "promiser" than any of Adams' precepts. Adams' external view of things derives from both a basically egotistical belief in the goodness and accuracy of his own perceptions and a selfless belief in the truths of Christian dogma. His excesses are comical and he can escape much of our censure because his instincts and intentions are good. But his method of understanding the world does not get off so easily.

In characters who are not as benevolent as Adams, the commitment to appearances is more sinister. All the innkeepers who judge by the appearance of clothes reflect Adams' philosophic commitment to physiognomy; all the deluded women who act from vanity reflect his vain pride in his scholarliness, his ability to write sermons, and his technique of brewing beer. These characters tend to take words as things, to believe in social formulas as immutable truths, and to worry more about the opinion of the world than about the moral validity of their actions. After the story of Leonora, each of the characters in the coach reacts in his own way. Mrs. Slipslop feels immediate sympathy with Leonora as another woman with a problem; Miss Graveairs treats her as a moral (or immoral) exemplum; and Adams introduces an appropriate classical analogy:

> "Poor woman!" says Mrs. Slipslop, "what a terrible *quandary* she must be in!" "Not at all," says Miss Grave-airs, "such sluts can never be confounded." "She must have more than Corinthian assurance," said Adams; "ay, more than Lais herself" (II, iv, p. 93).

Attention to surface meaning saves one from the need to search out more complex and therefore more difficult truths.

The difference between Adams and such characters is spontaneity. What appeals to us in Adams' character always emerges in response to a particular situation, without the mediation of preconceived form. Other characters are frozen by their preconceptions and substitute social formulas for sympathy. Adams' immediate sympathy with those in distress and his charity are never arguable; but they often are in conflict with his own precepts. When a specific event occurs, Adams will make doctrine coincide with spontaneous humanity; but when he argues abstractly, he is often as fatuous and as detached from the human reality of the immediate situation as is Trulliber or Barnabas. Wilson believes in the absolute villainy of the world; Adams believes in its absolute goodness. Each needs to temper his response to include the usually mixed nature of any situation. But their theories usually rule out other possibilities. In the puddle incident of Book Two, Adams takes visible fact to be the only truth. Such a scene does show his exuberant willingness to wade directly into the problems of the world, as he later rescues Fanny. But it also illustrates his defective sense of other possibilities:

> He therefore resolved to proceed slowly forwards, not doubting but that he should be shortly overtaken; and

soon came to a large water, which, filling the whole road, he saw no method of passing unless by wading through, which he accordingly did up to his middle; but was no sooner got to the other side, than he perceived, if he had looked over the hedge, he would have found a footpath capable of conducting him without wetting his shoes (II, ii, p. 78).

Adams *sees* one possibility and acts on it; he only *perceives* other possibilities through hindsight. The facts of the case exist purely. Adams does not appreciate how opinion, assumptions about the world, and a commitment to different kinds of knowledge can distort the seemingly immutable fact. He may act spontaneously; but he thinks in strictured patterns.[21]

Adams can be called the "hero" of *Joseph Andrews* because both his delusions and his virtues are at the center of Fielding's interest in the problem of knowledge.[22] We see all the characters in postures of deception and self-deception that illustrate their various inabilities to see clearly and perceptively and, therefore, to act. Fielding writes in *Joseph Andrews* a history that, unlike the public histories, *might* help the reader to understand the world. Too great a reliance on separate facts, he says, is as bad as a reliance on warped general assumptions; each feeds the other. Adams' blindness may be reflected in the blindness of other characters in the novel, but it is essential to recognize that he never hurts anyone by his excesses. Yet his good nature does not justify his faulty epistemology, however it may excuse it. The indicated solution is clear: to live in the world of *Joseph Andrews*, or a world like it, one must be able to integrate, as Adams cannot, the demands of spontaneity and context with those of form and generalization. Fielding never criticizes the doctrine supported by Adams. He criticizes how it is applied in the world and whether or not it is relevant. There is a good in Adams' behavior, but the greater concern of *Joseph Andrews* is with how this good has been needlessly hampered by Adams' view of the world.[n]

MANY OF FIELDING'S THEMES in *Joseph Andrews* grow therefore from a reaction against deficiencies in previous historiographical methods and purposes. Hume attempts to invoke the better self of history by a new approach to old problems. Fielding attempts to evolve a new form that will better serve history's professed ends. Through his narrative technique in *Joseph Andrews* he suggests how detail and context may properly be used to create a fictional world and thereby to understand an actual world. By using facts in *Joseph Andrews* to make particular points or complete specific causal progressions, Fielding implies that individual facts in fiction and in history should be used only in a frame of causal or circumstantial relevance. The narrator decides the relevance of fact. To emphasize this control, he occasionally mentions that he has left out something irrelevant. Later, in *Tom Jones,* Fielding extends this "technique of omission" and makes it more central to his interest in knowledge. But in *Joseph Andrews* he tends to concentrate on what facts should be left in and how they are related to both generalization and abstraction.[o]

Both facts and situations in *Joseph Andrews* must ultimately reveal the individual nature of the characters. But again Fielding is more interested in the process of under-

[n] Adams' conscious commitment to absolute precepts and his unconscious commitment to spontaneous action is partially resolved in his attitude toward the question of faith versus works. Throughout the novel he refuses to accept faith without works and continually argues with those characters who believe that religion should stay in the church. His goodness rests in his willingness to apply the idealistic solutions of Christianity to the problems he meets in the world, just as it is his weakness to believe that there is no situation that does not fit under his rubrics. In *Shamela* the hypocritical Parson Williams delivers a sermon praising faith over works.

[o] One example of the narrator's invocation of a standard of relevance occurs on IV, v, p. 249: "It would be unnecessary, if I was able, which indeed I am not, to relate the conversation between these two gentlemen, which rolled, as I have been informed, entirely on the subject of horse-racing."

standing itself than in what we finally learn. Facts about people must also meet the test of relevance. We do not, for example, learn Wilson's name until well into his story, for his name individuates him less than his story. The narrator rarely gives a proper name when he can help it. In this way, Fielding's characters function both as figures in a specific plot and as "representatives of general nature," whose names give the reader only the least idea of their individuality. Fanny, for example, has figured in the novel for three chapters before she is described. Her description finally comes not as an amalgam of detail that will make the novel more realistic, but in response to the logic of its narrative movement. Naturally enough, she must be described in the kind of romance terms that the narrator has already imposed upon the reader's expectations: " . . . reader, if thou art of an amorous hue, I advise thee to skip over the next paragraph; which, to render our history perfect, we are obliged to set down, humbly, hoping that we may escape the fate of Pygmalion . . ." (II, xii, p. 128). Thus, when we see the idealized description that follows, we have been already prepared for the possibility that the presentation colors the facts of the case and that the describer—the narrator—may be indulging in his own romantic fantasies.[p]

Most of the force of *Joseph Andrews* centers therefore in specific situations. The narrator uses facts to place a situation in a context of causality. In II, v, for example, Adams finds Joseph in the kitchen of the Tow-wouses' inn, being treated for a contusion. The narrator then backtracks to explain. He tells about the strange behavior of Adams' horse (which Joseph was riding), how Adams could have dealt with it, why Joseph could not, and the resultant fall and injury. In later novels, Fielding will make a larger point of retracing the causes which contribute to an occurrence.

[p] This chapter deals particularly with the distortions of reality worked by romantic rhetoric. Joseph's stylized Strephon-Chloe song is juxtaposed with his immediate physical response when he recognizes Fanny. Similarly, Adams accidentally drops his Aeschylus into the fire in his exuberance over the meeting.

In *Joseph Andrews* he is content to form little eddies of causality about situations in order to make them appear realistic not by their profusion of detail, but by the way in which they are related to the flow of events.

At the center of a situation are characters whose nature and ideas of the world are illuminated by it. As facts are lifeless without a context, so individuals are abstract stereotypes unless they can be displayed in situations. Fielding asserts in III, i, that he desires to show species, not individuals. But these "species" are not the formulas of the character-books. Their individuality emerges and is inductively revealed in context, not deductively (or pictorially) in stasis. When the stagecoach riders discover Joseph naked, the event is not an important link in a causal chain, but rather a situation that illustrates the nature of several characters through their reactions to it. Joseph's role in this scene is similar to the one he plays throughout the novel: the object of the attitudes of others.[23] We are directed to note how the people in the coach fall into extreme attitudes at the appearance of this extreme experience. Each passenger spins out a web of characteristic jargon to absorb the facts of Joseph's condition into their separate systems. The lawyer mouths legalism, the lady invokes moral abstractions, the gentleman is witty, and the coachman demands a shilling for the ride. Each hides behind his chosen forms and uses them to obscure what should be his clear human duty. The gestures of humanity that should have arisen spontaneously at the sight of Joseph are finally made, but only for reasons that accord with the private systems of the passengers. The lawyer decides that they should take in Joseph to avoid prosecution for his murder if he happens to die from exposure; the gentleman agrees, thinking Joseph's condition will be a good excuse for wit to impress the lady, ". . . till, partly alarmed by the threats of the one, and partly by the promises of the other, and perhaps being *a little* moved with compassion at the poor creature's condition, who stood bleeding and shivering with the cold, [the coachman] at length agreed . . ." (I, xii, p. 43). As if to counterbalance the reactions of the passengers, Fielding introduces the extreme action of the postilion. The harsh irony of his later transportation appropriately concludes a scene expressed in broad ironies, as if to illustrate the difficulties of decisions in a real world.

When Fielding reveals character, he exposes the masks and systematic deceptions through which people distort the meaning of facts and events and the nature of other people. There is more caricature in *Joseph Andrews* than in Fielding's other novels because here he is more interested in the minute distortions of everyday life and personality that are perpetrated by false views of the world. Lady Booby is the only character who seems to grow at all in the course of the novel. She begins like a Humian atomized "character" in whose mind Love, Honor, Pride, Pity, and Revenge debate about Joseph (I, ix, p. 36). Yet she is "the heroine of our history" (I, vii, p. 30). We gain a similarly reductive access to her mind in IV, iv; but she is the only character we get inside in even the most rudimentary way. Adams breaks from his forms by spontaneity. Lady Booby's laugh in IV, xiv, shows that she has achieved a more detached perspective. For a moment she has drawn back and seen the absurdities of everyone, including herself.[24] But Fielding has given her character at best only a sporadic complexity.

As no character really develops in the course of *Joseph Andrews*, there is also little development in the plot. Fielding never tries to mold events into larger patterns within the whole of *Joseph Andrews*. The connections between adjoining incidents are often fortuitous or nonexistent. Like Hume, Fielding may believe at this stage that an aesthetically organized form falsifies through its excessive rigidity. His doggedly episodic progress in *Joseph Andrews* certainly implies a severe scrutiny of any theory of history or human knowledge that dares to enforce pattern on more than just a small scale. Fielding ties together the frequently discrete episodes of *Joseph Andrews* by the thinnest and most coincidence-ridden thread of the kind of romance narrative he detested.[25] At the same time, whenever possible he explodes the typical narrative climaxes of all other literary forms. We are suspensefully titillated for several pages with speculation about the moment when Joseph will learn of Pamela's marriage to Mr. Booby; when the time comes, we find that a servant has already told him. *Joseph Andrews* is a kind of imitative form that attempts to mirror a world in which spurious unities are continually undermined and generalizations faced with counter examples.[26]

Fielding de-emphasizes the importance of tight causal pattern in *Joseph Andrews* because he wishes to view the pattern of life from the bottom, through the many complex facts of existence. Strict causality constitutes a species of explanation that can compel falsification as complete as any compelled by the unthinking use of institutional or doctrinal forms. Fielding assumes that there is a complexity in the world that inevitably defeats simplistic systematizing. Used appropriately, facts can confound the urge to insist upon rigid (and false) patterns. The fact-collecting editor or biographer assumes that the facts themselves completely determine and validate his general truths, whatever they may be. Their narrative forms are as deductive as those of the historians who write from political bias or the romancers who write from distorted ideas of human nature. To cleanse himself of such approaches, Fielding in *Joseph Andrews* deals with the minute details surrounding situation and character. Such an emphasis is not conducive to the discovery of larger patterns of development.[q]

The *a priori* systems of characters like Adams or any snobbish innkeeper, canting lawyer, or plenteous priest absorb all facts indiscriminately. But the true perceiver implied in *Joseph Andrews* should know the relevance of facts. He should use his assumptions about life and human

q The critics who interpret the novel as the illustration of an abstraction like charity often avoid the problem of structure and offer no rationale for the procession of episodes. See, for example, Battestin, Introduction to *Joseph Andrews* and *Shamela*. Compare W. B. Gallie, *Philosophy and the Historical Understanding*, p. 23: ". . . moral homilies are often bad or ruin good stories because they are too much like scientific proofs."

nature creatively rather than restrictively, without believing in their power to predict or control the daily events of his life. Systematic thought in *Joseph Andrews* not only limits a character's view of the world outside himself, but also limits his own potential humanity and, naturally, the reader's opinion of him. Such characters caricature themselves by, for example, their frequent use of jargon. Adams becomes a caricature partisan of the Ancients in the physiognomics discussion; Lawyer Scout spins out more and more legalisms as he continues to speak. Fielding's use of jargon as a frequent butt of satire in *Joseph Andrews* reflects his belief that deductive systems brandish words instead of understanding them and using them properly. For the narrow-minded man, forms are a trap and a refuge from empirically based thought. Facts do not revitalize his ideas; they become newly pinned butterflies in his collection. The unthinking application of generalities fostered by political institutions, law, or religious doctrine distorts not only the importance of individual acts and situations but also the meaning of words themselves. Words finally become things.

Fielding's ideal of knowledge in *Joseph Andrews* is therefore inductive. We may have general precepts before we act; but we must expose them to the qualifications of experience, rather than let experience be only a list of twisted exempla. Fielding puts his own construction on Bolingbroke's injunction that "history is philosophy teaching by example." He insists that there be a continual play between the generality and its manifestations in the world, with the former constantly at the mercy of the latter. A novel that contains an easily perceivable pattern falsifies the world as much as does a history with one theory or a person who applies a simplistic set of rules to the complexity of life. In *Joseph Andrews* Fielding emphasizes a totally inductive approach to the phenomena of life by making his seeming pattern—the discovery of Joseph's parentage—a ludicrous carry-over from the worst kind of romance. The reader must make sense of the multiplicity of incident through his own growing perception of how the world of *Joseph Andrews* works, not through any preconceived notions of how novels are constructed. As Fielding says early in the novel:

> It is an observation sometimes made, that to indicate our idea of a simple fellow, we say, "He is easily to be seen through": nor do I believe it a more improper denotation of a simple book. Instead of applying this to any particular performance, we choose rather to remark the contrary in this history, where the scene opens itself by small degrees; and he is a sagacious reader who can see two chapters before him (I, xi, p. 39).

The narrator himself breaks out of the forms that he has arranged for the occasion. He starts with a Preface loaded with reference to all sorts of literary authority, but in the course of the novel continually cites authors whose names he has "forgotten"; he attacks romance for its lack of reality and then introduces the overblown account of the discovery of Joseph's ancestry; he sets up the philosophical introductory chapter as a hallmark of his new form and then leaves it out in his final book. It is tempting to consider the famous Preface to be something of a blind for the Adamsian reader, if only because the narrator takes pains to dissociate himself from the kind of validation by the classics that it parades:

> Plato and Aristotle, or somebody else, hath said . . . [what they said plus a quotation from Virgil]. I would quote more great men if I could; but my memory not permitting me, I will proceed to exemplify these observations by the following instance . . . (II, xv, p. 144).

The often remarked disparity between the dicta of the Preface to *Joseph Andrews* and the body of the novel is therefore functional. It is another statement of the clash between precepts and experience, ideas and actions, with which the novel is preoccupied.

IF FIELDING DWELLS upon small parts of the novel's structure because he wishes to show the bad effects of literary pattern, what constitutes the unity of *Joseph Andrews?* This is a difficult question to answer because the main thrust of the novel seems to be often negative and destructive. Fielding attacks what is bad both in individual views of the world and in literary forms that pretend to embody the world. Yet he is himself caught in the paradox of his own making, for he has not quite decided what is good control and what is good patterning. The main positive value in *Joseph Andrews* is spontaneity and the ability to learn from experience. In literary terms, therefore, Fielding frequently asserts that the novel is in great part a recaptured reality. He remarks before the "roasting scene":

> Mr. Adams, from whom we had most of this relation, could not recollect all the jests of this kind practised on him, which the inoffensive disposition of his own heart made him slow in discovering; and indeed, had it not been for the information which we received from a servant of the family, this part of our history, which we take to be none of the least curious, must have been deplorably imperfect; though we must own it probable that some more jokes were (as they call it) "cracked" during their dinner; but we have by no means been able to come to the knowledge of them (III, viii, p. 207).[r]

Yet there exists a tension between the novel as recaptured reality and the novel as reconstructed reality. Fielding seems caught in an almost Humian dilemma: facts are potentially vitalizing; they have a kind of "objective" truth; yet "objective" narration pretends a point of view impossible for man. Fielding's comments on the use of words mirror this problem. Along with his satire of jargon he also satirizes any character for whom words have become

[r] Compare the narrator's remark after Joseph's speech on charity: "This was all of Mr. Joseph Andrews's speech which I could get him to recollect, which I have delivered as near as was possible in his own words, with a very small embellishment" (III, vi, p. 199).

real things. Adams again is a prime example. He cannot encompass the idea of verbal paradox because for him every word is an unalloyed reality. His son Dick tells the story of Leonard and Paul:

> "But, good as the lady was, she was still a woman: that is to say, an angel, and not an angel."—"You must mistake, child," cries the parson, "for you read nonsense." "It is so in the book," answered the son. Mr. Adams was then silenced by authority, and Dick proceeded (IV, x, p. 272).

Such a belief in the reality of words appears more malevolently in the severe deposition against Fanny and Joseph. They are to be sent to prison for cutting "one hasel-twig, of the value, he believes, of 3 halfpence, or thereabouts":

> "Jesu!" said the squire, "would you commit two persons to Bridewell for a twig?" "Yes," said the lawyer, "and with great lenity too; for if we had called it a young tree, they would have both have been hanged" (IV, v, p. 247).

But how does such criticism reflect on the writer who uses words to construct a plausible world?

Words, like facts, are not things in themselves but respond to the order that controls them. In *Joseph Andrews* Fielding has begun to move toward a distinction between the momentary, open-ended order of aesthetic form and the static order of institutional, political, and social necessities. Aesthetic form is an ideal for human action because it can order without compelling, explain without cataloguing, vary without fragmenting. Naturally, the perception of this form is reserved for the reader rather than the characters, and such perception might be on a different level from the perceptions of moral truths available to characters and reader alike. In *Joseph Andrews* Fielding makes the first steps toward a form in which the reader becomes the ideal perceiver. Within *Joseph Andrews*, and in the later novels, there is no character who is fully aware of what occurs, or who has no fault. As *Tom Jones* will show, Fielding's real hero is the best reader, not the best character. By Book IV of *Joseph Andrews* Fielding can rely on the reader to be more perceptive than any involved character because he has been led by the narrator so far through the novel. Fielding injects a parenthesis into the remarks of Lady Booby, who reminds Adams " ' . . . of the many great obligations you have had to this family' (with all which the reader hath, in the course of this history, been minutely acquainted) . . . " (IV, ii, p. 240).

The narrator and the reader are in complicity; they stand together on a plane of apprehension separate from that of the characters. The characters, says the narrator, are caught in time and space, while the reader and the narrator have no such limitations. The coachman refuses Mrs. Slipslop's request that he continue to chase after the fleet Adams: "But we will be more courteous to our reader than he was to Mrs. Slipslop; and leaving the coach and its company to pursue their journey, we will carry our reader on after parson Adams . . . " (II, vii, p. 109). Because of the greater awareness to which the narrator helps the reader, he can hopefully perceive a general but undistorted aesthetic pattern in what for the characters is immediate experience.

But Fielding fails to inform this relation between the reader and the narrator with any shaping power because he has an inconsistent narrative stance. The narrator at some times takes appearances for truth and at others seeks for the qualifications of truth necessary to understand a complex situation. If we overcriticize Adams for his foolishness and silly behavior, it is usually because the narrator has indulged himself in the *Caricatura* side of humor, which he had so criticized in the Preface. The swarm of facts that seem to cluster about Adams are often especially designed to make him ridiculous either in dress or general physical appearance. Adams in fact may be a trap for the reader who, like himself, judges by appearances, by the figure cut or by the ostensible countenance, rather than by the behavior that reveals inner character. It is difficult to find the narrator qualifying his ridicule of Adams in such situations:

It is not perhaps easy to describe the figure of Adams; he had risen in such a violent hurry, that he had on neither breeches nor stockings; nor had he taken from his head a red spotted handkerchief, which by night bound his wig, that was turned inside out, around his head. He had on his torn cassock and his greatcoat; but, as the remainder of his cassock hung down below his greatcoat, so did a small stripe of white, or rather whitish, linen appear below that; to which we may add the several colours which appeared on his face, where a long piss-burnt beard served to retain the liquor of the stonepot, and that of a blacker hue which distilled from the top (III, xii, p. 229).

The narrative voice emerges more often to ridicule than to mediate. Fielding remains an observer of the world he creates rather than a complete understander. We ourselves must interpret the actions of Adams as good and balance these good acts with his absurdities. In his effort to detach himself from setting up any figure in *Joseph Andrews* as an ideal of behavior, the narrator revokes his responsibility to coherence. Like Hume, he enters, but not enough. He has not completely thought out what the role of the narrator should be.

In *Joseph Andrews* Fielding successfully shows that facts alone are not sufficient to verify the existence of a fictional world. He concentrates instead upon the many ways in which they can be distorted by the deductive assumptions of individuals, whether benevolent or malign. Facts build situations and situations are the means through which the truth of individual character can be known. One might associate Fielding with Berkeley in his de-emphasis of the importance or even existence of phenomena separate from the mind. But facts do not breed large causes in *Joseph Andrews*. Fielding purges the novel of any general causes in order to present a world that must be appreciated moment by moment, even if these moments seem to have little connection. His own method of presentation, the sardonic narrator, reflects this essentially accumulative view of the world. The narrator never emerges as a coherent point of view, but rather as a satiric observer who punctures all pretenses. He proceeds as empirically as does the reader. In this way *Joseph Andrews* has the best and worst aspects of an imitative form. Fielding attacks the "objective" method of factual accumulation used by the antiquarian, the "biographer," and the Richardsonian "editor," because it hides deductive assumptions about how the facts should be selected and arranged. But he does not present a method to replace theirs. By the very existence of his narrator he does emphasize the need for a pattern, a definite point of view. He does recognize the fallacy that the fact collectors engage in when they assert the superior truth of their method. But *Joseph Andrews* is too involved in an attack against falsifying pattern for Fielding to present a coherent and appropriate pattern of his own. In *Jonathan Wild* he explores the possibility of pattern. If *Joseph Andrews* views life from the bottom, through the screen of factual *prima materia, Jonathan Wild* views it from above, from the God's-eye view of abstract pattern.

III. *Jonathan Wild:* The Varieties of Historical
    Explanation

Others apart sat on a Hill retir'd,
In thoughts more elevate, and reason'd high
Of Providence, Foreknowledge, Will, and Fate,
Fixt Fate, Free will, Foreknowledge absolute,
And found no end, in wand'ring mazes lost.
    Milton, *Paradise Lost*, II, 557–61

Indeed, most Historians, as well Christian as Pagan, have fallen into this idle Superstition, and spoken of ill Successes, unforeseen Disasters, and terrible Events, as if they had been let into the Secrets of Providence, and made acquainted with that private Conduct with which the World is governed.
    Joseph Addison, *Spectator* #483

While *Joseph Andrews* explored the private world of immediate experience, *Jonathan Wild* takes up the public, the structured, the institutionalized. Facts are less important in *Jonathan Wild* than they were in *Joseph Andrews*; Fielding is instead more interested in the kinds of patterns that pretend to encompass and supersede the minutely factual. *Joseph Andrews* dwelt on the proposition that actions could test abstractly-held principles. Action again usually contradicts principle in *Jonathan Wild*. But our attention is focused instead on the way principles are formulated.

Categories were also important in *Joseph Andrews*, but for the most part they were created for the painless absorption of private experience; they were prejudices that both blinded their possessor to what was actually happening and stifled his response to experience. The religious and doctrinal categories of Adams may occupy a much higher plane than the class prejudices of the many innkeepers, but they too are essentially based upon and designed for the private sphere of action. On the other hand, the categories of the characters—and the narrator—of *Jonathan Wild* are public categories, forms intended to comprehend and explain the entire history of the world, forms that are not only guides for action in the present, but also explanations of why people acted a certain way in the past and how they will act in the future. In *Joseph Andrews* institutional and public figures like judges, lawyers, and clergymen were frequently a source of the comic, while individual and spontaneous virtue provided a counterpoise to their dogmatic systematizing. In *Jonathan Wild* the nature of the public world is more fully examined, while private virtue—and private vice—become stereotyped and unrealistic. The thematic interests and narrative methods of the two novels are both parallel and ultimately complementary; they finally merge in *Tom Jones*.[27] As *Joseph Andrews* attacked the writers and historians who made too much or too little of fact, so *Jonathan Wild*, with its interest in larger forms of organization, attacks the historians and biographers who manipulate concepts like Providence, Fortune, Fate, or the Great Man for their own literary advantage. Like the "editor" novelist or the antiquarian, they pretend to an objectivity that they do not really have.

The characters in *Jonathan Wild* mirror this conceptual orientation in two ways. There are those, like Wild, who appreciate the rhetorical possibilities of transcendental explanations and manipulate them to achieve power. And there are those, like Heartfree, who accept such explanations as totally sufficient ways to comprehend the minutiae of the world into a coherent system. Both views are finally insufficient; neither Wild nor Heartfree has the inclusive perspective and the consequent freedom of action that Fielding believes is essential. Both become ultimately trapped by their patterns, Wild by his emphasis on rhetorical form and Heartfree by his providential explanations. *Jonathan Wild* finally implies, as had *Joseph Andrews*, that the ideal vision of events belongs only to the narrator and, hopefully, to the reader.[28]

IN SOME WAY or another every character in *Jonathan Wild* is trying to control others or to assert that he acts a particular way because he is controlled. When characters are tossed by circumstance, they console themselves by observing that their pain is not gratuitous, but part of some vast design; they thereby salve their feelings from the hurt caused by the momentary possibility of their own insignificance. They are readers of history who happen not to be statesmen but who still invoke the abstract categories of ecclesiastical or political history to rule their daily lives. Wild gains his ascendancy because he has some detachment from this obsessive belief in the pattern of life. His momentary ability to see beyond the crude generalizations of those around him makes him believe that he is in control of the present and the future. He believes wholeheartedly in the shaping power of his own will and his ability to impose it upon situations and circumstances. Wild has a very acute understanding of the ways by which appearances fool people, and he manipulates them for his own ends. He can appreciate the naive prejudices of others, like their belief in physiognomy or the truth of expensive show. But ultimately he cannot recognize that, although his knowledge of forms is more acute, it is not necessarily more accurate.

Wild's view of the world is a categorizing one. He is always ready to line people up according to one classification or another, as his conversations with the Count la Ruse emphasize. The Count is in fact most impressed by Wild's ability to grasp the abstractions of any situation. Wild gains control within his gang and in the outside world by his use of rhetoric and command of abstract argument. He achieves most of his success because the people he imposes upon have just those prejudices which he knows best how to manipulate. In his gang he appeals to their love of ostentation and their willingness to submit themselves to his "greatness." Outside the gang his manipulations are most effective with the Heartfrees.

Heartfree is the perfect foil to Wild because his belief in the absolute domination of Providence over every aspect of life fits in well with Wild's own ideas of how the world works.[s] In the momentary toils of their relation, Wild's epistemology fits him to be a manipulator, Heartfree's to be a victim. Although Heartfree's view of the world works less direct harm than Wild's, it is equally misguided. Both limit man's potentialities, and Fielding continually impresses us with Heartfree's culpability for his own mistakes. Heartfree is Adams without the qualifications of spontaneity and goodheartedness.[t] Not that Heartfree is mean

[s] The narrator calls Heartfree "a kind of a foil." I have used *Jonathan Wild* and *The Journal of a Voyage to Lisbon*, intro. A. R. Humphreys (London, 1932). Further citation will be included in the text.

[t] When Adams' spontaneity is thwarted, he often invokes providential explanation, for example, when he and Joseph are tied to bedposts and cannot help Fanny (III, xi, p. 224). In another situation he argues for a stoicism rooted in providential explanation until he is told that his eldest son has drowned; whereupon he "soon began to stamp about the room and deplore his loss with the bitterest agony" (IV, viii, p. 265). (Compare the similar account of the Stoic in *Rasselas*, ch. 18.) But Adams still will not give up the stoical argument and tells Joseph

in any way. He is emotional but passive, a believer in appearances who philosophically distrusts his own ability to act. The sumptuously equipped Count easily imposes upon his credulity:

> His house, his equipage, his appearance, but, above all, a certain plausibility in his voice and behaviour would have deceived any, but one whose great and wise heart had dictated to him something within, which would have secured him from any danger of imposition from without. Heartfree, therefore, did not in the least scruple giving him credit . . . (II, iii, p. 52).

Heartfree does not have such a "great and wise heart." Later, when faced by his mistake, he tries to excuse himself to Wild "by insisting on the figure and outward appearance of the count and his equipage" (II, viii, p. 69). It does not occur to him that his own insight into character might be at fault, because he did not choose to go deeper than these externals.[29]

Heartfree is fixed at the first stage described by Fielding in the "Essay on Characters." He has not proceeded beyond surface appearances. Like Adams, his belief in surface is not merely an innocent lack of knowledge; he has erected it into the only true way of seeing the world. His belief in appearances and "countenance" is directly related to a belief that no man can act freely, because everything that occurs is part of a vast plan. Heartfree is the perfect representative of a Christianity that asserts the unimpor-

---

who has questioned his inconsistency, that this child is an exception. Such providential explanation is enlarged to the public sphere in the letters Fielding "receives" from Adams that are published in the *True Patriot.* Here Adams interprets the success of the Rebels in the 1745 Rebellion to be "the just Judgment of God against an offending People." See the elaborate new edition done by Miriam Austin Locke (University of Alabama Press, 1964), #7 (17 December 1745), p. 81, col. 3. Fielding juxtaposes Adams' remarks with the "Present History of Great Britain," a purely reportorial account that attempts to find verifiable causal patterns. Adams in a later letter says that, since the Rebels are still around, the penances he suggested must have been inadequate (*True Patriot* #13[21–28 January 1746], pp. 127–28).

tance of this life, man's insignificant place in it, and his inability to do anything at all about his lot. Heartfree reacts to misfortune not by trying to act, but by philosophizing about the reward he will receive in the after life because of his sufferings on earth:

> How indifferent must such a persuasion make a man to all the occurrences of this life! What trifles must he represent to himself both the enjoyments and the afflictions of this world! How easily must he acquiesce under missing the former, and how patiently will he submit to the latter, who is convinced that his failing of a transitory imperfect reward here is a most certain argument of his obtaining one permanent and complete hereafter! (III, x, p. 111).

While Wild assumes a role of dominance, Heartfree takes one of subservience. While Wild strives for more power and control, Heartfree accepts without question a fatality of occupation, birth, and station.[u] In his children he hopes to eradicate even the minute striving that has "marred" his own life. He thinks he should entrust them to the "goodness and power" of God, much as he has entrusted himself:

> Nor matters it what state of life is allotted for them, whether it be their fate to procure bread with their own labour, or to eat it at the sweat of other. Perhaps, if we consider the case with proper attention, or resolve it with due sincerity, the former is much the sweeter. The hind may be more happy than the lord, for his desires are fewer, and those such are attended with more hope and less fear. I will do my utmost to lay the foundations of my

[u] Fielding's frequent qualifications of Heartfree's "philosophy" would seem to undercut attempts to make the novelist an advocate of Christian stoicism. Compare also Heartfree's ideas with Gibbon's presentation of Constantine's conversion to Christianity. That religion, Gibbon says, would justify "passive and unresisting obedience . . . in the eyes of an absolute monarch, the most conspicuous and useful of the evangelic virtues" (Bury, ed., II, xx, p. 313). Such a juxtaposition of politics and religion can illuminate the relationship between Heartfree and Wild.

children's happiness, I will carefully avoid educating them in a station superior to their fortune, and for the event trust to that Being in whom whoever rightly confides, must be superior to all worldly sorrows (III, ii, p. 89).

Fielding may believe the greater morality often rests with the exploited rather than the exploiter. But he also attacks Heartfree's acquiescence and passivity, which, in the face of events, inspires only self-pity. Wild's belief in his power to manipulate is reinforced by Heartfree, who so readily abandons himself to manipulation.

Mrs. Heartfree's adventures on the desert island restate in action her husband's philosophical reliance on the idea of Providence to account for the shape of his life. Like her husband, she believes that Providence is continually present, regulating every act and subsuming every fact.[v] Mrs. Heartfree's adventures also present the opportunity for broader satiric thrusts at providential explanation, a method that would be out of place in the more solemn urban sections of the novel. The juxtaposition of a satiric view of providential explanation with a fantastic travel adventure may also embody Fielding's attitude to works like *Robinson Crusoe*, in which providential talk plays such a large part. *Jonathan Wild* seems, in fact, to be at least partly Fielding's effort to place Defoe's kind of characters into a world where their attitudes toward life are qualified and even contradicted. Like Robinson Crusoe (and Pamela, for that matter), Mrs. Heartfree believes she is always being saved by Heaven from whatever trouble she falls into. But, more clearly in her case than in Crusoe's, she often invents or exaggerates the trouble, as well as her rescue. She sees

[v] This section is often treated as an excursus inserted for purely comic effect. Fielding seems to strengthen such an interpretation in the Preface to the *Miscellanies*. He says that in *Jonathan Wild* he generally wishes to inculcate the advantages of goodness ". . . confining myself at the same time within the rules of probability. (For except one chapter, which is visibly meant as a burlesque on the extravagant accounts of travellers, I believe I have not exceeded it.) " See *The Works of Henry Fielding, Esq.*, ed. James P. Browne, 11 vols. (London, 1903) , XI, p. 93. The Preface is not printed in Henley.

herself, and is presented by Fielding, as a romantic heroine, whose virtue is constantly being attacked, only to be rescued at the last minute. The Count la Ruse tells her that he will protect her: "The kind accents which accompanied these words gave me some comfort, which was assisted by the repossession of our jewels by an accident so strongly savouring of the disposition of Providence in my favour" (IV, ix, p. 153).

It is difficult to see far enough behind her story to ascertain how much she is embroidering or inventing for her husband's benefit. Her story is, after all, a personal narrative. But every once in a while something untoward slips out. Her concern for her chastity is paralleled and qualified by her concern for her jewels. After she fends off the romantic hermit, her sailor companions decide to look for liquor in his cave: "The sailors searched the whole cave, where finding nothing more which they deemed worth their taking, they walked off with the bottle and immediately emptying it without offering me a drop, they proceeded with me towards the town" (IV, xi, pp. 158–59).

The only truly odd incident in the story, allowing for exaggeration and incidental satire, is the presence of the Count la Ruse on the shore where Mrs. Heartfree landed. In most ways, this seems to be more the hand of chance than anything else. He is not there to effect any elaborate rescue for Mrs. Heartfree. He does not take a pre-ordained place in a causal chain that returns her to England. Only her jewels are returned through this accidental meeting. Yet Mrs. Heartfree sees in the whole series of adventures the hand of Providence protecting her personally from horrors, an interpretation that fits well with her idea of herself as the continually attacked romantic heroine. She ends her story with a capitalized coda, calling her adventures " . . . a strong instance of what I am persuaded is the surest truth, THAT PROVIDENCE WILL SOONER OR LATER PROCURE THE FELICITY OF THE VIRTUOUS AND INNOCENT" (IV, xi, p. 161).

Fielding's concern with the Great Man theory of history in *Jonathan Wild* parallels his interest in providential explanation. Fielding certainly detests that "greatness" that is based only on military valor. But his interest in the idea of the Great Man goes much deeper than this commonplace moral judgment. Fielding in *Jonathan Wild* approaches the theory of the Great Man as he approaches Providence, in terms of their effect on the individuals who try to live by them.[30] Neither allows for the operations of chance, which can disrupt the simple causal patterns assumed by those who believe either in the controlling hand of God or in the necessary success given by Fortune to the Great. In *The Champion* for December 6, 1739, Fielding had attacked Richelieu's belief in the power of human beings, especially great public figures, to control the procedure of events and to make "the Event of almost every Scheme to depend on a wise Design":

> For my own part, I differ so entirely from these Great Men, that I imagine Wisdom to be of very little Consequence in the Affairs of this World: Human Life appears to me to resemble the Game of *Hazard*, much more than that of *Chess*; in the latter, among good Players, one false step must infallibly lose the Game; whereas, in the former, the worst that can happen is to have the odds against you, which are never more than two to one; and we often see a blundering Fellow, who scarce knows on which side the Odds are, dribble out his bad Chance upon the Table, and Sweep the whole Board, while the wisest Players, and those who stick close to the Rule, lift up their Eyes and curse the Dice.[31]

In *Joseph Andrews* Fielding finds the chess analogy more suitable because it emphasizes the complexity of factors that can often upset the best combination of skill and planning:

> But human life, as hath been discovered by some great man or other (for I would by no means be understood

to affect the honour of making any such discovery), very
much resembles a game at chess: for as in the latter, while
a gamester is too attentive to secure himself very strongly
on one side the board, he is apt to leave an unguarded
opening on the other; so doth it often happen in life . . .
(I, xvi, p. 58).[32]

Similarly, in *Jonathan Wild,* plans are made and then
thwarted by the most minute circumstances, which the plotter had neglected to take into account because he had believed so wholeheartedly in his ability to control.

Fielding therefore attacks the Great Man theory of history, as anatomized by historians and practiced by men
acting on their examples, for its assertion of complete human control. Like Hume, he does not believe in the idea of
the "event-making man" and allows only the "eventful
man" to be a possibility in the world.[33] Tacitus, he says,
wrongly insists on the power of the Great Man to work his
own ends. And Fielding ridicules Cardinal Wolsey, who
wanted to strike the word "unfortunate" from his dictionary because he believed every man totally made his own life.
To this belief in the unimpeded working of the human will,
Fielding opposes the occurrence of arbitrary and often perverse chance, which, he says, the Great Man more often
takes advantage of than controls. Like Hume, he considers
Cromwell to be the great example of a man who takes advantage of situations that already exist: "He certainly had
very little Hand in procuring the War, of which he after-
ward made so glorious a Use; indeed, he seems to have had
a wonderful Address in turning the wise Schemes and Actions of others to his own Honour and Advantage; but as
these could not be attributed to his own Foresight, so might
Chance have favoured him in those Opportunities of working his own Ends out of them."[34]

He next speaks of Cromwell's military success, but then
returns to his main theme:

But still, I say, he owed all this principally to Chance;
namely, to the Death of those great Men whom the long

continuance of the Civil War had exhausted; those who
began that War against the Crown for the sake of their
Liberties and Properties, and would have disdained to
have seen the Nation enslaved to the absolute Will of a
Subject in Rank very little above the common Level. . . .
. . . To conclude, whoever looks on *Cromwell* to be that
whom I have here represented, (and what I have here said,
are Facts transcribed from the Historians of those Times)
must agree that he was the Child of Fortune; and, as Mr.
Cowley seems to think, an Object rather to our Surprise
than Admiration.[35]

Fielding's attack on the Great Man theory, as prosecuted
in *Jonathan Wild*, forms part of his general denial that
history provides either examples of political behavior or
fleshed-out moral precepts. *Amelia* deals more directly with
the possibilities for redefining heroism. But in *Jonathan
Wild*, as in *Joseph Andrews*, Fielding's approach is primarily
critical; he is interested in how the "modern idea of heroism" distorts the perception of the characters who believe
it. Fielding's metaphor for "modern heroism" is the completely external: the act that has no meditative depth and
the reliance upon will interpreted only as power.[w] Modern
heroes like Wild are the masters of the external. They are
heroes of pageant and display who manipulate their followers through shared conceptions of heroism. Wild continually makes analogies between himself and the classical
heroes, and the narrator, playing the role of an ardent admirer, follows along:

w In the more individually oriented world of *Joseph Andrews*, "heroism" is often expressed as physical strength, the private counterpart of
military prowess. Adams, for example, hits Fanny's attacker over the
head with his crabstick. But the attacker is one of the "persons of
heroic calling" and his head is "three times as thick as those of ordinary men, who are designed to exercise talents which are vulgarly
called rational." Nature has fitted this man for heroism ". . . and, indeed, in some who are predestined to the command of armies and em-
pires she is supposed sometimes to make that part perfectly solid"
(II, ix, p. 116) .

He was a passionate admirer of heroes, particularly of Alexander the Great, between whom and the late king of Sweden, he would frequently draw parallels (I, ii, p. 11).

The name of this youth, who will hereafter make some figure in this history, being the Achates of our Aeneas, or rather the Hephaestion of our Alexander, was Fireblood (III, iv, p. 92).

But Wild's control does not mean that he himself is free, for he assumes that the superficialities he manipulates are ends in themselves. At first, in the chapter "Of hats" (II, vi), he tries to draw a strict distinction between telling someone the world is organized in a particular way and believing it yourself. Wild's men wear different hats in remembrance of their disparate original professions, and cock them in two different ways to denote the present division of the gang into two parties. Wild decides to stop their dissension by making a distinction between hats and the abstract principles they may stand for—as if he were writing a criticism of *A Tale of a Tub*:

> Do you think the first inventors of hats, or at least of the distinctions between them, really conceived that one form of hats should inspire a man with divinity, another with law, another with learning, or another with bravery? No, they meant no more by these outward signs than to impose on the vulgar, and, instead of putting great men to the trouble of acquiring or maintaining the substance, to make it sufficient that they condescend to wear the type or shadow of it. You do wisely, therefore when in a crowd, to amuse the mob by quarrels on such accounts, that while they are listening to your jargon you may with the greater ease and safety pick their pockets; but surely to be in earnest, and privately to keep up such a ridiculous contention among yourself must argue the highest folly and absurdity (II, vi, p. 65).

By the end of the novel, however, when Wild is in prison, he has himself come to believe in the substantiality of the external form. He expresses his victory over Roger Johnson by stripping his rival of his clothing and then strutting around in it as the new head of Newgate. As befits this later part of the novel, the narrator gives a more sober and detached estimate of the meaning of this act:

> To speak sincerely, there was more bravado than real use or advantage in these trappings. As for the nightgown, its outside indeed made a glittering tinsel appearance, but it kept him not warm, nor could the finery do him much honour, since every one knew it did not properly belong to him; as to the waistcoat, it fitted him very ill, being infinitely too big for him; and the cap was so heavy that it made his head ache. Thus these clothes, which perhaps (as they presented the idea of their misery more sensibly to the people's eyes) brought him more envy, hatred, and detraction, than all his deeper impositions and more real advantages, afforded very little use or honour to the wearer; nay, could scarce serve to amuse his own vanity when this was cool enough to reflect with the least seriousness (IV, iii, pp. 134–35).

The last qualifications make it improbable that Wild will ever regain enough perspective to make such a detached judgment. The externals he manipulated so well earlier in the novel have finally turned against him. He has begun to believe in them as a coherent system of their own, after he had denied any other system but the measure of himself.

This Swiftian emphasis on dress forms part of a larger theme that runs through *Jonathan Wild*: the relation between the essential nature of a word, a principle, or a man and the external sign that denotes it. The confusions that arise where words are taken to be things, a subtheme in *Joseph Andrews*, becomes central to *Jonathan Wild*. But these words are no longer the easily satirized jargon of Fielding's first novel. Instead they are the cant terms of a public world, easily manipulated abstractions that have no meaning of their own. In the introductory chapters Fielding introduces us to the satiric possibilities of this idea by glossing the argot of the thieves for the uninitiated reader. But satiric fun has laid the groundwork for more serious themes when we discover that the thieves use many words that we use ourselves as jargon—"love," "honor," "respect." Both the thieves and, Fielding implies, the readers use these words only as gestures because their abstraction has removed them from any human relevance. To mean anything, they must be glossed in terms of context and motivation rather than as immutable truths.

To PARALLEL THOSE CHARACTERS who try to manipulate abstractions in order to understand the multiplicity and confusion of their lives, the narrator of *Jonathan Wild* tries out various techniques of writing history. In the first chapter he associates the ability of men to act with the means by which the historian details and explains their actions. Abstracting, moralizing, generalizing, searching amid the varieties of historical explanation, the narrator is more oppressively present in *Jonathan Wild* than he was in *Joseph Andrews*. In the first novel he was a detached observer who interspliced the narrative with his reflections and interpretations for momentary satiric effect. He did not draw general patterns from the world of the novel because his role did not demand it. The narrator of *Jonathan Wild*, on the other hand, is present as an interpreter. His mere ubiquitousness enforces the feeling that somehow he is controlling the narrative and manipulating it for his own heavily moral ends. The satiric technique of *Joseph Andrews* was often the ridiculous detail, the bit of overblown jargon, the farce of appearance. In *Jonathan Wild* it is the elevation of mock gravity, the extension to absurdity of stilted seriousness.[36] The Richardsonian editor and the Defoe-like biographer are criticized when the narrator introduces the conjectures of "a friend of mine, who had a long intimacy with the Wild family" (III, vii, p. 103). "Very authentic information" abounds as Wild is put into prison (p. 132) and footnotes reveal the provenance of documents relating to

Wild's words (p. 156n). Finally a whole chapter is devoted to a dialogue between Wild and the ordinary of Newgate:

> The ordinary of Newgate had frequent conferences with him, and greatly would it embellish our history could we record all which that good man delivered on these occasions; but unhappily we could procure only the substance of a single conference, which was taken down in shorthand by one who overheard it. We shall transcribe it, therefore, exactly in the same form and words we received it; nor can we help regarding it as one of the most curious pieces which ancient or modern history hath recorded (IV, xiii, p. 163).

But Fielding uses this omni-interpretive narrator as an ironic device itself. One of the basic claims of historians he attacks is the assertion that the patterns they find in history are actually there. By having his oppressive narrator find similar patterns, Fielding emphasizes the way in which a historian's own didactic ends dictate what "inherent" pattern he finds in history, whether his ends are political, moral, or religious. The overpowering importance of the interpretive and patterning narrator in *Jonathan Wild* undermines the pretence that the historian or biographer presents only the facts. The satires of historical and biographical method in *Jonathan Wild*, therefore, usually concentrate upon the false assumptions that lie behind the manipulation of facts. The first chapter, for example, relates the criminal biography and the tradition of the Great Man by praising both the exemplary nature of such great figures and the general ability of men to control events: "As it is necessary that all great and surprising events, the designs of which are laid, conducted, and brought to perfection by the utmost force of human invention and art, should be produced by great and eminent men, so the lives of such may be justly and properly styled the quintessence of history" (II, i, p. 3).

In the Preface to the *Miscellanies* Fielding disclaims that he is presenting another circumstantial biography in *Jonathan Wild*:

. . . my design is not to enter the lists with that excellent historian, who from authentic papers and records, &c. hath already given so satisfactory an account of the life and actions of this great man. I have not indeed the least intention to deprecate the veracity and impartiality of that history; nor do I pretend to any of those lights, not having, to my knowledge, ever seen a single paper relating to my hero, save some short memoirs, which about the time of his death were published in certain chronicles called newspapers, the authority of which hath been sometimes questioned, and in the Ordinary of *Newgate* his account, which generally contains a more particular relation of what the heroes are to suffer in the next world, than of what they did in this.[37]

In *Jonathan Wild* Fielding examines the assumptions about history and the nature of historical truth that lie behind the biographical method. Wild's personal story and the veiled allusions to Walpole, as well as the moralizations about the "good man" and the "great man," have a supplementary importance at best. In 1752 Fielding revised *Jonathan Wild* to soften the anti-Walpole content not, I would say, in order to generalize his attacks, but because he no longer saw the ex-Prime Minister as a special case. Through his narrator Fielding goes behind the Wild story into the assumptions of the writers who would seize upon it as a vehicle for didacticism, an exemplified truth that can be profitably related to the problems of the reader. *Jonathan Wild* vividly shows that much of history-writing is the reductive imposition of one man's point of view upon a complex world, and that the patterns which historians claim to find in the world are usually imported there by them.

Fielding uses his narrative voice in two major ways: the narrator believes in the patterns developed by the historians; but he also introduces uncertainty, chance, and sarcastic complexity. These two stances may be compared to the two distinguished in *Joseph Andrews*: that of the

Hogarthian narrator, who is interested primarily in the pictorial and external; and that of a more complex and qualifying narrator, who looks beyond appearances. In both cases one stance illustrates a fault by taking it seriously and exaggerating it, while another seeks to find the basis of the fault in the perceptions of the characters.

The narrator's attempts to pick his way, seriously and satirically, through different modes of historical interpretation appear in a full-dress presentation towards the center of *Jonathan Wild*. Cast adrift in a small boat by the French captain, Wild decides to drown himself, and thus assert his will in the fact of misfortune: ". . . he proceeded immediately to put his purpose into execution, and, as his resolution never failed him, he had no sooner dispatched the small quantity of provision which his enemy had with no vast liberality presented him, than he cast himself headlong into the sea" (II, xi, p. 78).

In the next chapter the narrator examines the strange fact that two minutes after Wild jumped into the sea, he was "miraculously" replaced in the boat. The narrator first denies that there is an actually miraculous or mythological way of telling the story. Wild was returned ". . . without the assistance of a dolphin or seahorse, or any other fish or animal, who are always as ready at hand when a poet or historian pleases to call for them to carry a hero through the sea, as any chairman at a coffee-house door near St. James's to convey a beau over the street, and preserve his white stocking" (II, xii, p. 79). He congratulates himself on avoiding the miraculous, for ". . . indeed we are much deeper read in natural than supernatural causes." The actions of Nature are more relevant: "Whatever Nature, therefore, purposes to herself, she never suffers any reason, design, or accident to frustrate." The deification of Nature has replaced the more pagan Miraculous. But this explanation also becomes swamped, like Wild, in a sea of qualification. Nature's "purposes" are vague and even irrelevant. They are less a real mode of explanation than a faint glimmer in the midst of a smokescreen of rhetoric:

Indeed, the true reason for the general ignorance of mankind on this head seems to be this; that, as Nature chooses to execute these her purposes by certain second causes, and as many of these second causes seem so totally foreign to her design, the wit of man, which, like his eye, sees best directly forward, and very little and imperfectly what is oblique, is not able to discern the end from the means. Thus, how a handsome wife or daughter should contribute to execute her original designation of a general, or how flattery or half a dozen houses in a borough-town should denote a judge, or a bishop, he is not capable of comprehending. And, indeed, we ourselves, wise as we are, are forced to reason *ab effectu*; and if we had been asked what Nature had intended such men for, before she herself had by the event demonstrated her purpose, it is possible we might sometimes have been puzzled to declare; for it must be confessed that at first sight, and to a mind uninspired, a man of vast natural capacity and much acquired knowledge may seem by Nature designed for power and honour, rather than one remarkable only for the want of these, and indeed all other qualifications; whereas daily experience convinces us of the contrary, and drives us into the opinion I have here disclosed (II, xii, p. 80).

The narrator reveals that Nature had whispered in Wild's ear and told him to go back to that boat. He then congratulates himself for avoiding the "Prodigious" in explanation by introducing such "natural" reasoning.

The narrator of this chapter has donned the mask of a "great man" historian. He asserts the existence of pattern —here the "plan of Nature"—as if it were an innate part of the world. Yet it is clear that he employs his pattern primarily as a literary technique for saving his hero from the charge of cowardice. The "Nature" that saves Wild is the secular equivalent of the "Providence" continually invoked by Heartfree. Through his pedantic hyperbole

Fielding satirically implies the literary sources of his "pattern"; truth is not a criterion:

> Thus we think this passage in our history, at first so greatly surprising, is very naturally accounted for, and our relation rescued from the Prodigious, which, though it often occurs in biography, is not to be encouraged nor much commended on any occasion, unless when absolutely necessary to prevent the history's being at an end. Secondly, we hope our hero is justified from that imputation of want of resolution which must have been fatal to the greatness of his character (II, xii, pp. 380–81).

For such omnivorous believers in absolute pattern, every detail is grist. Shortly after Wild reaches land, he succeeds in borrowing enough money by confidence tricks so "that he was enabled to provide himself with a place in the stage-coach; which (as God permitted it to perform the journey) brought him at the appointed time to an inn in the metropolis" (II, xiii, p. 83). The parenthesis adds nothing to the narrative except a dig at those whose taste for explanation is so providential that every detail, despite its irrelevance, is subsumed into their theory. The joke in *Jonathan Wild* is that all these theories are continually vying, through the narrator, to get credit for the procession of events. The story of Wild is studded with assertions of pattern that purport to explain, but on closer inspection reveal a poverty of imagination and technical ability in those writers who have recourse to them. As the narrator remarks, ". . . Fortune, like a lazy poet . . . " (IV, xiv, pp. 168–69).[x]

The existence of accident in the world furnishes ammunition for the most direct attack on the belief that the Great Man is aided by Fortune or Providence. Accident interferes with the plots of Wild increasingly as the novel continues.

---

[x] Compare P. H. Meyer on Voltaire: "Related to the inordinate use to which Voltaire puts the concept of opinion is the unwarrantably large part attributed to chance as a determining factor in history throughout his *Essai*" ("Voltaire and Hume as Historians," pp. 57–58). Hume at first believed that the reliance on chance as an explanation indicated only a lack of knowledge. See above, p. 33.

The elaborate plot against the rich young gentleman in the stagecoach is almost offhandedly thwarted by circumstance. Wild sends Fireblood out to ambush the young man: "Fireblood returned from his enterprise unsuccessful. The gentleman happened to go home another way than he had intended; so that the whole design miscarried" (III, vi, p. 98). Through such accidents Fielding reminds us that one can control only so much; if one proceeds under the illusion of absolute control, he is doomed to be thwarted by accidents.ʸ In the *Champion* Fielding wrote that Wild desired to keep his gang and operations secret; nevertheless he became famous: "But Reputation is not always the Fruit of Design; Chance hath in this, as in all other wordly Affairs, a very considerable Dominion."[38] When Wild finally is thwarted by a few accidents, his whole system breaks down. He once seemed to be a man of will, but we now discover he is only so because he is self-centered, not because he is self-sufficient.

Fielding's narrator in *Jonathan Wild* does not finally embrace any pattern as completely as do some of the characters. Instead he tries out many, to see how they work and to what extent they are valid as explanations. He follows this procedure in order to bring the reader along in an understanding of the forces at work in the novel. Fielding primarily focuses on what previous authors have made of Wild's life and how their methods of explanation are related to the world of the reader, in which precepts are extracted from the examples of history and (ideally) applied to daily life: "To confess the truth, my narrative is rather of such actions which he might have performed, or would, or should have performed, than what he really did; and may, in reality, well suit any other such great man, as the person himself whose name it bears.[39]

Such an approach goes beyond superficial didactic moralism to explore the assumptions of didacticism itself: how does the didactic author mediate between his materials

---

ʸ The possibility exists that, when Fielding mentions "accidents," he may be punning on "accidence." This interpretation would give an added dimension to the way Wild's rhetoric turns back upon him.

and his reader? *Jonathan Wild*, like *Joseph Andrews*, offers only a partial answer to this problem. Fielding in *Joseph Andrews* alludes a few times to the increasing knowledge of the reader. *Jonathan Wild* utilizes the relation between the reader and the narrator more extensively, until it has almost a "plot" of its own. The earlier sections of the novel treat the reader as the typical appreciator of criminal biography; they assume that his sympathies are naturally with Wild. Of course, this assumption is carried on with the broadest of irony, but it nevertheless has some force. The reader may be against Wild morally, but Wild is still the most interesting character, the controller, the man to admire, however his talents may have gone astray. The reader is often called "great" to parallel the hero (e.g., II, vii, p. 67). This "great" reader is also interested in causes and circumstance, and how Wild molds them for his purposes. For "more sagacious" readers (II, vii, p. 71) the narrator recounts circumstances and Wild's dispassionate control of them, for example, the plot to ruin Heartfree: "So he postponed all endeavours for this purpose till he had first effected what, by order of time, was regularly supposed to precede this latter design; with such regularity did this our hero conduct all his schemes, and so truly superior was he to all the efforts of passion, which so often disconcert and disappoint the noblest views of others" (II, viii, p. 71). The reader is lured with the rhetoric of control, in which no obstacle is conceived to stand between the cause, Wild's will, and the effect, Heartfree's ruin.

When Wild's plots begin to be thwarted by accident, the narrator withdraws somewhat, and the reader's identification with his hero is in doubt. Wild hopes to find a ship in Deal to attack the Frenchman's ship. He persuades a passing fisherman to take him there: "The fisherman took his advice, and soon arrived at Deal, where the reader will, I doubt not, be as much concerned as Wild was, that there was not a single ship prepared to go on the expedition" (II, xiii, p. 82). From this point on, the narrator assumes in the reader a greater antipathy to Wild than before. He allows himself to evaluate psychologically Wild's methods of manipulating people (II, v, p. 94). Yet he still does not openly condemn Wild, for this is again not his purpose. He wishes to bring the reader instead to an understanding of the way in which historians and other writers often present a false picture of the world, even while they pretend to tell the truth.

ALMOST EVERY CHARACTER in *Jonathan Wild* is caught in a web of self-imposed pattern, a system of total belief from which they cannot get free. Like Adams, they do not have the sense of other possibilities that is necessary to live in the world. Fielding associates their limited vision with their sedulous absorption of the "truths" of public history. The characters of *Jonathan Wild* are singleminded because they have limited themselves. Their literary flatness results from possessing simplistic views of the world that turn around and reduce their human possibilities; and these views are exemplified and promulgated by popular interpretations of history. Fielding does not deny that systematic explanation may frequently be relevant, but he attacks its absolute use. The effort of characters in *Jonathan Wild* to live by unitary systems of explanation has suppressed both the real variety of the world and the vital potentiality of human beings to work in it.[z]

[z] Fielding's late piece of hackwork "Examples of the Interposition of Providence in the Detection and Punishment of Murder" (1752) might be cited to prove that Fielding accepted providential explanation to some degree. Wilbur Cross remarks: "Fielding, I fear, was rather credulous when it came to a supernatural story" (II, p. 270). The "iron chain of causes" is more strongly emphasized here than in any of the novels. But Fielding's subject is horrible crime, not the common flow of life. And even there God's punishment is not the end of the story, for every revelation of crime must be circumstantially accepted by a court of law. Letters and evidence appear; divine justice must be brought into the sphere of human understanding represented by law: "He afterwards made a proper confession before a magistrate; the body was searched for and found, and the man was hanged in chains where the murder was committed" (Henley, XVI, p. 124).

I stress the historiographical origin of the restrictive patterns in *Jonathan Wild* because I believe that Fielding characterizes their restrictiveness in terms of the imposition of what is usually only a literary pattern onto the spontaneity and flux of daily life. *Joseph Andrews* and *Jonathan Wild* negatively spend most of their time attacking views of the world and methods of explaining events that distort present and future action. But implicit in these explorations is the need for a formal structure of explanation that can clarify and pattern without restricting. Hume believed the answer lay in objectivity and detachment. But Fielding finds his solution in the assertion of artificiality and involvement. Properly used, aesthetic pattern can furnish a flexible frame that avoids the faults of other patterns. Reacting against those who use literary methods of organization while denying them, appalled by the pretence that jargon either does not exist or is inherent in the subject, Fielding prescribes instead a sensitivity to complex and contingent form and an appreciation for fictive pattern. The oppressive interpreter of *Jonathan Wild* becomes the genial and expansive narrator of *Tom Jones. Joseph Andrews* and *Jonathan Wild* have cleared the way. In *Tom Jones* Fielding asserts that the most obvious and artificial structure is also the most liberating. Because it does not claim to be necessary, it therefore allows the material the freest play and gives the truest and most relevant representation of life. Previous authors had used techniques of history, like the accumulation of factual detail or the resonant absolute pattern, to give their works a feeling of truth and an aspect of reality; in *Tom Jones* Fielding presents his own program and practice. In it he fully expresses all the moral themes that received only partial treatment before, because he was interested more in the means than in the content of their expression. After the explorations of *Joseph Andrews* and *Jonathan Wild*, Fielding in *Tom Jones* achieves a form that embodies the vital interdependence of moral truth and the literary techniques that express it.

IV. *Tom Jones*: THE NARRATIVE STANCE

Narrative or historical truth must needs be highly estimable; especially when we consider how mankind, who are become so deeply interested in the subject, have suffered by the want of clearness in it. 'Tis itself a part of moral truth. To be a judge in one, requires a judgment in the other. The morals, the character, and the genius of an author must be thoroughly considered; and the historian or relater of things important to mankind must, whoever he be, approve himself many ways to us, both in respect of his judgment, candour, and disinterestedness, ere we are bound to take anything on his authority.

Shaftesbury, *Characteristics*

Both *Joseph Andrews* and *Jonathan Wild* contained much discussion of the illusion cast by historical narrative and the methods used to create it. But Fielding's treatment of these problems was fragmentary. Because his preoccupations were so vast, involving the nature of the world around us and how we see it, there often appeared to be very little difference between satirizing and partially assenting to a particular point of view. Fielding can, for example, both attack and employ the pose of the antiquary, slowly accumulating mounds of data. In *Tom Jones*, however, such satire takes a subordinate place. The achievement of *Tom Jones* is the delicacy and complexity of the narrative control, which unites the spontaneity of *Joseph Andrews* with the pattern of *Jonathan Wild*, the interests of unexpected plot with the satisfaction of completed form.

Fielding remarks while he tells of the effects of gossip on the relation between Tom and Sophia Western: " . . . I am not writing a system but a history. . . ."[a] In *Tom Jones* he is centrally concerned with defining the role of the historian-narrator and the relation that this historian has to both the world he presents and the reader for whom he

[a] *Tom Jones*, afterword by Frank Kermode (New York, 1963), XII, viii, p. 553. I have used this edition because it is readily accessible and there is as yet none more definitive; Kermode does include some important variant readings (pp. 852–54). All citations will be included in the text.

presents it. Fielding's insistence upon the individuality of his narrative voice frees him from the falsification of system. In Shaftesbury's terms he has "judgment, candour, and disinterestedness," but certainly not depersonalized objectivity. Fielding in *Tom Jones* implies what Hume, seemingly secure in his detachment, never considered: only by admitting that his general pattern is arbitrary can the historian be free to demonstrate what he believes to be specifically true. Pattern by its nature falsifies. But we cannot collect knowledge in an infinitude of separate bundles; there must be some means of ordering, however provisional. In the midst of the tightly organized pattern of *Tom Jones* Fielding continually implies that there are many facts that may be irrelevant to his purposes, but perhaps relevant to someone else's. Beneath the artificial form is the impression of provisional statement. Fielding frequently says "I will not venture to determine." Even though he may have assured the proper answer by what has gone before, such a statement can convey the sense of an open-ended judgment, which is always ready to examine and be changed by new evidence. The world of *Tom Jones* is palpably a created world. It is not a mirror of the actual world; it is an analogy to it, more ordered and definite, better planned and articulated. It is a device created by the narrator as an object lesson for the reader. The action of *Tom Jones* is not the same as real life; it cannot be, if it is meant to help the reader understand and appreciate his own world.

Fielding redefines the essence of historical understanding to be the appreciation of the manipulations the narrator performs in full view of the reader. He uses the world of *Tom Jones* to make sense of a world that, by itself, in discrete bundles of detail, impression, motive, and action, never appears quite as intelligible as the fictional one.[40] Only the narrator can guide us through its length, tying together beginning, middle, and end in a complex mesh of relationship. Usually our attention is directed more toward the process of interweaving than to the elements that are united. The narrator proceeds on two levels at once: he views things at the same pace and with the same developing knowledge as the reader; but he also continually emphasizes that he knew all along how things would turn out and has guided us primarily for our own best advantage. When at the end of the novel we learn the truth of Tom's parentage, we are not expected to turn back to Bridget Blifil's protestations at the beginning to savor what must surely be the longest-range irony in literature. We are invited instead to admire again the way the narrator has given us only the relevant facts, only those that move the plot as he wishes, with control and discretion.

In *Tom Jones* Fielding attempts to exploit the full potentialities of a fictional form while he tells you how he works and invites you to learn by his method. The process of reading *Tom Jones* is a learning process for the reader; he is led and sometimes pushed by the narrator into the narrator's created world, for the purposes of entertainment and the growth of his perceptions. In *Tom Jones*, to see well is first to appreciate the artifice of the narrator in creating his world. Fielding admonishes both reader and critic not to carp at parts before they have seen the whole:

> First, then, we warn thee not too hastily to condemn any of the incidents in this our history as impertinent and foreign to our main design because thou dost not immediately conceive in what manner such incident may conduce to that design. This work may, indeed, be considered as a great creation of our own, and for a little reptile of a critic to presume to find fault with any of its parts without knowing the manner in which the whole is connected, and before he comes to the final catastrophe, is a most presumptuous absurdity (X, i, p. 440).

The blatant artifice of Fielding's form emphasizes his unwillingness to commit himself to any system that claims all-inclusiveness. In the introductory chapters and throughout the novel he presents his plans and methods both as a writer—a creator of reality—and a teacher—a preceptor who will make the reader appreciate reality better through the experience of reading *Tom Jones*.

In *Joseph Andrews* and *Jonathan Wild* the concentration on "relevance" implied a statement about fictional technique while it also attacked the indiscriminate array of facts presented by chronicling antiquarians and "realistic" novelists. In *Tom Jones* Fielding uses "relevance" to define the radical sense of contingency on which the world of the novel is built. The tight plot of *Tom Jones*, which Coleridge admired so much, implies a play of possibilities that its form for a moment encompasses.[41] The narrator can explain this world because he has created it. Yet, in order that the novel retain its status as the mirror of a less explainable world, he suggests more questions than he answers. And most of these provisional questions and answers revolve around the tangle of human motives. Why does Blifil continue to court Sophia, when he knows she hates him and he actually also hates her? "I answer, for that very reason, as well as for several others equally good, which we shall now proceed to open to the reader" (VII, vi, p. 291): (1) because of his animal desires, Blifil considers Sophia "a most delicious morsel," and her distress over Tom's plight has made her even more delectable; (2) the idea of subduing her even though she hates him has a great attraction; (3) the prospect of supplanting Tom makes him feel triumphant; (4) one reason "which few readers will regard with any great abhorrence," he is after Squire Western's estate. With a similar approach, the narrator considers Black George's debate with himself whether or not to give the money from Allworthy and Sophia to Tom (VI, xiii, pp. 270–71), and Honour's hesitation whether to run away with Sophia or to expose her (VII, viii, p. 298). No causes are sufficient, although many are relevant, and the solution often occurs through the appearance of a new cause, some fortuitous accident.

THE AUTHORITY of the narrator of *Tom Jones* rests not on his "objectivity," but on his demonstrated personal worth.

He is a historian who clearly uses special methods to relate the otherwise discrete characters and actions under his observation. We sense his personal force not through exhibitions of caprice or prejudice but because we believe his assertions that he personally experienced the kinds of life he describes in the novel. We accept his judgments not only because he is experienced but also because he possesses narrative talents that are more important than experience, sympathy, and empathy: invention, judgment, and learning (IX, i). His literary talent naturally needs the fuel of his sensibility, but sensibility without aesthetic order is useless. The narrator stands between his own scattered empirical observations and the consciousness of the reader, furnishing through the play of his creative imagination provisional patterns of explanation that can help the reader's understanding. Neither Fielding's method in *Tom Jones*, nor the truths he wishes to inculcate, are absolute. He never implies that a certain set of moral precepts are sufficient for every situation. Some critics have claimed that *Tom Jones* "shows" that even the most warmhearted person needs prudence and discretion. But Fielding actually spends most of his time attacking the kind of oversimplification that insists upon swallowing up the variety of life into moral rubrics. Has anyone ever questioned the value of discretion and prudence?[b] Critics are often puzzled by the energy Fielding expends affirming the goodness of the good and the badness of the bad. But this emphasis is puzzling only if we take the novel to be static and endlessly exemplary. In *Tom Jones* Fielding tries to find a form for uncertainty, a structure for spontaneity, a pattern for contingency. His main interest is not in who is good and who is bad. He con-

[b] Perhaps even this moral theme also has historiographical relevance. Myron Gilmore describes the Ciceronian concept of virtue, in which "prudence, one of the four cardinal virtues, was divided into three parts: the memory of things past, the consciousness of things present and the foreseeing of things to come" ("Renaissance Conception of the Lessons of History," p. 83). Building on this idea, Jean Bodin made a distinction between three kinds of history—divine, natural, and human—that corresponded to three kinds of knowledge—"faith, science, and prudence" (p. 93).

centrates instead on the way we transmute the mixed and complex impressions of the world into personal standards for action. The narrative process of *Tom Jones* gradually reveals the difficulties of extracting the truth from observed situations.

The way the narrator leads the reader through the world of *Tom Jones* is an essential element of the meaning of the novel.[42] He is typically interested in the reader's reaction to the events of the plot and how the characters act. He explains and he questions. He qualifies and he allows the reader to interpret as he pleases. The narrator attempts to give the reader both the immediacy of occurrence and the privilege of mediation. He early brings the reader into the story, or at least into the world of the novel, by involving his judgment in the process of events.[c] The reader is first invited to become aware of the mixture of description and presentation in the narrator's own method. Allworthy is described in fulsome language climbing a hill in an early morning walk, "a human being replete with benevolence, meditating in what manner he might render himself more acceptable to his Creator by doing most good to his creatures" (I, iv, p. 35). The narrator then draws up short and by a metaphor involves the reader both in the world of the plot (Allworthy's) and the world of the plot's meaning (the narrator's):

> Reader, take care; I have inadvisedly led thee to the top of as high a hill as Mr. Allworthy's, and how to get thee down without breaking my neck I do not well know. However, let us e'en venture to slide down together, for Miss Bridget rings her bell and Mr. Allworthy is summoned to breakfast, where I must attend, and, if you please, shall be glad of your company.

c The narrator of *Jonathan Wild* uses the attributed attitude of the reader toward Wild as one of his ironic techniques. There is less of this kind of reader-narrator relation in *Tom Jones*. It appears most clearly in the narrator's remarks about the common love narrator and reader share for Sophia, and in his beliefs about the reader's desire to see Tom wind up on the gallows.

The narrator expects the reader to appreciate equally well the high hill of his own rhetoric as well as the exaggerated rhetoric of the characters. Mock epic passages frequently end "To speak plainly. . . ." All overblown language, whether the narrator's or a character's, is usually qualified in some way. Metaphors and similes are dissected to discover their real relation to the plot; the moral jargons of Thwackum and Square are placed against our knowledge of the actual events and their individual natures. The narrator may compare Tom's departure from Paradise Hall to Adam's from Eden. But he destines such high rhetoric primarily for imminent deflation. Toward the end of the departure chapter, the narrator implies that the worst characteristic of poetic rhetoric is its penchant for exaggeration and ambiguity:

> At last the Ocean, that hospitable friend to the wretched, opened her capacious arms to receive him; and he instantly resolved to accept her kind invitation. To express myself less figuratively, he determined to go to sea (VII, ii, p. 278).

By his own self-qualifications and by his attitude toward all his characters, the narrator inspires the reader with a sense of his judicious presentation and his ability to point out the most important characteristics of the events he surveys. Against his ideal of inclusive knowledge he plays a kind of reductive didacticism that would remain unconscious of other possibilities. This often appears in the chapter titles: "A hint to justices of the peace concerning the necessary qualifications of a clerk" (VII, ix). Other chapters contain broadly ironic remarks on the nature of publicans (VIII, vii, p. 361), the behavior of innkeepers and servants (X, iii, p. 448), and the handling of daughters (XIII, iv, p. 593). This is the social-guidebook view of the world. Fielding also similarly satirizes the moral-handbook method of organizing experience: "Containing many rules, and some examples, concerning falling in love; descriptions of beauty, and other more prudential inducements to matrimony" (I, xi); "Containing among other things, the ingenuity of Partridge, the madness of Jones, and the folly of Fitzpatrick" (X, vi). At this point we might be reminded that the "editor" of *Pamela* mentions that the novel contains not only moral exempla but also instruction in household management. The richness of Fielding's account in the chapters themselves is enhanced by the flatness of the character-book psychomachia of the chapter titles.

The narrator early asserts his personal authority as the best interpreter and generalizer about the events of *Tom Jones*: "Reader, I think proper, before we proceed any farther together, to acquaint thee that I intend to digress through this whole history as often as I see occasion: of which I am myself a better judge than any pitiful critic whatever" (I, ii, p. 31). But his knowledge, art, and insight are all at the service of the reader, the development of whose complex understanding of the world is the goal of the novel:

> . . . for as I am, in reality, the founder of a new province of writing, so I am at liberty to make the laws I please therein. And these laws my readers, whom I consider as my subjects, are bound to believe in and to obey; with which that they may readily and cheerfully comply, I do hereby assure them that I shall principally regard their ease and advantage in all such institutions; for I do not, like a *jure divino* tyrant, imagine that they are my slaves or my commodity. I am, indeed, set over them for their own good only, and was created for their use and not they for mine (II, i, pp. 65–66).

The perceptions of the narrator are greater than those of any character in the novel, but they should not be understood therefore to be, in the usual critical phrase, "omniscient." The knowledge and perceptions of the narrator become in the course of *Tom Jones* the object of the reader's own development, an achievable epistemological ideal. He seems omniscient because he controls the world of *Tom Jones*, dispensing facts, causes, and reasons as he sees fit to further the reader's insight. But he cannot be completely omniscient. *Tom Jones* is a special case of perception in which our knowledge of a complete aesthetic world emphasizes the impossibility of ever completely knowing or judging the actual world. For all the seeming narrative control, much of the explanation is open-ended and some is wrong. Once again we see two aspects to the narrator: the writer who has created and now explains a world; and the good perceiver whose penetration and judgment are goals which the reader is expected to approximate through the course of the novel's length.

THE READER IS WARNED early that he may expect some help, but that he is ultimately expected to exercise his own judgment, rather than be led passively by the narrator. The narrator has, for example, just made a general observation drawn from Bridget Blifil's behavior to the baby Tom:

> As this is one of those deep observations which very few readers can be supposed capable of making themselves, I have thought it proper to lend them my assistance; but this is a favour rarely to be expected in the course of my work. Indeed, I shall seldom or never so indulge him, unless in such instances as this, where nothing but the inspiration with which we writers are gifted can possibly enable any one to make the discovery (I, v, p. 38).

Soon the narrator begins to disparage the reader who has been too easily deceived by the externals of action and has not paid enough attention to the subtleties of motivation that the narrator has uncovered. Often this reader is identified with the gossip of the townspeople, that winds its way through the novel as ubiquitously as Virgilian *fama* and *rumor*. Like the gossips, this reader indulges in a crude and often ludicrous form of attributed motive. Gossip is the normal mode of perception in the early stages of the novel.[d]

d Virgil's idea of the relation between *fama* and history, in which the two terms are as frequently contrasted as they are identified, may

The narrator has not yet begun to lead the reader concertedly along the path to greater understanding. He mentions for example the rumor that Allworthy is the father of Jenny Jones' baby: "But as we cannot possibly divine what complexion our reader may be of, and as it will be some time before he will hear any more of Jenny, we think proper to give an early intimation that Mr. Allworthy was, and will hereafter appear to be, absolutely innocent of any criminal intention whatever" (I, ix, p. 49).

The reader should not judge simply on the slim basis of what he knows. Partridge and his wife are saved from starvation by some unknown benefactor: "As this support was conveyed to them by an unknown hand, they imagined, and so, I doubt not, will the reader, that Mr. Allworthy himself was their secret benefactor, who, though he would not openly encourage vice, could yet privately relieve the distresses of the vicious themselves when they became too exquisite and disproportionate to their merit" (II, vi, p. 86).

Slowly but surely the reader is educated in the difference between opinion and facts, how even the narrator's personal feelings might cause him to color events:

> Though I called him poor Partridge in the last paragraph, I would have the reader rather impute that epithet to the compassion of my temper than conceive it to be any declaration of his innocence. Whether he was innocent or not will perhaps appear hereafter; but if the historic Muse hath entrusted me with any secrets, I will by no means be guilty of discovering them till she shall give me leave (II, vi, p. 84).

The later reluctance of the narrator to blame Sophia for anything, including her measure of vanity and romanticism, can therefore be fully understood by the perceptive reader, who has learned not to expect "omniscience." The narrator always explains exactly how he injects himself into

---

be restated in Fielding's view of the interpenetration of gossip and historical event (the 1745 Rebellion). See below, pp. 176–77.

the world of *Tom Jones* and he expects his readers to develop good general categories for appreciating his methods.

The process of reading *Tom Jones* is a learning process. Questions are left to "the reader's conjecture" (III, ix, p. 122); he is asked to supply from his own experience the best idea of Sophia's perfections (IV, ii, p. 131); he is encouraged to deduce Sophia's liking for Tom and detestation of Blifil from what the narrator has already said (IV, v, p. 137). The narrator shames the reader into some specific interpretations (IV, xi, p. 162) and flatters him into others (IV, xiv, p. 174). He can also draw the reader up short by attributing wrong deductions to him, as if he is not yet fully schooled in the world. Honour pays Tom a visit as he convalesces from the broken arm received when rescuing Sophia from a runaway horse:

> Among other visitants who paid their compliments to the young gentleman in his confinement Mrs. Honour was one. The reader, perhaps when he reflects on some expressions which have formerly dropped from her, may conceive that she herself had a very particular affection for Mr. Jones, but in reality it was no such thing (V, iv, p. 186).

Similarly, the reader's faulty generalizations about the character of Square are exposed when Tom discovers that Square is also one of Molly's visitors: "I question not but the surprise of the reader will be here equal to that of Jones, as the suspicions which must arise from the appearance of this wise and grave man in such a place may seem so inconsistent with that character which he hath, doubtless, maintained hitherto in the opinion of every one" (V, v, p. 192).

After both of these statements the narrator shows the reasons why the reader's deductions have been wrong. Such demonstration does not involve facts the reader should have remembered, but expresses instead the general lesson of relevance and contingency. It condemns both hasty generalization from insufficient detail and the tendency to

make literary characters obey a harsher standard of coherence and seeming consistency than one expects from
people in daily life.

By about halfway through the novel the narrator expects
the reader to be able to make a few more complex judgments on his own. The reader's viewpoint has been separated from the gossip of the townspeople, now localized in
the kitchen and purveyed by Partridge and Mrs. Honour.
The reader is hopefully ready to show a penetration into
events greater than that of any character. The narrator
arranges an examination. An unknown woman catches up
with Sophia shortly after she has left Upton: "This unexpected encounter surprised the ladies much more than I
believe it will the sagacious reader, who must have imagined
that the strange lady could be no other than Mrs. Fitzpatrick, the cousin of Miss Western, whom we before mentioned to have sallied from the inn a few minutes after her"
(XI, ii, p. 484). To understand this much the reader should
have grasped the narrator's principle of coherent narrative, in which there is a strict economy of incident; nothing
irrelevant to his purposes is ever mentioned and every detail is ultimately a part of the pattern. He is expected in
other words to have learned the conventions of the form
of *Tom Jones*. But at the same time he is expected to have
understood the principles of actuality which that form is
intended to illuminate.

To test this knowledge the narrator shortly arranges another problem. After Harriet Fitzpatrick tells Sophia of
her adventures and Sophia reciprocates, the narrator
seems to chide Sophia with affectionate irony for her lack
of candor:

> One remark, however, I cannot forbear making on her
> narrative; namely, that she made no more mention of
> Jones from the beginning to the end than if there had
> been no such person alive. This I will neither endeavour
> to account for nor to excuse. Indeed, if this may be called
> a kind of dishonesty, it seems the more inexcusable from

the apparent openness and sincerity of the other lady. But so it was (XI, viii, p. 510).

Such an estimate of Sophia seems wilful obtuseness on the part of the narrator, a severe qualification of his previous insight into motives and their relation to truth. By her halting narrative and abrupt shifts of topic, it is fairly clear that Harriet is hiding something. But the reader is invited to understand more than the narrator reveals, at least for a moment. As the chapter goes on, the narrator reveals the actual circumstances behind Harriet's escape from confinement, the complicity of the Irish peer, and his bribery of the person delegated by her husband to watch her. Then he ridicules the reader who had not perceived that something important was left out of the story she told to Sophia:

> This circumstance [the bribery by the Irish peer], however, as the lady did not think it material enough to relate to her friend, we would not at that time impart it to the reader. We rather chose to leave him awhile under a supposition that she had found or coined or by some very extraordinary, perhaps supernatural means had possessed herself of the money with which she had bribed her keeper than to interrupt her narrative by giving a hint of what seemed to her of too little importance to be mentioned (XI, viii, p. 515).

In passages such as these the reader is invited to see behind the artifice of character and perceive intentions and truths without the explicative help of the narrator.[43] There is no narrator in life, and it is for being a good perceiver of the world around him that the reader is being prepared. The narrator acts like an epistemological crutch in *Tom Jones* to emphasize that no such aid is present in the world. We must ultimately rely on the breadth of our sympathies and the complexity of our understanding to live well. *Tom Jones* aims to develop such sympathy and understanding through the reader's participation in the process of the novel. Shortly following the problem of Sophia's candor, for example, Fielding makes a demand on the active use of the reader's intellect and sympathies at least as strong as any exacted by twentieth-century poetry. The narrator first makes a few comments on the uses of description in prose-writing:

> And now, reader, as we are in haste to attend our heroine, we will leave to thy sagacity to apply all this to the Boeotian writers and to those who are their opposites. This thou wilt be abundantly able to perform without our aid. Bestir thyself, therefore, on this occasion; for though we will always lend thee proper assistance in difficult places, as we do not, like some others, expect thee to use the arts of divination to discover our meaning, yet we shall not indulge thy laziness where nothing but thy own attention is required; for thou art highly mistaken if thou dost imagine that we intended when we begun this great work to leave thy sagacity nothing to do, or that without sometimes exercising this talent thou wilt be able to travel through our pages with any pleasure or profit to thyself (XI, ix, p. 520).

Througout *Tom Jones* the narrator plays with the reader's reactions and beliefs about the "design" of the novel. He weaves a fabric in which the problems of literary presentation are inseparable from those of moral action and in which an eclectic and elastic literary technique is a model of the complex view of the world for which the "good" readers should strive.

FIELDING DEVELOPS THE RELATION between literary form and empirical understanding by concentrating on the problem of causality. Early in the novel the narrator often apologizes for including a "childish" or "trifling" incident that might compromise "the dignity of history." His later assertion that everything fits into his plan (X, i, p. 440) reflects ironically on such statements. They become jibes at public historians who emphasize only the great events and often miss the interrelation of small and great that makes a causal pattern. The narrator crows about his artistic management of the scene at Upton. But such a scene is also part of the reader's education in causality:

> If the reader will please to refresh his memory by turning to the scene at Upton in the ninth book, he will be apt to admire the many strange accidents which unfortunately prevented any interview between Partridge and Mrs. Waters when she spent a whole day there with Mr. Jones. Instances of this kind we may frequently observe in life, where the greatest events are produced by a nice train of little circumstances, and more than one example of this may be discovered by the accurate eye in this our history (XVIII, ii, p. 792).

The causal relations are so intricately exact because the view of events is retrospective. The narrator has made and ordered this pattern for our delectation and education. It is not a transcript of all the parts of life. It is instead an artificial model that for the moment has been cleansed of most of life's irrelevancies.[44]

The imperceptive characters in the novel impose such patterns absolutely, even though they may have only partial knowledge of the situation. Gossip and kitchen opinion are private equivalents of the "records" and "reports" that unthinking historians and novelists have taken as total truth; at base they are formed by the opinions of men. False literary causalities parallel false causalities in life. The narrator often plays with this kind of imputed causality, dictated by self-interest, natural embroidery, or merely man's inherent urge to distort. He pokes fun, for example, at his own tendency to romanticize Sophia. While traveling to London, Sophia, "with a voice much fuller of honey than was ever that of Plato, though his mouth is supposed to have been a beehive," asks the guide to let them turn toward Bristol rather than London:

> Reader, I am not superstitious nor any great believer in modern miracles. I do not, therefore, deliver the follow-

ing as a certain truth, for indeed I can scarce credit it myself; but the fidelity of an historian obliges me to relate what hath been confidently asserted. The horse, then, on which the guide rode, is reported to have been so charmed by Sophia's voice that he made a full stop and expressed an unwillingness to proceed any farther (X, x, p. 473).

This is romance causality. The narrator can knowingly indulge in it because it is in part deserved. Similarly, Tom and Sophia can indulge in the most extreme romantic rhetoric because they are really in love. The substance ratifies the show.

But when such romanticizing begins to falsify what actually happened, a sense of proportion is in order:

> Perhaps, however, the fact may be true and less miraculous than it hath been represented, since the natural cause seems adequate to the effect; for as the guide at that moment desisted from a constant application of his armed right heel (for like Hudibras he wore but one spur), it is more than possible that this omission alone might occasion the beast to stop, especially as this was very frequent with him at other times (X, ix, p. 473).

To romanticize Sophia's personality is one thing; to allow such romanticization to distort our perception of the world is quite different. The tone of the second paragraph resembles the heavy-handed, tautological elaboration of the obvious used in explaining something to the grotesquely ignorant. Rhetoric can lead one into a causal swamp. Fielding wants to purge his readers of such misapprehensions of the action of the world, just as he ridicules similarly fanciful causalities in the short discussion of the "amazing natural fact" of the letter in the stomach of the pullet (XVI, iii). After the narrator speculates on the discoveries of the Royal Society in such matters and their occurrence in classical ages, he finally presents the real reason: simply enough, someone put it there.

The impulse to evolve fanciful and romantic explanations when simple ones will suffice is, however, only peripheral to the real object of Fielding's attack. More dangerous are the monolithic interpretations of all experience that flatten the variety of life into harsh paradigms and exempla. Even the benevolent can have this bent. We accept Allworthy's frequently tedious sermonizing because, like Tom's talk of romance, it expresses real feeling. But in the early chapters the narrator remarks that the progress of the novel —its particular pattern of causes and effects—owes as much to Allworthy's false perceptions and generalizations as to Tom's lack of perception (III, vii, p. 117).

Allworthy is traditionally one of Fielding's "good men," although he actually loses this epithet for the greater part of *Tom Jones,* and regains it only at the end. His goodness does not completely save him from criticism. In fact, he tends to generalize on goodness until his abstractions blind him to the particulars before his face; in a humorous example of this tendency, his prolonged meditation on babies at the sight of young Tom makes him forget that he is running around in his nightshirt. Yet Allworthy can be an admirable character despite his stock of sermonizing platitudes, because he has the capacity to change. His Christianity can potentially encompass the vast variety of human situations. He understands that charity must be expressed in action; and he tries, sometimes unsuccessfully, to avoid a total commitment to principles that ignore the phenomena of real situations (II, v, p. 79). In Abraham Adams the theoretical formulation and the intuitive sympathy are often at odds; in Allworthy they are ultimately complementary. New information can change Allworthy's opinion, while Adams frequently rejects facts that do not fit his systems. Allworthy's distortions are never so willful; they are usually only misguided.

Many minor characters in *Tom Jones* share the tendency to overgeneralize. The satire of surgeons in the novel is aimed not at their jargon (as it was in *Joseph Andrews*), but at their high-sounding and vague generalizations, which are usually irrelevant to the case before them. More fully presented characters have a slightly more complex tendency to categorize and dismiss. Both the landlady and the Quaker (VIII, ii) treat Tom well as an individually appealing and interesting young man. But when they find out that he is a bastard, they treat him scornfully. He has exemplified one of their abstract categories of evil and must be completely disdained. Accordingly they pigeonhole and dehumanize him.

The Man of the Hill section elaborates many of these themes in some detail. The Quaker with his excessive moralizing, the lieutenant with his excessive concern for "honor," the landlady with her excessive deference to class —all are good characters flawed by a tendency to generalize too much upon one aspect of life to the detriment of their larger sympathies. The Man of the Hill is the apotheosis of such a view. His complete generalizations render him incapable of acting. His excessive pessimism about man's nature extends into public life. He is almost paranoid in his insistence upon the evil of the world and does not quite believe it when Tom assures him that the histories have recorded the Glorious Revolution accurately. The Man of the Hill has generalized about the venality of men from his own experience and then reimposed these generalizations upon all the succeeding phenomena that come his way. Here is what he considers to be "A Brief History of Europe. . . .":

> In Italy the landlords are very silent. In France they are more talkative, but yet civil. In Germany and Holland they are generally very impertinent. And as for their honesty, I believe it is pretty equal in all those countries (VIII, xv, p. 404).

His generalizations flatten and reduce any insight into human nature he might have gained through experience.

Tom does learn from his confrontation with the Man of the Hill. He has the capacity to learn, and his journey is therefore more genuinely picaresque than Joseph's. He sharpens his own view of the variety of life when he faces the absolute generalities of the Man of the Hill. Thinking means abstraction to the Man of the Hill. He reads only "true philosophy" and despises those who have any attachment to the particular over the general (VIII, xiii, p. 397). His ideas are finally put to the test when he and Tom hear the screams of Mrs. Waters, who is being attacked by Northerton. Tom races to her rescue; the Man of the Hill, lost in meditation, does not move.

Closely involved with the Man of the Hill's commitment to absolute generalization is his belief in the providential theory of history. It is significant in the light of the treatment of Providence in *Joseph Andrews* and *Jonathan Wild* that the main characters in *Tom Jones* who share such views and apply them to explain public events are the hyperphilosophic Man of the Hill (VIII, xiv, p. 401), the ignorant Partridge (XII, viii, p. 552), and the villainous Blifil (XVII, ii, p. 755).[e] Like Heartfree, the Man of the Hill couples a belief in Providence with a belief in the insignificance of man before God (VIII, xv, p. 406). And, also like Heartfree, his belief in the insignificance and depravity of man's will before the power of Providence renders him incapable of acting. In the words of Tom, Fielding asserts that such constructions are usually derived from self-interest and then raised into innate patterns of history. Even those believers in Providence who may be sincere are at least glancingly criticized in *Tom Jones*. Events are coming to a climax when Allworthy happens to run into Black George while paying a visit to Old Nightingale. The narrator describes the encounter in these terms: "Here an accident happened of a very extraordinary kind; one indeed of those strange chances whence very good and grave men have concluded that Providence often interposes in the discovery of the most secret villainy in order to caution men from quit-

---

e Both the Man of the Hill (VIII, x, p. 377) and Partridge (VIII, iii, p. 349) are also physiognomists, perhaps to indicate the similarity between the philosophy and the ignorance that rely on the same modes of perception. Mrs. Whitefield (VIII, viii, p. 365) is also a physiognomist, but this is more in keeping with her profession.

ting the paths of honesty, however warily they tread in those of vice" (XVIII, xi, p. 795).

No matter how sincere its basis and how respectable its spokesmen outside the novel, the providential view in *Tom Jones* is at best supererogatory and at worst ignorantly or meretriciously self-serving. Even the "grave and good men" are shown to be adherents of an irrelevant mode of interpretation. Christian stoicism is an evasion of the complex problems of knowing and acting. In "On the Recent Interpositions of Providence" the revealed crime must be circumstantially and legally ratified by the institutions of human justice. In *Tom Jones* Providence has even less of a role to play. Allworthy must make proper and conscious use of his meeting with Black George if it is to have any real importance.

Most characters in *Tom Jones*, and in fact most characters in Fielding, use abstractions both to shield themselves from the confused variousness of the world and to mask their own ignorance and venality. Instead of responding directly to human situations, they rhetorically inflate and then manipulate terms like "charity," "honor," and "love." Discussion takes the place of actions; exempla stand for individual characters. There are few moments when one character is not misunderstanding another character's actions or attitudes. Sophia's arm is bled because she fainted (IV, xiv). Actually she is worried about Tom's broken arm, not her own narrow escape. Mrs. Partridge is already so suspicious of Partridge and Jenny Jones that anything they do supports her suspicions (II, iii). No matter what Sophia says or does, the landlord interprets it, because of his previous assumptions, to be further proof that she is Jenny Cameron (XI, vi, p. 503).

FIELDING'S MANIPULATION of causality and his preoccupation with its importance reflect his feeling for the extra piece of information that may change everything. Although he continually argues the possibility that the next instant will bring a new element that may disrupt a well-oiled system of explanation, he does not therefore imply that the previous formulations are venal, precipitate, or necessarily irresponsible. He indicates instead that the total belief in any formulation is wrong. Formulations are good until they fail. Some only obscure understanding and are therefore more patently wrong than others. The narrator considers his prime didactic purpose in *Tom Jones* to be the inculcation of the sense of contingency in explanation. To make an analogy to the puddle scene in *Joseph Andrews*: *Tom Jones* appears to be the narrow country road of necessitous plotting; but it carries within it the anticipation of possibilities behind the hedge. Fielding continually forces the reader to ask "What is a good reason? "What is a good explanation?" "What is relevant among the welter of possibilities?" Philip Stevick uses the image of the spider web to describe Fielding's causality.[45] But the lines are only apparently so straight and intersecting. Fielding believes instead that no explanation is forever fixed. Some causes explain more at some moments; some explain more at other moments.[f] Many times in *Tom Jones* we seem to get the whole story and we (and often the narrator) make judgments upon the basis of what we know. Then, some time later, the narrator introduces new information. His method catches the contingency of our acquaintance with the world, in which no judgment is absolute.[46] The new fact does not necessarily invalidate the generalizations brought to bear on the basis of the previously known facts; it does compel a new assessment of a particular situation. Eight hundred pages after we have received an elaborate explanation of why Bridget Blifil treats Tom well, we discover the all-encompassing reason

---

[f] The narrator has told us, for example, that Molly Seagrim's sister Betty envied Molly and did certain things for that reason. At one point she tells Tom that Will Barnes was Molly's first lover. This vengeful animosity toward her sister requires a stronger explanation; accordingly, the narrator tells how Molly had stolen Will Barnes from Betty: "Hence had grown that implacable hatred which we have before seen raging in the mind of Betty, though we did not think it necessary to assign this cause sooner, as envy itself was alone adequate to all the effects we have mentioned" (V, vi, p. 197).

why she should behave that way. Although this new reason may invalidate certain conclusions or conjectures, it does not, for example, importantly change our estimate of Bridget's character; she is still unattractive.

Fielding's method does try to keep us open to new experience and knowledge. Although in retrospect the world—or *Tom Jones*—may seem to follow a tight causal economy, in prospect we are as confused as Partridge. The answer is not passive belief in an ultimate order, but an active search for understanding. Fielding explores the general behavior of men *through* the variety of life, not by merely demonstrating his generalities by examples. In his way he partakes of the process that Ernst Cassirer believes is typical of the Enlightenment: ". . . as the center of gravity of thought shifts from definition to description, from the species to the individual, mechanism can no longer be considered as the sole and sufficient basis of explanation; there is in the making a transition to a conception of nature which no longer seeks to derive and explain becoming from being, but being from becoming."[47]

If *Tom Jones* has any didactic purposes, they involve the inculcation of a methodology of perception rather than specific moral principles. Fielding appears to believe that if we perceive properly, we will naturally act properly. Tom, for example, has shown in straight narrative his refusal to bandy Sophia's name in public. Sophia hates him for what she believes to be his continual flaunting of her name in public. The narrator first attempts to quiet his readers who believe such a contradictory state of affairs to be "unnatural" by reminding them he is "not writing a system but a history." Then he offers a few preliminary formulations of how the contradictory attitudes are justified and how they may be reconciled:

> Now, perhaps the reflections which we should be here inclined to draw would alike contradict both those conclusions, and would show that these incidents contribute only to confirm the great, useful, and uncommon doc-

trine which it is the purpose of this whole work to inculcate and which we must not full up our pages by
frequent repeating, as an ordinary parson fills his sermon by repeating his text at the end of every paragraph
(XII, ix, p. 554).

What is this doctrine? The next paragraph provides the
answer: "We are contented that it must appear, however unhappily Sophia erred in her opinion of Jones, she had sufficient reason for her opinion, since, I believe, every other
young lady would in her situation have erred in the same
manner."

As I have tried to suggest, the "great, useful, and uncommon doctrine" is the idea that one may have enough reason—sufficient reason—for an opinion, but never necessary reason. Plausible reasons are not always true. The
only way to protect against foolish behavior on the basis of
sufficient but wrong reasoning is to be aware of the nature
of epistemological contingency, of the path on the other
side of the hedge.

"Accidents" are what Fielding calls the events in *Tom
Jones* that disrupt ignorantly applied causalities to imply
the fabric of actual contingency from which the pattern of
the novel is drawn. They existed, as we have seen, in both
Joseph Andrews and *Jonathan Wild*. In *Tom Jones* they
achieve their full epistemological significance. Characters
blame Fortune, Fate, or Chance for the "accidents" that
thwart their long-range plans. Instead of being open to
contingency, they deify abstract historical explanation in
order to escape personal responsibility. As in *Jonathan
Wild*, the characters who come off worst are those who believe either in their full power of control or in their full
submission to control. The progress of the plot of *Tom
Jones*, for all its retrospective tightness, occurs by "accident": the "accident" of the falling cloth that reveals Square
in Molly's room (V, v, p. 191); the "accident" by which
Sophia goes to change her hair ribbons and therefore fails
to meet Tom by the canal (VI, vi, p. 246); the "accident"

of Partridge's arrival to help Tom at the Upton fight (IX, iii, p. 421); the "mere chance" by which Tom goes to London the same way as Sophia (XII, iii, p. 532); the "other cross incidents" that hinder Tom from meeting Lady Bellaston but allow him to see Sophia (XIII, xi, p. 620); the "lucky circumstance" of Squire Western's entrance into the very room where Fellamar is attacking Sophia, "the only accident on earth" that could have saved her (IV, v, p. 682). Such examples could be freely multiplied. They occur in almost every chapter. In fact, the typical pattern of a chapter in *Tom Jones* begins with an elaborately abstract attitude or a complex situation, which is then severely qualified by the introduction of a "strange accident" or "trifling incident" at the chapter's conclusion.

But these "accidents" are not the uncaused or gratuitous eruptions of an arbitrary universe.[48] The narrator spends much time justifying them with a profusion of circumstantial detail and analysis. Squire Western's fortuitous entrance, for example, is followed by several pages that attempt to account for his being there at that particular time. The narrator makes a procedural point, while the reader receives the maximum in entertaining surprise. Coincidence in *Tom Jones* emphasizes the control of the narrator and attunes the reader to the often strange concatenations of events that he may expect from life. By producing the necessary explanation only *after* the effect has been achieved and the scene witnessed, the narrator reveals that the elaborate patterns we make of history are only retrospectively ironclad and knowable. Any system that we employ to yield predictions is doomed to failure if it is not elastic enough to encompass accidents and "trifling incidents."

Fielding, like Hume, believes that causality is more important as a means of explanation rather than an inherent characteristic of nature. Chance and accident are continual possibilities for which absolute systems of causal pattern can never allow. The damage accidents can do to an absolute explanation for the world is shown in minature by the puppet-show (XII, v–vi). The puppet-master is the lowest type of aesthetic patterner. He wishes to present an unqualified and direct moral imperative. Accordingly, he excises the "low" parts from Vanbrugh and Cibber's *The Provok'd Husband*, showing only "the fine and serious part." The narrator comments that the show was performed "with great regularity and decency"; it was "a grave and solemn entertainment," "a rational entertainment." However, the lessons that the show is supposed to inculcate have an exactly opposite effect. The maid of the inn is discovered embracing one of the clowns right on the puppet-show stage. This situation illuminates some of the characteristics of Fielding's narrative I have already discussed. In XII, v, the narrator discourses very solemnly on the puppet-show, outlines the puppet-master's program, and records Tom's objections to the method, ending with another harangue by the puppet-master on the didactic superiority of his technique. In XII, vi, he immediately qualifies the abstract discussion of XII, v, by presenting an actual situation. The narrator then emphasizes the general rule he finds in such a juxtaposition:

> Nothing indeed could have happened so very inopportune as this accident; the most wanton malice of Fortune could not have contrived such another stratagem to confound the poor fellow while he was so triumphantly descanting on the good morals inculcated by his exhibitions. His mouth was now as effectually stopped as that of a quack must be if in the midst of a declamation on the great virtues of his pills and powders, the corpse of one of his martyrs should be brought forth and deposited before the stage as a testimony of his skill (p. 544).

"Accidents" are the intrusion of the facts of actuality upon the embalmed abstractions of system, either philosophical or aesthetic. They seem accidental only because we have somehow been lulled into feeling that the generalities of a character, of the narrator, or of our own preconceptions and assumptions, are applicable and relevant in every case. It is not necessary to posit an arbitrary force behind actuality to explain accidents; they are thrown off by the complex and various nature of the world. The clear thinking and perceptive reader should have expected them all along.

The ideal of clear perception is closely related to the ability to be spontaneous. Tom's spontaneity and appreciation for the individuality of a particular person in a particular situation is set against the conventional and formalized reactions of the other characters, presented in purified form by the Man of the Hill. Tom recognizes the self-centered origin of the Man's abstract "pure philosophy":

> . . . I believe as well as hope that the abhorrence which you express for mankind in the conclusion [of your remarks] is much too general. Indeed you here fall into an error which, in my little experience, I have observed to be a very common one, by taking the character of mankind from the worst and basest among them, whereas indeed, as an excellent writer observes, nothing should be esteemed as characteristical of a species but what is to be found among the best and most perfect individuals of that species. This error, I believe, is generally committed by those who, from want of proper caution in the choice of their friends and acquaintances, have suffered injuries from bad and worthless men, two or three instances of which are very unjustly charged on all the human race (VIII, xv, pp. 406–407).

Similarly, Tom attacks the Man of the Hill's providential fatalism by opposing to it the unpatternable but nevertheless understandable occurrence of chance:

> If there was indeed much more wickedness in the world than there is, it would not prove such general assertions against human nature, since much of this arrives by mere accident, and many a man who commits evil is not totally bad and corrupt in his heart. In truth, none seem to have any title to assert human nature to be necessarily

and universally evil but those whose own minds afford them one instance of this natural depravity, which is not, I am convinced, your case (p. 407).

Despite Tom's disclaimer, it is clear that he condemns the epistemological orientation of the Man of the Hill as one-sided and distorting. Providence, Chance, Fate, or Fortune are irrelevant beside what a character makes of the opportunities life presents. Through clear perceptions and free acts men can break from the causal chains others have imposed upon them.

In *Tom Jones* most of the causal impositions are attempts to control or regulate the behavior of Tom and Sophia. Characters from Blifil to Squire Western to Mrs. Western have elaborate plans for Sophia. She thwarts them all by running away from home; she makes a decision and then carries it out. Allworthy thinks Tom was "sent by Fortune" to his care, but the operative cause is the machinations of his sister Bridget. "Accidents" in this context are the actions of as yet free characters that can upset the reductive strictures of others. Inflated by their belief in their own insight, characters like Mrs. Western, Thwackum, and even All-worthy believe they are seeing clearly and interpreting correctly; but they are actually imposing limited conceptions both of personality and the relation between motives and actions. As the polarized views of Thwackum and Square are suspect by their very extremity, so the opposition of Squire Western and his sister implies that each could benefit from the view of the other. He sees clearly only what is in front of him, but cannot place it in any coherent pattern of interpretation. She sees only at a distance, and even at a distance she does not see very well (VI, ii, p. 230). Both use themselves as generalized standards of behavior and are dumbfounded when these standards are insufficient for understanding others. As the narrator indicates, the true understanding of others is retained only by those characters who have both sufficient empathy to understand another person and sufficient detachment to separate personal prejudices from the realities of a situation.

The ability to react freely and spontaneously is rooted in an appreciation of the complex natures of others. When Adams in *Joseph Andrews* hears three accounts of the Promiser's behavior, he believes he has heard about three different men. Like the early Hume, deluded characters in *Tom Jones* frequently seek for a spurious "consistency" in others. Blifil, the Westerns, Thwackum, and all the others who attempt to control Tom and Sophia, proceed from assumptions about human characters that are as simple-minded as their assumptions about causal explanation. The characters in *Tom Jones* who think of themselves or others as totally consistent are invariably wrong. As in the condemnation of simple-minded causality, Fielding does not say that human character is a chaotic and unintelligible shambles. He says merely that abstract systems of character, like abstract patterns of cause, are more binding than liberating, more irrelevant than useful, more false than true. He reasserts a point like the one he made about the practice of physiognomy in the "Essay on the Knowledge of Characters": perhaps the greatest physiognomist would never make any mistakes; but until he appears we need a kind of understanding that can work for all of us, not merely the most perceptive.

We have already noticed in Fielding's novels the growing frequency of situations in which human sympathy is thwarted by the stereotyped ideas of character—Tom's bastardy, for instance. Characters also limit themselves, as well as others, by such stereotypes. They use the simplistic opinions of the "world" to excuse themselves from personal responsibility: Black George steals Tom's £500 and Fellamar tries to rape Sophia because they believe it is expected of them, as impoverished tenants or town beaux. When characters try to fathom the motives of others, they usually project their personal natures, instead of trying to understand someone else's individuality. Lack of self-knowledge is intimately related to inability to understand others. Both are variations of the wrong-headed postulation of consistency of personality. The egocentric Man of the Hill uses the image of the self as a polished steel ball. He praises the study of philosophy and religion for their help in his achievement of his present mental state:

> They do indeed produce similar effects with exercise, for they strengthen and confirm the mind till man becomes, in the noble strain of Horace,
>
> Fortis, et in seipso totus teres atque rotundus,
> Externi ne quid valeat per laeve morari;
> In quem manca ruit semper Fortuna.
>
> Here Jones smiled at some conceit which intruded itself into his imagination, but the stranger, I believe, perceived it not ... (VII, xiii, p. 397).

Whether Tom may be reminded of the self-contained worlds of Thwackum and Square, with perhaps a jibe at Thwackum's fatness, is unclear.[g] But the inadequacy of the Man's self-image as a description of Tom himself is picked up much later by the narrator: ". . . poor Jones was one of the best-natured fellows alive and had all that weakness which is called compassion, and which distinguishes this imperfect character from that noble firmness of mind which rolls a man, as it were, within himself and, like a polished bowl, enables him to run through the world without once being stopped by the calamities which happen to others" (XIV, vi, p. 648).

Opposed to the image of the polished surface is Fielding's use of the various categories of the mind and passions to give an indication of the complexity of character. This is certainly generalization of a sort. Yet when Fielding uses these categories, his generalizations are not deductive, but a mixture of the inductive with the codified impressions of

[g] The quotation is from *Satires*, II, vii, ll. 86–88. Tom may be musing on the fact that in context the remarks are made by Horace's slave Davus, who, through the customary freedom of Saturnalia, is revealing to his master the self-indulgence that lies beneath Horace's praise of stoic virtue and the customs of the ancient Romans.

the past. Alongside his generalizations about character we must continually keep in mind Fielding's insistence on their individuality. He maintains a delicate balance between his emphasis on the relevance of change and context, and his impulse to generalize about human nature. His urge to show "true" human types from the "book of nature" is at least as strong as his attack against the oversimplification of human character. Because he is trying to criticize and construct at once, it is often difficult to disentangle the strains of "good" and "bad" generalizations. But the key, as in all of Fielding's "philosophy," is the balance between abstraction and particular, type and context, essence and appearance.

To aid the development of his understanding, the reader himself may be implicated in the same faults of perception possessed by the characters. Throughout *Tom Jones* Fielding draws our attention to what are seeming inconsistencies in a character's behavior, only to demonstrate later that we thought them inconsistent because of a falsely reductive view of the integrity of that particular personality. The presence of Square in Molly's bedroom is only one such instance. Similarly, the narrator appeals to our knowledge of our own "inconsistent" behavior—"so uncertain are our tempers and so much do we at different time differ from ourselves"—so that we should not place impossibly stringent patterns on the behavior of characters we find in novels (VII, ix, p. 301).[h] As we have seen, a typical personage in *Tom Jones* is the otherwise good character—the landlady, the lieutenant, the Quaker, Uncle Nightingale— who has one blind spot. The reader must be on guard against any categories that reduce the complexity of human character; he must be able to see beyond the literary manipulation of character as he sees beyond the simplified causal world of *Tom Jones*.[49] To perceive both the com-

[h] Compare Hume's remark on Henry VIII: ". . . he was so different from himself in different parts of his reign, that . . . his history is his best character and description" (*History of England*, III, xxxiii, p. 308). See above, p. 71.

plexity of character and its coherence is palpably an act of understanding, in which sympathies must be mediated and supplemented by reason:

> . . . we must admonish thee, my worthy friend (for, perhaps, thy heart may be better than thy head), not to condemn a character as a bad one because it is not perfectly a good one. If thou dost delight in these models for perception, there are books enow written to gratify thy taste; but as we have not in the course of our conversation ever happened to meet with any such person, we have not chosen to introduce any such here. . . . Nor do I, indeed, conceive the good purposes served by inserting characters of such angelic perfection or such diabolical depravity in any work of invention, since from contemplating either, the mind of man is more likely to be overwhelmed with sorrow and shame than to draw any good uses from such patterns . . . (X, i, pp. 441–42).

Acts of villainy may be done by the best of men as acts of good may be done by the worst; innate depravity as well as complete goodness is equally untenable. Fielding's concept of "conservation of character" attempts to preserve the diversity of an individual personality by establishing a coherent relation of character and action comprehensible to the perceptive observer. As he did in "On the Knowledge of Characters," Fielding in *Tom Jones* continues to believe that action is the clearest indication of character. But he has complicated this idea by trying to show how the postulations of "consistency" that we bring to literature and life often blind us to the complexities that are actually there.

Appropriately enough, Tom and Sophia, who do not try to manipulate or impose understanding, are the most free in action and the most spontaneous in response. Tom's manner of perception in at least one instance can stand as a model for the reader. The scene is the party before the day of the marriage of Nightingale and Betty Miller. All the company but Tom are apprehensive about one thing or another. The narrator has often remarked that, when someone dissembles, that person usually has no awareness either of himself or of others. The narrator observes now that the atmosphere has changed from their previous meeting: "This alteration was not, however, greatly remarked by any present; for as every one was now endeavouring to conceal their own thoughts and to act a part, they became all too busily engaged in the scene to be spectators of it" (XIV, x, p. 667). Tom's willingness to help others, coupled with his lack of involvement in the specific situation, allows him to understand what the others do not: "Jones, who was the least concerned in this scene, saw the most."

Fielding's view of the relation of character and causality is never as simple as is Hume's in the Stuart volumes of his *History*. In *Tom Jones* he further emphasizes the difficulty of precisely deducing character from action, or vice versa. Because his methods must be relevant to daily life and behavior, he criticizes the reductive hindsight of the public historian. Even though Hume asserts the difficulty of entering the mind of a historical personage, he exercises his prerogative and often does so. Fielding, on the other hand, frequently disclaims such a privilege. Such a method is not open to the reader in his daily life; and *Tom Jones* in some way attempts to approximate our immediate knowledge of the world. The narrator of *Tom Jones* may be an ideal of perception, and the world of *Tom Jones* may be an ideal model of the world. But this ideal world teaches the reader to learn in a world less perfect, and the narrator often imposes upon himself the epistemological limitations that are part of any person's immediate perceptions. When he goes beyond such limitations, he tells you so and he points out the artificial forms he has created in order to do it.

To COUNTER the spuriously complete system, the narrator's world in *Tom Jones* is a palpable imposition, a methodology of learning. Unmediated, the facts of history, public or private, make no sense. There must always be some point of view. To pretend the objective detachment and rhetoric of the chroniclers, the Richardsonian editor, or the "criminal" biographer is to attempt to hoodwink the reader. Fielding may wish to uncover general moral truths, but his interests go beyond moral precepts and exempla. He wants primarily to emphasize the atmosphere of epistemological uncertainty in which we live. History should not be written for statesmen, but for the common reader, whose goal should be to approximate in his own life the sympathies and perceptions of the historians. Fielding turns to novels because he believes that "real" history, what Marc Bloch has called "eventish" history, has been discredited by partisan historians. Hume's detached approach is an attempt to remedy the situation. But Fielding rejects the form itself. His attack against chronologers in *Joseph Andrews* expands in *Tom Jones* to an attack against all who believe that the essence of human history lies in the chronological lists of public events. His attack against Great Men in *Jonathan Wild* emerges more clearly in *Tom Jones* as an attack against historians who foist such ideas on the reader.

The elaborate time scheme of *Tom Jones* is in a way a booby trap for the chronologers. By the conclusion of the novel, the reader, in his greater knowledge, should be able to penetrate the artificiality of the time scheme to a larger and less temporally based appreciation of the variety of human nature. The narrative voice in *Tom Jones* frees the action from the artificialities of chronology. The least interesting aspect of *Tom Jones* should be its potential verifiability in calendar time. Time imposes its false causalities in the same way as many of the characters. All critical assertions that attempt to tie *Tom Jones* to a fictional method that has been called "so faithful to fact that it checks with the almanac for 1745" have remained on the surface of Fielding's presentation.[50] They assume he has the same conception of the role of the historian that we have seen him ridicule in *Joseph Andrews*.[51]

Tom Jones eschews the straight lines of public history because its own movement is basically circular. It contains references to a world beyond its pages, from the 1745 Rebellion through Mrs. Whitefield (who actually did run the Bell Inn at Gloucester) to various unnamed but alluded-to tastemakers and tradesmen. But in *Tom Jones* a great "public event" like the '45 Rebellion has little "reality" or "meaning" beyond that imposed upon it by different characters for their own interests. In the kitchen of the puppet-show inn (XII, vii, pp. 549–50), everyone makes of the Rebellion what they wish. The landlady at Upton decides to become a Jacobite because Sophia was gracious to her and she believes Sophia is Jenny Cameron, the mistress of Bonny Prince Charles. The Whig and Jacobite terms used by Squire Western and Mrs. Western are obviously only counters for their incessant private quarrels. Fielding implies that public history is bankrupt because it concentrates so much upon great events that it devalues daily life. When it does treat human beings, as in the biographies of great men, it either subordinates them to abstract theories of historical meaning or caricatures complex personalities under reductive moral or political rubrics. Mrs. Western is the great reader of public history in the novel; she is the pre-eminent "political" person, always in touch with the great events, personalities, and current abstractions of the public world. Yet more than any other character she confuses and obfuscates by her inability to have even the slightest perception of the private motives and actions in play about her.

The point of *Tom Jones* is not that the novel can be made to adhere to an externally verifiable scheme of geography and historical event. Fielding implies by his jocular play with Sophia's muff that a physical object, a public event, or a public person carries a weight of imputed meaning often at complete variance with its "innate" meaning.[1] Revolving around the scenes at Upton, the aesthetic

[1] Maurice Johnson traces the appearance of the muff in *Tom Jones* and the situations it induces. He mentions the possibility of a slang interpretation, but goes no further. See "The Device of Sophia's Muff in *Tom Jones*," *MLN*, 74 (1959), pp. 685–90, reprinted in *Fielding's Art of Fiction* (Philadelphia, 1965). Eric Partridge in his *Dictionary of Slang and Unconventional English* says that "muff" had the same obscene connotations in the eighteenth century that it has today. Again

pattern of *Tom Jones* works against and finally overcomes its nominal chronological pattern. Tom is really no more (or no less) worthy of Sophia at the end than at the beginning. The bulk of *Tom Jones* is a complex exercise in misunderstanding. Its artificial form, involuted plot, and freight of meditation have been constructed to make us perceptive readers of novels and therefore perceptive experiencers of life. The goal of the novelist-historian is the discovery of basic truths about human nature; his method is the examination of the pattern of cause and effect. Similarly, the goal of the reader is to live well and perceptively; his understanding of the world around him should presuppose a network of sufficient, but not necessary, relations. The episodic structure of *Joseph Andrews* tended to ridicule discernible causal pattern. *Jonathan Wild* imposed iron laws of causality as an instrument of similar ridicule. One of the essentials of the narrator's control in *Tom Jones* is his mastery of the patterns of cause. But these are not the linear causes of public history, nor are they merely the evidences of a deified Fortune.[52] *Tom Jones* places causality in proper perspective as a method for understanding rather than an illusion or a necessary pattern.

Tom Jones consolidates the insights of *Joseph Andrews* and *Jonathan Wild* and presents a world in which the claims of detail and the claims of pattern are given their proper roles. It schools the reader in a fresh response to the world. Fielding searches for general truths about man, but he demands that these general truths be in a continually self-correcting interplay with the particulars from which they are derived. He attacks the generality about human behavior that has broken away from the contexts that formed it and now exists without possibility of change. But

Fielding is playing with the many constructions that can be placed upon words. Perhaps the *locus classicus* for this kind of joke is the "china" scene in *The Country Wife*. For a similarly ironic use of the meaning imposed on a physical object, see the discussion of Amelia's "cordial," below, pp. 206–07.

he argues for an empirical attitude, rather than a slavish devotion to the minutiae of the world. The important facts in the world of *Tom Jones* are the facts of human action and personality, not the descriptive details of a neutral empirical world. The important contexts are composed of the interactions of different personalities, not the moments of calendar time. The truths of human behavior which Fielding contemplates remain free of time because he believes in the continuity of human reactions throughout the ages, no matter how complex a specific individual may be. But this continuity implies vital change, not systematic sameness. Fielding focuses his renovation of reality on private life because he believes that the practice of public history has served primarily to distort people's appreciation of the world and how it works. He condemns the pretense to impartiality and objectivity that makes either conscious or unconscious distortion. Because Fielding's approach is constructive, he treats the world in *Tom Jones* with less bitterness than he did in either *Joseph Andrews* or *Jonathan Wild*. The conflict between theory and practice, always suspect and often venal in *Joseph Andrews*, in *Tom Jones* is considered to be almost inevitable and natural, not an aberration, only something to watch out for.

The source of Fielding's vitality in *Tom Jones* is his reliance upon the unexpected and the individual. They can revitalize, he shows, the atrophied abstractions and stereotypes that have been the common currency of previous writers. To stretch the mind of the reader Fielding emphasizes not only the present diversity, but also the diversity to come. His ideal is a complex and coherent whole; but along the way he points out the dangers of shortcuts to unity. Fielding's characters in *Tom Jones* stand between exempla and real individuals. Many of their traits are presented generally, as types, but we know them not abstractly but through action. No one really changes in *Tom Jones,* although Tom himself realizes many of his potentialities. Allworthy and Sophia criticize Tom not because of anything he has done but because they have either misinterpreted what they have heard about him or accepted what was untrue. Tom's major fault is that he gets into situations that are likely to be misinterpreted by imperceptive people. He is a pure character, cut off from all causes. In the circumstances of Tom's birth—the son of the nasty Bridget Blifil and the nonentity Mr. Summer—Fielding ridicules hereditary causation. Cut off from cause, Tom is unfortunately the perfect receptacle for the causes imposed by others. If his character does become refined (I would not say "developed"), it may be only an extra treat for Allworthy and Sophia. Perhaps it can be said that what was present at the beginning of the novel is present at the end. But we have changed. Through our contemplation of the self-contained and self-authenticating world of *Tom Jones* we have learned methods of knowing, of clearly apprehending the reality around us. Fielding achieves our learning through the device of his narrator, the mediator of historical materials that without him might be disjointed and meaningless. He defines in the narrator of *Tom Jones* the model historian who constructs from the materials of observation, learning, and authority an appropriate causal pattern, without necessity but with plausibility, and totally fitted to the varied world in which we must live.

V. *Amelia*: THE PRIMACY OF PRIVATE HISTORY

Not sedulous by Nature to indite
Wars, hitherto the only Argument
Heroic deem'd, chief maistry to dissect
With long and tedious havoc fabl'd Knights
In Battles feign'd; the better fortitude
Of Patience and Heroic Martyrdom
Unsung. . . .
    MILTON, *Paradise Lost*, IX, 27-33

Through its strict narrative control, *Tom Jones* presents a laboratory world that will hopefully prepare the reader for the actual world. *Amelia* may be the test for which *Tom Jones* has prepared Fielding's reader. *Amelia* often seems permeated with a sense of despair, in contrast to the hearty optimism of much of *Tom Jones*. But it is not more real than *Tom Jones* because it imports Richardsonian gloom and moral themes. Through its form it conveys a sense of the uncertainty of real life, which *Tom Jones* could give only intellectually. The world of *Amelia* is more shaky and uncertain than that of *Tom Jones*. It has none of the carefully built foundation of the earlier novel; we enter *in medias res*. Fielding attempts in *Amelia* a novel that puts us more on our mettle than we were in *Tom Jones*. But *Amelia* is not a venture into unmediated realism. The world of Fielding's last novel is a more real and more uncertain world than he has ever created before, but it is still a created world, embodied in a work of literature.

The narrator of *Amelia* does not give us much help. Instead he invites us to test the categories and methods learned from *Tom Jones* in a less controlled world, one which more closely resembles our own lives. Fielding's narrative voice has also changed. He is now more eager to make the reader sensitive to the actual world than to tie up situations into neat bundles in the fictional world.[53] In many ways the major technique in *Amelia* extends the one Fielding uses in the section of Tom Jones where Mrs. Fitzpatrick tells her story: the reader is invited to discern character by comparing a character's account of himself with his subsequent action.[54] *Amelia* proceeds outward from the limited narrations of Miss Matthews and Booth that form the first half. The narrator gradually reveals his omniscience and begins to pull the reader up short more often, especially that reader who has been imperceptive enough to believe any of the first-person narrators wholly. In the later books the narrator is more concerned than he was earlier to justify and explain actions and bring the story up to date with flashbacks. Our knowledge becomes a little more extensive than that of the characters because we must finally have a perspective on them. We know that the Methodist stole Booth's snuffbox, although Booth does not; we similarly

know more than Booth about the womanizing nature of
the lord who promises him preferment.ʲ

Fielding makes the world of *Amelia* seem less created
than the world of *Tom Jones* because he is now more concerned with the relation of private perceptions to the world
of external society—the world of public figures, public
events, and public institutions. *Tom Jones* presents a private world that in various ways impinges or is impinged
upon by the public world, the world of history-book events
like the Battle of Preston Pans or a particular Garrick performance of *Hamlet*. Mediating between the reader and the
world of *Tom Jones* is the narrator, a partially private, partially public personality, who not only can invoke authority from the Bible, the Latin Elegists, and the Greek philosophers but also can reveal something of his private
life by comparing Sophia Western to his late wife, Charlotte
Cradock (IXII, i, p. 581). *Tom Jones* assumed that the
private world was naturally prior to the public world; the
true importance of the 1745 Rebellion was in what individuals made of it. Private affairs and a "private history" like
Tom Jones are more relevant to learning how to lead a
good life and be a good person than public affairs and "public history" can ever be.

Amelia focuses more clearly on the way public life and
the institutions of society threaten the individual: mere
spontaneity and exuberance are not sufficient to meet their
attacks. If *Joseph Andrews*, *Jonathan Wild*, and *Tom Jones*
ask whether worldly innocence and moral virtues are self-
sufficient values, *Amelia* answers no. The relation between
public and private life in *Amelia* embodies the major concerns of the earlier novels in a new organization that attempts to make them more relevant to the actual life of the
reader. In *Amelia* there is no longer a question of retreat
to the country to preserve innocence or good nature. Fielding's previous references to a Golden Age had always been
vexed. Adams calls Wilson's retreat "the way people lived

ʲ *Amelia*, intro. A. R. Humphreys, 2 vols. (London, 1962), I, v, p.
22; IV, ix, p. 205. Further citations will be included in the text.

in the Golden Age" (III, iv, p. 193); but the scene is shattered by the hunting squire. The gypsies' system of absolute monarchy, the narrator of *Tom Jones* finally decides, can never really work.[55] In *Amelia* there is hardly even the shadow of such a Utopian solution. Booth and Amelia, like Tom and Sophia, do go away to the country at the close of the novel. But their retreat is more clearly a jibe at romantic solutions, which artifically dissipate conflict.[56] Characters from the country—like Robinson, Murphy, and Amelia's sister Betty—are both more venal and less attractive than Black George or Molly.

Amelia does not offer the irresponsible solutions of romantic retreat or political Utopia. Harrison's speeches and actions argue instead that private virtue can ultimately reinvigorate public life or, by extension, that the truths discovered through the private mode of fiction can purge the venality of the public mode of history. Perhaps one reason for the relative failure of *Amelia* is that Fielding wishes to build a firmer link to the real world of action, and the novel suffers the strain. *Amelia* is as much a creation as *Tom Jones*, but less self-contained in its implications. In his last novel Fielding experiments with the relation between the private world of the individual and the public world of society, between the private world of a work of art and the actuality on which it is based and to which it must refer. Despite its flaws, *Amelia* is his most profound exploration of these themes.

MISINTERPRETATION is as rife in *Amelia* as it was in *Tom Jones*. Most characters in both novels cannot and do not see the need to take a flexible attitude toward the materials of experience. In an effort to make sense of what they do not immediately understand, they interpret events according to their own predilections. At the lowest level in *Amelia*, as in *Tom Jones*, are the distortions of gossip, for example, the story of Booth hiding in the wine-basket, as reported by Miss Matthews (I, v, p. 74). A more benevolent image for this kind of interpretation appears when Amelia and Booth listen to the gurgles of their first child:

> Our imaginations suggested a hundred agreeable circumstances, none of which had, perhaps, any foundation. We made words and meaning out of every sound, and in every feature found out some resemblance to my Amelia as she did to me (III, xi, p. 144).

But most of the imposed interpretation in *Amelia* is neither so pleasant nor so good-natured. And the misinterpretations of innocence are often not very benevolent in their effects. Thus Amelia and Booth's belief that Mrs. Ellison and Atkinson are going to be married helps blind the Booths to her venality (and the reader is taken in as well). Their misinterpretation is in fact not wholly innocent, for it springs from a vice which even the best characters have, the firm belief in their ability to fathom the characters of others. Booth interprets James' kindness to him as a support for the doctrine of the passions; virtue and religion cannot explain it, since James has neither (III, v, pp. 113–14). By seizing so readily on something that seems to support his own theory of personality, Booth blinds himself to actuality. Miss Matthews' projection of her own jealousy on to Amelia makes her draw back when Amelia meets Booth in prison. Amelia ascribes this reticence only to a dim recollection of the scandal in which Miss Matthews has been involved. But the damage is done: if Miss Matthews had not been so eager to ascribe her own motives to another, she might have been able to stay with Booth somewhat longer. Similarly, James tries to get Atkinson to act as his pimp with Amelia because in a similar position he would do the same himself:

> . . . an opinion which the serjeant might have pardoned, though he had never given the least grounds for it, since the colonel borrowed it from the knowledge of his own heart. This dictated to him that he, from a bad motive, was capable of desiring to debauch his friend's wife;

and the same heart inspired him to hope that another, from a rather bad motive, might be guilty of the same breach of friendship in assisting him. Few men, I believe, think better of others than of themselves; nor do they easily allow the existence of any virtue of which they perceive no traces in their own minds . . . (VIII, viii, p. 92).

The misinterpretations of Booth are particularly important because many characters, including himself, believe that his problems are the result of the repressive influence of the public world upon the individual, the refusal of a corrupt society to recognize merit. Booth is a soldier, a character with both a public and a private life, who must resolve his conflicts within that dual frame. His final conversion is only a summation of the process through which he has learned to sort out the separate demands of public and private life, and it is an emblematic act more for the reader than for him. His "philosophy" is as much an equivocation as are the beliefs of more venal characters. But because Booth is a better person, he is less to blame when he gives in to it. Booth believes in the same kind of necessary pattern in history as does Robinson; but he declines to call its originator God (I, iii, p. 14). Booth's brand of fatality is impersonal and its medium is the passions of the individual: ". . . [he] declared himself to be of the same opinion with regard to the necessity of human actions; adding, however, that he did not believe men were under any blind impulse or direction of fate, but that every man acted merely from the force of that passion which was uppermost in his mind, and could do not otherwise" (I, iii, p. 15).

Tied closely to this doctrine is Booth's belief in the power of Fortune, particularly Ill Fortune. The characters of *Amelia* float in a capricious universe and perpetually call on Fate, Providence, Fortune, or Ill Chance to order what seems to them to be incomprehensible. Booth appeals to his doctrine of the passions, and characters like Bondum the bailiff invoke the sanction of established institutions. Both are trying to salve their feeling of individual inadequacy as much as they are making a conscious refusal to accept responsibility. In *Amelia* the hypostatized projections of human inadequacy, which take the form of theories of history and behavior, have cut themselves off from their human origins and appear to many characters as malevolent gods, who sport with man at their arbitrary will. Many of the characters in *Amelia*, unlike Booth, have made some adjustment to what they believe are the necessary "rules" by which society operates. Like characters in previous novels, they project their own ideas upon their environment and then get them back; their beliefs become self-justifying. Fielding in the course of the novel broods over all such views of reality, showing how they warp and inhibit the spontaneous response to situations and other people. At best, such views are hindsight excuses for weakness, not innate truths about history and character; they are not perceptions of the inner workings of the world, but socially countenanced evasions of true perception and responsibility.

Characters in *Amelia* often believe they are at the mercy of adamant impersonal causes. Miss Matthews, for example, says that all her woes are the result of "one false step" (I, viii, p. 337), using the rhetoric of Richardsonian iron-chain causality both to heighten the language of her story and to excuse herself from too much personal responsibility for her actions.[k] Later, when she believes Booth has been

k See Richardson's "Hints of a Preface to Clarissa" in *Clarissa: Preface, Hints of a Preface, and Postscript*, ed. R. F. Brissenden, *Augustan Reprint Society, 103* (1964), p. 10: "Clarissa takes but one false step in the whole Piece. . . . But this single Step was of the utmost Consequence." Compare *Tom Jones*, I, ix, p. 50: Allworthy has decided to turn Jenny Jones out rather than send her to Bridewell, as the "mob" wishes: "So far from complying with this their inclination, by which all hopes of reformation would have been abolished, and even the gate shut against her if her own inclinations should ever hereafter lead her to choose the road of virtue, Mr. Allworthy rather chose to encourage the girl to return thither by the only possible means; for too true, I am afraid, it is that many women have become abandoned and have sunk to the last degree of vice by being unable to retrieve the first slip."

killed by Colonel James in a duel, she again uses a niggling causal explanation to revoke responsibility:

> She looked on James as the tool with which she had done this murder; and, as it is usual for people who have rashly or inadvertently made any animate or inanimate thing the instrument of mischief to hate the innocent means by which the mischief was effected (for this is a subtle method which the mind invents to excuse ourselves, the last objects on whom we would willingly wreak our vengeance), so Miss Matthews now hated and cursed James as the efficient cause of that act which she herself had contrived and laboured to carry into execution (V, viii, p. 249).

Mrs. Bennet, another woman who has taken part in a sordid situation, similarly uses the "one false step" argument: ". . . it is now my stedfast opinion that the woman who gives up the least outwork of her virtue doth, in that very moment, betray the citadel" (VII, vii, pp. 37–38). Later, however, she seems to have regained some of her belief in her power to manipulate, as shown by her marriage to Atkinson, her arguments with Harrison about the role of women, and her use of the peer to get her husband a commission. The figure of Mrs. Bennet with her rationality and classical learning is a foil to Miss Matthews and her passion, despite the extent to which Mrs. Bennet will fall back on Miss Matthews' mode of explanation when she finds herself in a similar situation.

With many other characters in *Amelia*, Billy Booth too often bemoans his fate and the seeming "directed" circumstances that bring about particular turns of ill luck. Such a view is basically egotistical; it assumes that the entire force of the universe, either directed by God or some more abstract power, is turned against the poor individual:

> . . . poor Booth imagined that a larger share of misfortunes had fallen to his lot than he had merited; and this

led him, who (though a good classical scholar) was not deeply learned in religious matters, into a disadvantageous opinion of Providence. A dangerous way of reasoning, in which our conclusions are not only too hasty, from an imperfect view of things, but we are likewise liable to much error from partiality to ourselves; viewing our virtues and vices as through a perspective, in which we turn the glass always to our own advantage, so as to diminish the one, as greatly magnify the other (I, iii, pp. 14–15).

When Booth is feeling expansive, he can dispense with Fortune and "several other imaginary beings" as the spawn of superstition (II, vii, p. 80). But more often he cherishes the belief that he is a victim of Fortune. He tells Miss Matthews how Harrison turned against him and Amelia: "Our happiness was, perhaps, too great; for fortune seemed to grow envious of it, and interposed one of the most cruel accidents that could have befallen us by robbing us of our dearest friend the doctor" (III, xii, p. 152).

When he tells more of the story, however, it becomes clear that the "cruel" accident he refers to—Harrison's appointment as a traveling tutor to his patron's son—is not really causally operative in the way Booth says it is. It merely sets the stage for Booth's own mistakes in conducting his farm, mistakes that he might have avoided if Harrison had been present to counsel him, but mistakes that were still the products of his own will, not the simple result of Harrison's absence. But Booth's imperceptions are easier to accept than Heartfree's, or even Tom's. His "ruling passion" theory of character at least emphasizes the uniqueness of the individual in a world that frequently dispenses with individual value. The *Essay on Man* was not written for this venal society; its theories unfortunately belong to the past. Yet Booth's use of abstraction can be appropriate, even though he frequently uses the doctrine of the ruling passion to excuse a lack of self-control. When we first see him, he is employing his philosophical bent to ease his mind while in prison. His philosophy, "of which he had no inconsiderable share" (I, iii, p. 11), is being used for a particular purpose in a particular situation.

Words like Providence, and Fortune, and Chance are used by many characters to justify what is seemingly unexplainable. For people who cannot bear the presence of caprice in the world, they are a handy means to collect discrete data into one rhetorically (and perhaps philosophically) manageable bundle. Mrs. Bennet describes this kind of personality, without realizing its nature, when she speaks of her first husband:

> If his breakfast was not ready to a moment—if a dish of meat was too much or too little done—in short, if anything failed to exactly hitting his taste, he was sure to be out of humour all that day, so that, indeed, he was scarce ever in a good temper a whole day together; for fortune seems to take a delight in thwarting this kind of disposition, to which human life, with its many crosses and accidents, is, in truth, by no means fitted (VII, v, p. 26).

The point here is surely plain. Life with "its many crosses and accidents" is not an intellectual formulation made by someone who wants to understand the world; it is an attempt to justify a certain kind of personality, perhaps an involuntary quotation from something her husband once said. Such abuses of words are drawn with somewhat broader outlines in the character of Major Bath. Every incident that comes his way is immediately considered in the light of his "honor," an abstraction that is as totally demanding in the necessary response to it as Booth's doctrine of the passions. When a duel is in the air, everything is irrelevant, even humanity, so demanding are the abstractions by which Bath has chosen to present his personality and structure his actions. The abstract concept, originally designed to be a generalized explanation and description, now cut off from its roots in situation and context, is perfectly illustrated in the "honor" of Colonel Bath, "who, with all the other principles of honour and humanity, made no more of cutting the throat of a man upon any of his punctilios than a butcher doth of cutting sheep" (XII, iv, p. 286).

Harrison can, however, appropriately use providential language to comfort Booth and Amelia in their troubles (III, x, p. 140), because it is validated by his own actions. He does not think that Christian stoicism in adversity should preclude action in the world; his theoretical beliefs are usually closely related to his actions. Robinson, the other major user of providential explanation in *Amelia,* has more common difficulties with abstract language. There is obviously a relation between his belief in Providence's arbitrary ways and his professional gambling, but which came first is uncertain. Robinson's adherence to historical necessity, like that of Amelia's sister Betty, indicates primarily self-serving, personal desires, hidden in abstract and generalized language. Robinson uses his language to convince Booth he is a philosophically minded person and worthy of trust:

> I perceive, sir, you are but just arrived in this dismal place, which, is indeed, rendered more detestable by the wretches who inhabit it than by any other circumstance; but even these a wise man will soon bring himself to bear with indifference; for what is, is; and what must be, must be. The knowledge of this, which, simple as it appears, is in truth the height of all philosophy, renders a wise man superior to every evil which can befal him . . . (I, iii, p. 13).

> . . . there was something in the manner of Robinson which, notwithstanding the meanness of his dress seemed to distinguish him from the crowd of wretches who swarmed in those regions; and, above all, the sentiments which he had just declared very nearly coincided with those of Mr. Booth . . . (I, iii, p. 14).

Providential language for sister Betsy self-righteously supports her trickery of Amelia:

"Sister, here is a great alteration in this place since you saw it last; Heaven hath been pleased to take my poor mother to itself."—(Here she wiped her eyes, and then continued)—"I hope I know my duty, and have learned a proper resignation to the Divine will; but something is to be allowed to grief for the best of mothers; for so she was to us both; and if at last she made any distinction, she must have had her reasons for doing so. I am sure I can truly say I never wished, much less desired it" (III, xi, pp. 145–46).

By manipulating abstractions and surface appearances, individuals take part in public society. Their allegiance to institutions that lack any human content complements the general superficiality of their views of the world. Like many "public" histories, *Amelia* deals with individuals meshed with institutions, although no one in the novel, except perhaps Harrison, consciously considers the problem in this light. All the other characters are trying to work out individual solutions, either of accommodation, manipulation, or opposition. Characters excuse themselves from responsibility by invoking the "necessary" workings of public life even more frequently than they invoke the action of impersonal causes or uncontrollable passions.

These characters typically appeal to the "demands" of an institution and rely on the appearances by which "society" judges. Justice Thrasher's belief that the truth never appears "in sordid apparel" constitutes his idea of the necessary philosophy for his role (I, ii, p. 10). For the jailer a legal question is similarly reducible to a question of manners: ". . . certainly it can never be imagined that a lady who behaves herself so handsomely as you have done ever since you have been under my keys should be guilty of killing a man without being very highly provoked to do it" (I, x, p. 51).

People like Mrs. James, who aspire to the higher orders of society and conceive of themselves as "public" persons, model their reactions on those of actresses: "Neither Miss Bellamy nor Mrs. Cibber were ever in a greater consternation on the stage than now appeared in the countenance of Mrs. James" (V, viii, p. 246).

Colonel James too can "dress out" his countenance whenever the situation demands. The physiognomic imperceptions of *Joseph Andrews* now have more malevolent implications. But the reader is again invited to look behind the mask. Blear-eyed Moll is "one of the merriest persons in the whole prison," a fact that the narrator feels is "productive of moral lesson" (I, iii, p. 13).

The reader is also invited to look through the personal affairs into the public issues. Public and private life are not separated in *Amelia*; we are shown instead the analogy between them. The second chapter of the novel introduces this theme. The narrator makes a few jibes at the chronicle form, then pauses to discuss institutions more generally:

> On the first of April, in the year——, the watchman of a certain parish (I know not particularly which) within the liberty of Westminster brought several persons whom they had apprehended the preceding night, before Jonathan Thrasher, Esq., one of the justices of the peace for that liberty. But here, reader, before we proceed to the trials of these offenders, we shall, after our usual manner, premise some things which it may be necessary for thee to know (I, ii, p. 5).

It is necessary for the reader to know that many writers have observed that human institutions are by their nature incapable of achieving "consummate perfection." Thrasher is an example of this observation. Even though he represents the law, he knows nothing about legal history or theory. In addition, he is even worse than ignorant, for he is venal. The narrator remarks that, if Thrasher had been merely ignorant, wrong and right would at least have shared decisions fifty-fifty.

Thrasher is only the first in the parade of inadequate institutional representatives who populate the novel. Often such characters are not dishonest; their perceptions are merely inadequate to the position they hold. Like Bondum the bailiff, when faced by a problem of equity, they complain that they are only doing their jobs. They do not appreciate the difference between general law and individual case; their view of their jobs ignores the concept of equity. Fielding believes such blindness parallels the blindness that allows philosophical abstractions to fix responses. The narrator informs us that Bondum the bailiff is not really a bad person and in the process uses the same metaphor of slaughter he used to describe Bath's conception of "honor":

> Here the reader may be apt to conclude that the bailiff, instead of being a friend, was really an enemy to poor Booth; but, in fact, he was not so. His desire was no more than to accumulate bail-bonds; for the bailiff was reckoned an honest and good sort of man in his way, and had no more malice against the bodies in his custody than a butcher hath to those in his: and as the latter, when he takes his knife in hand, hath no other design but of the joints into which he is to cut the carcase; so the former, when he handles his writ, hath no other design but to cut out the body into as many bail-bonds as possible. As to the life of the animal, or the liberty of the man, they are thoughts which never obtrude themselves on either (VIII, i, p. 60).

The world of *Amelia* then is a world of venal or imperceptive institutional representatives who imply inadequate institutions behind them. Since the institutions only operate as they are embodied as individuals, it is ridiculous to say that they remain pure while their representatives are corrupted. Although the system of law receives most of Fielding's concentration, no institution of society is exempt: the aristocracy, the army, and the clergy. The fact that the lascivious peer is never named contributes to his status as a generalized representative. Colonel James (and to an even greater extent, Trent) reveal the manipulations necessary to achieve success in the military world. Harrison and the young man in orders argue the same problems in a religious context. The criterion of success in the world of *Amelia* is the ability to rise amid the corruption of institutions. None of the "successful" characters ever questions the system; they accept its faults and change themselves to fit in with them. Thus a major sub-problem in *Amelia* is policy, the means by which the individual must compromise or change his values in order to conform to a venal public world. The father of the young man in orders expects his son to be politic even to the impolitic Harrison. After Harrison leaves, the young man complains that Harrison has gotten the better of him in argument:

> "What of that?" cries the father; "I never told you he was a wise man, nor did I ever think him so. If he had any understanding, he would have been a bishop long ago, to my certain knowledge. But, indeed, he hath been always a fool in private life; for I question whether he is worth £100 in the world, more than his annual income" (IX, x, p. 161).

Yet, despite his low opinion of Harrison, the old gentleman knows he has a position in the church and must be pacified: "Indeed, Tom, thou art as great a simpleton as himself. How do you expect to rise in the Church if you cannot temporize, and give in to the opinions of your superiors?" (p. 162).

Policy makes the corrupt institutions of the world of *Amelia* work. Merit has no place in the system. When Harrison petitions the lord for a military position for Booth, the lord naturally expects a political favor in return. This nobleman gives the most philosophical exposition in *Amelia* of the necessary venality of human institutions, and he asserts that policy is the only means of getting along with them to one's advantage. To believe that merit would always be served, he says, is "mere Utopia . . . the chimerical system of Plato's commonwealth, with which we amused ourselves at the university; politics which are inconsistent with the state of human affairs" (XI, ii, p. 228). The noble-man rejects the examples of good states drawn from history because they are "irrelevant" to England. Like Booth quot-ing Othello, and Bath on Hotspur (X, v, p. 190), he is will-ing to pick and choose among the authorities to find the most congenial:

> "To apply maxims of government drawn from the Greek and Roman histories to this nation is absurd and impos-sible. But, if you will have Roman examples, fetch them from those times of the republic that were most like our own. Do you not know, doctor, that this is as corrupt a nation as ever existed under the sun? And would you think of governing such a people by the strict principles of honesty and morality?"

This is fatalistic history with a vengeance. Nothing can be done about things because they are the inevitable results of the necessary degeneration of society and the necessary corruption of the individual. (The nobleman later com-pares a nation's history to the life of a man.) Despite his many statements about divine Providence, Harrison has no such fatalistic view of things:

> "If it be so corrupt," said the doctor, "I think it is high time to amend it: or else it is easy to foresee that Roman and British liberty will have the same fate. . . ."

If human institutions are not infallible, they are not there-fore completely venal.

What is called fate or historical necessity is a made thing, amended or effected by will, just as the novel that pretends to be a transcript of life is actually a made literary object. People who claim to be forced into actions by circumstance or necessity are either hypocrites or fools. As if to mock the nobleman's high-flown justification of his use of policy, the story of Trent almost immediately follows. Trent's scur-rilous career is completely a matter of choice and he battens on corruption. Accordingly, Trent believes that this is the way of the world, the only method by which a deserving young man can rise. Other possibilities do not occur to him, and he considers Booth to be a fool for trying to get anywhere by merit alone. The young man in orders values the clergy so highly not for its moral and religious role but because he has chosen to associate himself with it. His father exemplifies the man who consciously conforms to warped institutions for his own benefit. Both have essentially the same view of the relation of men and institutions; the old man is only a little more cynical. Like Booth, the young man has too great an opinion of his own understanding, particularly his knowledge of classics. He supports the clergy as an institution because he sees it as a projection of himself. Booth's self-conceit does not go this far, perhaps only because his own efforts to rise have been unsuccessful.

FIELDING'S IDEAL for the world of *Amelia* involves the revitalizing of public institutions through individual reflection and action, to counter the way individual ignorance and incompetence have degraded them. Against the young man in orders who will brook no insult to the clergy as an institution, Harrison opposes the reforming power of the individual and the individual conscience. The young man believes that any attack on the clergy supports the atheists, while Harrison argues that sensible and specific criticism is always beneficial. The good character must take situations and individuals on their own merits, without adducing through self-interest or self-pity a vague theory of history or character to pigeonhole them. As in earlier Fielding novels, the perceptive character must be willing to admit the existence of "accidents." Such "accidents" in *Tom Jones* often occurred at the ends of chapters, confusing the careful planning of the characters or the careful abstractions of the narrator. In *Amelia*, instead of being part of an epistemological manifesto, such "accidents" constitute the very materials with which the narrator must work; they are the rule, rather than the exceptions. The first sentence of chapter one informs us that *Amelia* will be about "the various accidents which befel a very worthy couple after their uniting in the state of matrimony" (p. 3). These accidents would seem to be the direct result of the "utmost malice" of Fortune (or, if the couple were not so worthy, Providence). But the narrator points out that Fortune has been convicted "by the public voice . . . of many facts in which she had not the least concern." Similarly, Fortune has been honored for false reasons. The invocation of Fortune denies the power of will, man's ability to shape the materials of his environment: "Whoever, therefore, calls such a man fortunate [a man who has retrieved the ill consequences of foolish conduct], is guilty of no less impropriety in speech than he would be who should call the statuary or the poet fortunate who carved a Venus or who writ an Iliad" (pp. 3–4).

The "ART OF LIFE" is the ability to perceive the possibilities of pattern and to extract them from the irrelevancies. In a sense Fielding has reversed his position on Wolsey, who would strike "unfortunate" from his dictionary. The perceptive man may control his life with understanding. And the perception for which the reader of *Tom Jones* was schooled is paralleled again to that of the organizing creative artist: "Life may as properly be called an art as any other; and the great incidents in it are no more to be considered as mere accidents than the several members of a fine statue or a noble poem" (p. 4).

The existence of chance confounds simple causality. Yet chance is not always arbitrary, no matter how it may appear. The more ludicrous "accidents" emphasize Fielding's belief in the limitless possibilities of life, the extent to which the unexpected can occur. A trifling event happens and it is quickly absorbed into the process of life, perhaps spawning a complex causality. In IX, vi, occurs "as surprising an accident as is perhaps recorded in history." Atkinson dreams that Colonel James is about to stab Amelia if she does not give in to his demands. Atkinson wakes up and, still in his dream, starts to battle with his wife. She faints. Atkinson sees his mistake and begins to sprinkle water over her. Hearing the uproar, Booth runs upstairs to find the Atkinsons' bed seemingly awash in blood. Atkinson looks down and begins to rave that he has killed his wife:

> "O sir!" cries the serjeant, "I dreamt I was rescuing your lady from the hands of Colonel James, and I have killed my poor wife" (p. 136).

Amelia enters and her "delicate nose" detects the truth: the sergeant has by mistake doused his wife with cherry brandy, not water. This minor error has not only engendered the whole uproar, but also has revealed to Booth the intentions of James, of whom Booth has previously no suspicion. In an appropriate metaphor for Fielding's general attitude toward accidents and the way they generate causes, all has come about because of a dream and a mistake in the dark. Causality in *Amelia* is often a farcical and gratuitous concatenation of events. The important factor is what Booth does with his knowledge. Because of Booth's high opinion of James, he does not apprehend the full import of Atkinson's outburst; it merely makes him a little suspicious and not always ready to ascribe to James the highest motives. The amazing "accident" has had its power substantially dissipated because Booth does not know how to take advantage of it.

The one character who can use generalizations elastically and respond spontaneously to new situations is Dr. Harrison. He admits that Amelia's revelation that James made advances to her is a blow to his vanity; he thought more of James than that. But he is flexible enough to change his views in terms of the new evidence. He imposes his own interpretation on the toys that the peer has given the Booth children. But he soon sees that "ocular demonstration" (in his phrase) is not enough. We appreciate Adams' "innocence" in *Joseph Andrews* because that world is more enclosed; the test of good faith and trust might be enough. But if one wishes to work in the world of *Amelia* and not compromise one's standards, the inadequacies of innocence are more blatant. Harrison can remain flexible without the need for the use of policy or excessive suspicion of the motives of others. Like Allworthy, he is presented first as a categorizer of individuals: for example, in his condemnation of Booth merely because Booth is a soldier and all soldiers are naturally ill-mannered fortune hunters (II, iv, pp. 68–69). Yet he is flexible enough to confront his generalization with Booth's individual nature and change his first impressions (II, vii, p. 83). His view of human nature is sufficiently various to admit aberrations and differences. He knows what is necessary for the occasion. In his role as a parson, for example, ". . . he so well knows when to soothe, when to reason, and when to ridicule, that he never applies any of those arts improperly, which is almost universally the case with the physicians of the mind, and which it requires very great judgment and dexterity to avoid" (III, ii, p. 102).

Harrison is, in fact, the only character in *Amelia* who appears to be able to have a successful relation to society without resorting to policy or hypocrisy. Unique among Fielding's characters, he can both criticize his age and live within it. He has none of the providential pessimism of Adams in the *True Patriot*, for example, and he does not advocate a return to the primitive Christian conditions that Adams might approve. His ideal for the "true Christian disposition," as he describes Amelia, includes empathy and respect for others (X, viii, p. 146). But he can also appreciate the deficiencies in Amelia's view of the world, which, despite its moral goodness, does not give full value to the uncertainties of experience. Amelia praises the beauties of Vauxhall Gardens:

> "I could not have, indeed, imagined there had been any-thing like this in the world." The doctor smiled, and said, "You see, dear madam, there may be pleasures of which you could conceive no idea till you actually enjoyed them" (IX, ix, p. 152).

In many ways Harrison represents a conflation of Fielding's good men with the kind of epistemological good sense possessed previously only by the narrators.[57]

Harrison's character may also embody an effort to apply the values of Amelia to the world of Booth. Because of his "philosophy" and general epistemological innocence, Booth cannot take advantage of situations. In a way strangely reminiscent of Adams, Booth is the real innocent in the social world, walking around the masquerade at Ranelagh without a mask. Even Amelia holds her counsel, but Booth, once he has decided according to his philosophy, moves blithely forward. When the Jameses invite them to dinner, he does not notice Amelia's distress, because of his own lack of suspicion. And suspicion is the reserved judgment that the people of policy consider essential for working in society: " . . . this, indeed, is the great optic-glass helping us to discern plainly almost all that passes in the minds of others, without some use of which nothing is more purblind than human nature" (IX, ii, p. 116).

Amelia's innocence may be more suited to her sphere, but she also has her limitations. She is definitely quite vain. Her disfigured nose lends a comic element to her characterization that serves (or should serve) to warn us away from idealizing her too much.[1] Booth is a little more obviously frail. Yet these two characters represent the values that Fielding believes can regenerate and renew the outworn institutions of their world. Amelia may be self-centered, but she is not egotistic; she attempts to establish value in her own world. Against the restrictive abstraction of public history, Amelia and, to a certain extent, Booth represent ideals of spontaneous and elastic reactions to experience. This capacity is no different from that prized in the earlier novels. In *Amelia*, however, it is tied to an institutional base. Just as individual differences and vitality can regenerate static institutions, so the figure of Amelia represents

[1] Philip Stevick, in "The Augustan Nose," *UTQ*, *34* (1965), pp. 110–17, comments that the association between syphilis and the lack of a nose was an eighteenth-century commonplace. He believes that Amelia's broken nose is a "gross miscalculation" on Fielding's part. It is more likely that the detail is another one of Fielding's jibes against an excessive commitment to appearances.

an attempt to rest value in the institution that is the most accurate projection of individual values—the family.[m] Fielding's earlier attacks on public history as a guide to individual behavior concentrated on the "heroes" of history, the martial and political Great Men who pretended that physical force implied metaphysical excellence. Amelia's "heroic" role as wife and mother restates the conflict between private and public history as a conflict between essentially female and essentially male values. Fielding, like Richardson, situates ultimate value in a woman. The military hero is the supreme example of the person who distorts the world by imposing his egocentric perception upon others. Feminine heroism subordinates the self to others and does good in particular, private situations, rather than in vast public contexts. Physical heroism must be either replaced by or coupled with ethical heroism. Fielding relates Amelia to the "she-heroes" of Otway and Rowe by allusions in the text. But more important are the many references to Antony and Cleopatra, Dido and Aeneas, and Alexander and Statira.[n] These references state

[m] Compare Sabine Nathan, "The Anticipation of Nineteenth-Century Ideological Trends in Fielding's *Amelia*," *Zeitschrift für Anglistik und Amerikanistik, 6* (1958) , p. 396: Amelia is against playing cards because ". . . it is vital to prove how much more sane, healthy, and religious is the family compared to society—two institutions which were from this time growing to be irreconcilable." Nathan cannot, however, quite reconcile Amelia's credulity with her status as an ideal (pp. 406–08) , and he finds a similar problem in the character of Harrison. On the family as a center of value superior to the state and its institutions, compare Fielding's remarks in the *Lisbon Journal*, p. 194: "And though I disclaim all pretence to that Spartan or Roman patriotism which loved the public so well that it was always ready to become a voluntary sacrifice to the public good, I do solemnly declare that I have that love for my family."

[n] There have been some attempts to assert that the structure of *Amelia* is minutely related to that of the *Aeneid*. See, for example, Lyall H. Powers, "The Influence of the *Aeneid* on Fielding's *Amelia*," *MLN*, *71* (1956) , pp. 330–36. The method naturally enough does violence to both works; the parallel between separate books becomes more and more tenuous; and the parallels between characters do not achieve even that distinction: "For Booth and Aeneas both have destinies to fulfill which involve Amelia and Lavinia respectively. . . . Booth and Aeneas share a common destiny: each is seeking to provide a secure

again the different claims of the male public world and the female private world, claims that may be reconciled in the figure of Harrison.

But Harrison is no complete paragon. His view of adultery as the usurpation of property is peculiarly harsh and unhuman (X, ii, p. 172). Fielding takes time to poke much fun at his hostility to Mrs. Bennet's classical learning.⁰ Harrison's false judgment of James may be exposed; but the way in which his country-gentleman friend has played on his vanity, since it is not relevant to the main movement of events, is never openly discussed, although we see it in their conversation. These deviations from ideal goodness and perception in the character of Harrison again illustrate basic concerns of *Amelia*. As usual, Fielding tries to accomplish many things at once. More than any of the three preceding novels, *Amelia* attempts to present a fully qualified world, without absolute judgment, in which the statement and its necessary disclaimer exist almost simultaneously. It is not enough to show that we must look to individual virtue to revitalize the institutions that have become degraded through individual egotism. At the same time we are shown the complexities of individual character, the contradictions and uncertainties we must know so that we might understand and thus be free of them. Despite the simple ideas certain characters have of their own personalities and why they act in special ways, the reader can see the contradictions, and the response to arbitrary circumstances.

---

foundation for his progeny, and each already has some family to care for" (p. 331). The mock-epic implications of such analogies seem irrelevant to Fielding's purposes. A more fruitful comparison of the *Aeneid* and *Amelia* might follow the lines of a distinction between the male world of war and history and the female world of emotion and domesticity. For a similar view of Virgil, see Adam Parry, "The Two Voices of Virgil's *Aeneid*," *Arion*, 2 (1963), pp. 66–80. In Fielding's view the problem of relative values is no longer so ambiguous; the desire to enter public history and fulfill "destiny" has lost any legitimacy it may have had for Virgil.

⁰ Mrs. Bennet gets her share of criticism also. As in *Tom Jones*, neither masculinists (Squire Western) nor feminists (Mrs. Western) get the nod.

John Coolidge says that Booth is like a character in *Tom Jones*: his actions are deducible from his nature.[58] Whatever the merits of this observation in regard to the earlier novel, in *Amelia* it seems beside the point. That he acts according to his nature is Booth's explanation of his character, not necessarily ours. Context and circumstance always mediate the relation between character traits and subsequent action. The demands of moral codes are relevant to action, but their influence need not be overpowering. Booth may have the best intentions in the world and the greatest love for Amelia, but these must be understood in relation to the situations in which he finds himself:

> We desire, therefore, the good-natured and candid reader will be pleased to weigh attentively the several unlucky circumstances which concurred so critically, that Fortune seemed to have used her utmost endeavours to ensnare poor Booth's constancy. Let the reader set before his eyes a fine young woman, in a manner, a first love, conferring obligations and using every art to soften, to allure, to win, and to inflame; let him consider the time and place; let him remember that Mr. Booth was a young fellow in the highest vigor of life; and lastly, let him add one single circumstance, that the parties were alone together, and then, if he will not acquit the defendant, he must be convicted, for I have nothing more to say in his defense (IV, ii, p. 161).

Other characters have similarly mixed motives. In the course of Booth's narrative Miss Matthews insults Amelia to put herself in a better light. But she also respects Amelia as a woman and often calls her heroic, especially when Booth tells of the Bagillard incident (III, ix, p. 137). Colonel James' generosity is genuine, even though he is a bad husband. (Generosity, we might remember, was a prime virtue in *Tom Jones*.) In short, no one factor is enough for a sufficient or necessary interpretation of another person. Even the presence of vices is not a sure clue, because the context of a bad personality makes them worse, while in a good per-

sonality their effect may be nil: "Ambition scarce ever produces any evil but when it reigns in cruel and savage
bosoms; and avarice seldom flourishes at all but in the basest
and poorest soil" (VI, i, p. 261).ᴾ Harrison points out that
man has a basically good nature, which becomes distorted
by "bad education, bad habits, and bad customs." For this
distortion he blames "the governors of the world," including the clergy (IX, v, p. 131). We see in the example of
Robinson at the end of *Amelia* that, if a man has no will
to change his character, no matter what he may wish, he
will fall back into the old ways of distortion: "So apt are
men whose manners have been once thoroughly corrupted,
to return, from any dawn of an amendment, into the dark
paths of vice" (XII, ix, p. 311).

Harrison then is sanguine about men's ability to bring
together private virtue and public life. He is Booth and
Amelia, the marriage of male martial virtue with female
ethical virtue. The only enemy is contentment with corruption, based on false views of history. Harrison quotes
Livy to the nobleman to show the circularity of a belief
that the state and society are corrupt by historical necessity. Favoritism in filling office insures the corruption of
the state and solidifies the excuse that favoritism is the only
way. In such a system there is no incentive for good people
to go into public life and discontent appears in the nation.
The rule of Cromwell, says Harrison, was good because of
its strict use of the merit system. The pessimistic nobleman
asks him if people become rogues through choice or by
the necessities of the system. Harrison answers:

"Perhaps the opinion of the world may sometimes mis-
lead men to think those measures necessary which in
reality are not so. Or the truth may be, that a man of
good inclination finds his office filled with such corrup-

ᴾ There is a great similarity between Trent's advice to Booth to use
Amelia as a means of gaining a commission (X, vii, p. 203) and what
Mrs. Atkinson actually does to advance her husband (detailed in the
argument with Amelia in X, viii). Yet Trent is obviously a 'bad'
character, while the Atkinsons are 'good.'

tion by the iniquity of his predecessors, that he may despair of being capable of purging it; and so sits down contented, as Augeas did with the filth of his stables, not because he thought them the better, or that such filth was really necessary to a stable, but that he despaired of sufficient force to cleanse them" (XI, ii, p. 231).

The mythological reference proleptically implies that a hero with ingenuity and physical power will accomplish the cleansing. The concept of heroism with which *Amelia* replaces the classical ideal emphasizes good action controlled by good perception.[q] The play between theory and practice is a constant in Fielding's descriptions of "good men": Adams represents their frequent inconsistency; Heartfree exists only in a world of theory; Allworthy believes optimistically that theory and practice are the same. Only Harrison has both the ideals and the worldly experience necessary to bring them together.

BEHIND THE STATUS QUO justifications of institutions Fielding perceives the simple causalities fostered by public history. *Joseph Andrews* attacked the idea that the impression of actuality was conveyed by the indiscriminate collection of empirical detail. The presentation of the 1745 Rebellion in *Tom Jones* stressed the necessary subjectivity of all observation. In *Amelia* Fielding implies a distinction between an empirical method and an empirical attitude, between the facts that bind and the facts that liberate. As in his examination of physiognomy, he implies that false generalizations frequently derive from false specifics, distorted by a screen of deductive assumptions. Yet the reader does need good provisional generalizations to protect him from the purely factual, the conspiracy of data that threatens to

[q] Ian Watt ascribes such a conception of the new hero primarily to Richardson (*Rise of the Novel*, p. 244). As I have tried to imply through some of my epigraphs, Fielding clearly derives from Milton many of his ideas about a domestic and Christian heroism that stands in opposition to the martial and political heroes of public history. See also below, p. 209.

take from the individual his power of will and change. We must steer between absolute generalization and unalloyed detail. Simple description belongs in the primitive Hogarthian mode of the early jail scenes; and even there, in the figure of Blear-eyed Moll, Fielding underlines its deceptions. Similarly, the London of *Amelia* has few place names and little to distinguish it from any other city.[r] Gibraltar and the Gibraltar campaign have little existence apart from Booth's wounds.

The reader who searches for the detail is gulled as a worshiper of the ephemeral. Amelia complains to Mrs. Atkinson about Booth's arrest by the bailiffs:

> In this situation Mrs. Atkinson was doing her utmost to support her when a most violent knocking was heard at the door, and immediately the serjeant ran hastily into the room, bringing with him a cordial which presently relieved Amelia. What this cordial was, we shall inform the reader in due time. In the meanwhile he must suspend his curiosity; and the gentleman at White's may lay wagers whether it was Ward's pill or Dr. James' powder (VIII, ix, p. 97).

The first chapter of Book X recounts the actions of Harrison and his false assumptions about the "ocular demonstration," while the narrator rebukes anyone who rests too much importance on such methods. On his way to ask Amelia to explain things, Harrison then meets Atkinson: "The doctor took his old servant into a coffee-house, where he received from him such an account of Booth and his family, that he desired the serjeant to show him presently to Amelia; and this was the cordial which we mentioned at the end of the ninth chapter of the preceding book" (p. 113). In another

---

[r] See, for example, the refusal to describe Vauxhall Gardens, except to note Amelia's appreciation of it (IX, ix, p. 152). The only physical descriptions of Amelia and Booth are in the exaggerated terms of Colonel and Mrs. James (XI, i, pp. 222–23), although Amelia is also described through the poetry of Waller, Suckling, and Milton. The lack of geographical description is noted by Wright (*Fielding: Mask and Feast*, p. 48).

apt metaphor Fielding has placed value not in an object, but in a person.

Fielding's growing feeling for the complexities of individual character and his distaste for the exemplum contributes to his attack on public history. In his novels he favors the idea that there is a generalizable human behavior, but insists on deriving this behavior from the private history that is its base. To do so is the highest gift of both the writer and the perceiver. As Fielding writes in *Tom Jones,*

> Thou art to know, friend, that there are certain characteristics in which most individuals of every profession and occupation agree. To be able to preserve these characteristics and at the same time to diversify their operation is one talent of a good writer. Again, to mark the nice distinction between two persons actuated by the same vice or folly is another; and as this last talent is found in a very few writers, so is the true discernment of it found in as few readers . . . (X, i, 441).[8]

Through his novels he has pursued this ideal of perception, the constant interaction of the general and the individual. *Amelia* represents its most complex realization. In this perception, public history has little role. And Fielding makes public history finally merely another metaphor for the individual.

He announces this revaluation early in the novel, when the narrator attempts to express the complexities of the personality of Miss Matthews. The entire passage becomes a farce of deduction. At first the narrator tries the method of precursors and exempla:

> . . . it may be necessary to whisper a word or two to the critics, who have, perhaps, begun to express no less astonishment than Mr. Booth, that a lady in whom we had remarked a most extraordinary power of displaying softness should, the very next moment after the words were

[8] Note the shift in emphasis from the "species, not individuals" of *Joseph Andrews* (III, i) .

out of her mouth, express sentiments becoming the lips of Dalila, Jezebel, Medea, Semiramis, Parysatis, Tanquil, Livilla, Messalina, Agrippina, Brunichilde, Elfrida, Lady Macbeth, Joan of Naples, Christina of Sweden, Katharine Hays, Sarah Malcolm, Con Philips, or any other heroine of the tender sex, which history, sacred or profane, ancient or modern, false or true, hath recorded (I, vi, p. 28).

But such "heroic" figures account only for the unattractive side of her character. A more apt metaphor for human complexity draws upon the theories of climatic determinism that are also used to explain the nature of nations. Fielding therefore adduces a great part of the political history of eighteenth-century England to the task of understanding and explaining the character of Miss Matthews:

We desire such critics to remember that it is the same English climate in which, on the lovely 10th of June, under a serene sky, the amorous Jacobite, kissing the odoriferous zephyr's breath, gathers a nosegay of white roses to deck the whiter breast of Celia; and in which, on the 11th of June, the very next day, the boisterous Boreas, roused by the hollow thunder, rushes horrible into the air, and, driving the wet tempest beside him, levels the hope of the husbandman with the earth, dreadful remembrance of the consequences of the Revolution. Again, let it be remembered that this is the selfsame Celia all tender, soft, and delicate, who with a voice, the sweetness of which the Syrens might envy, warbles the harmonious song in praise of the young adventurer; and again, the next day, or, perhaps the next hour, with fiery eyes, wrinkled brows, and foaming lips, roars forth treason and nonsense in a political argument with some fair one of a different principle (p. 29).

The hyperbolic silliness in these passages implies the inability of such methods to "explain" Miss Matthews and punctures the pretense that public history helps us at all to know character.

Through the characters of Amelia, Harrison, and Booth, public history has been made finally subordinate to private history. Fielding has drawn upon historical methods and concerns, but has finally completely rejected the matter of history. He invokes no ideal of progress when he emphasizes the ability of the individual to revitalize the institution. Public history represents to him the accumulation of falsehoods numerous enough to give the impression of truth. Booth's "conversion" can be explained by no idea of progress. Any explanation for it must rest instead on a feeling for something mysterious and protean at the base of human character. Both Fielding's insights and his ideals emphasize the effort to grasp that mystery through a process of continual interaction and reconciliation, criticism and dialectic.

Amelia and Booth finally leave the social world for the countryside, but this is not a solution indicated for all. Fielding rests no special value in any particular time or place; he finally rejects any pastoral Golden Age. Booth and Amelia can go to the country because they do not have to, just as Sophia and Tom can engage in romantic rhetoric because they have the real thing. In two places in *Amelia* Fielding speaks of an ideal retreat. First he describes Amelia in terms of Milton's Eve:

—Adorn'd
With what all Earth or Heaven could bestow
To make her amiable.

. . . .

Grace was in all her steps, Heaven in her eye,
In every gesture, dignity and love (VI, i, p. 258).

Later Mrs. Bennet describes the perfect marriage: "A match of real love is, indeed, truly paradise; and such perfect happiness seems to be the forbidden fruit to mortals, which we are to lament having tasted during the rest of our lives" (VII, v, p. 25).

Such absolute perfection is an impossible ideal; but in the novel's last chapter Amelia and Booth fulfill it as much as is humanly possible, not because of the literary convention of the benevolent countryside, but because the relation of Amelia and Booth embodies the best potentiality for individual growth.

In the last chapter Amelia and Booth pleasantly realize what they deserved from the beginning of the novel. The end of the novel's larger concerns—and perhaps Fielding's farewell to the novel form—occurs two chapters before. The concatenation of accidents, coincidences, goodness and venality, plots and counterplots that finally result in the happiness of Amelia and Booth emphasizes the arbitrary nature of their deliverance. There may be a personal truth involved, but where is the social truth? Lady Mary Wortley Montagu complained that her cousin's novels would "encourage young people to hope for impossible events, to draw them out of the misery they chose to plunge themselves into, expecting legacies from unknown relations, and generous benefactors to distressed virtue, as much out of nature as fairy treasures."[59]

Amelia and Booth may emerge victorious, but what about other deserving characters, like Trent's father-in-law and Bob Bound, who did not and will never have the same chance? The answer is a cautious ideal. *Amelia* gives the closest scrutiny to the perversions and distortions of law. Presiding over the beginning of the novel is Justice Thrasher, the embodiment of corruption, perverse social institutions, and personal egoism. But, like Hume, Fielding has a great hope for the ability of law to translate private virtue into public good. Like the historian in Hume, the meditative and reformist narrator of *Amelia* defines himself, by his expositions of legal theory and practice (through several learned footnotes), as an expert in law. To balance Thrasher, there appears toward the end of the novel another justice, whose excessive concern for the law nettles Harrison somewhat, but who is still an honest man trying to do a fair job. With his help, all the problems are solved and everyone is happy. It is difficult not to see this unnamed good-natured justice as a surrogate for the narrator, for the reader, and for Fielding himself. Like them, he finds out the facts and tries to make a just decision. Here in the last of Fielding's novels is the ideal hinted at in the first—the justice who rules in terms of equity, mediating the claims of generalized law and individual situation. Like Jonson's Adam Overdo, this justice learns, although through a less severe experience, to sort out the claims of principles and individual behavior. And, again like Jonson's hero, he gathers all the characters together, because of admiration for Amelia or "reflection on the remarkable act of justice he had performed, or whatever motive . . . I will not determine," and celebrates the hope of a reinvigorated and ordered society by inviting everyone to dinner.[60]

FIELDING'S NOVELS attack and qualify the false orders of public history and the inflated rhetoric of causal connection. Physical detail, landscape, even chronology itself are stripped away or subordinated to the search for forms flexible enough to be used in understanding the world about us. Fielding's precise plots are often traps for those who have an over-precise or over-systematized view of life. True freedom in the novels of Fielding seems to imply the ability to approximate the breadth of sympathy possessed by the narrator, to understand the styles of everyone and even to try them out, but to know finally that they are at best only partial truths. In contrast to Hume's ideal of the detached and objective judge, Fielding emphasizes the clear, but ultimately personal, perceptions of an individual confronting a specific situation.[61]

The process of Fielding's fiction attempts to free the reader from the false forms imposed by other literary structurings of actuality. It is no chance that the narrative form of his novels is often a circular one, in which we discover at the end what we should have known from the start. Both the excessive subjectivity of romance and the excessive objectivity of public history are sham orders that can pervert and distort human values.[t] Through his fictional practice Fielding wishes to foster a method for perceiving the variety of the world rather than categories that can only reduce it. His personal narrative voice is an attempt to establish an author-reader relation modeled on, but fuller and more complex than, the relation of the epic poet to his audience. Fielding's epic poet is not interested in the great exploits of heroic figures, but in the probable lives of people much like his readers.[u] The community of sympathy and understanding he wishes to establish is independent of the categories of accumulating time, political events, and military battles. Through the medium of his narrative voice he attempts to bring his readers back to an ideal of perception fragmented by the rush of moral prejudice and partisan history. He tries to help them to return to a time when there was a community of "good-natured" readers and less separation between literature and life.

[t] Georg Lukács does not appreciate that Fielding turns away from public history. He believes that Fielding does grasp to a certain extent the "increasing concreteness of the novel . . . [in] the historical peculiarities of characters and events." See *The Historical Novel*, trans. Hannah and Stanley Mitchell (New York, 1963), p. 20. However, since the true consciousness of historical existence must arrive with the French Revolution, a comment on "the concrete historical moment" like Fielding's treatment of the 1745 Jacobite Rebellion in *Tom Jones* passes unnoticed.

[u] Ian Watt says that the public and collective nature of the epic was not fitted to the form of the novel (*Rise of the Novel*, p. 240). But Fielding plays with the relation of the novel to a more public epic form as he does with its relation to a more public form of history.

$\mathcal{F}IVE$ | Gibbon:
PUBLIC HISTORY AND THE
SHAPING SELF

Les exemples des grands hommes ne prouvent rien.
Essai sur l'Étude de la Littérature

The present is a fleeting moment; the past is no more; and our
prospect of futurity is dark and doubteful.
The History of the Decline and Fall of the Roman Empire

. . . many crude lumps of Speed, Rapin, Mezeray, Davila, Ma-
chiavel, Father Paul, Bower &c. passed through me like so many
novels.
Memoirs of My Life

I. INTRODUCTION

WHILE THERE ARE no proofs of specific influence, it is evident
from Gibbon's works and letters that he admired Hume
and Fielding. In *The History of the Decline and Fall of
the Roman Empire* he shares their preoccupations and
reflects their assumptions about the relations between narrative fiction and history. Every long work, except one that
has been heavily revised, is necessarily a work visibly in the
process of composition. While Gibbon works with his materials, his attitudes and emphasis change; his ideas take on
different shapes. This process in Hume's *History* involved
the gradual discovery that the cumulative process of time
could furnish the essential coherence of history. Gibbon, it
might be said, begins with such an assumption. But he also
has with him the experience of imaginative unity in the
novels of Fielding, especially *Tom Jones*; the pseudo-chro-
nology of its structure argued for methods of understanding

and narrative organization that could cut across the order of time. While Hume is wary because interpretation is ultimately subjective, Gibbon gradually embraces that subjectivity and transcends it by his acceptance. The past is his material, but history is what he has created; the pattern he perceives is not innate, but is instead the provisional coherence imposed by one perceptive individual. The shape of history in the *Decline and Fall* is pre-eminently a construction, a literary work with aesthetic rather than systematic order and coherence. In the course of the *Decline and Fall* Gibbon's controlling presence becomes more and more palpable, ordering, assorting, varying, and qualifying. By its conclusion the *Decline and Fall* has become an enclosed object, to be contemplated as much for its formal and detailed beauty as for its accurate transcription of what was.

Gibbon, therefore, directly concerns himself with the historian's role. The historian becomes an important figure only towards the end of Hume's *History*, as Hume begins to adjudicate historians of the past. For Gibbon such adjudication is an integral part of his practice and the story he is telling. The past is to a great extent what past historians thought it was. Paralleling his interest in the development of his own role is his interest in the historians of the past, whose accounts of their own times he assimilates into his narrative. Through their works he entertains their points of view and thus can peer directly into the history of a particular era. Next to the public figures the historians are the characters most fully and frequently described in the *Decline and Fall*. But their vision is ultimately faulty. The true heroes that emerge through the process of Gibbon's history are literary men, like Boethius, who can view their contemporaries clearly, with a vision undistorted by public controversy or private interest. To achieve his own narrative stance, Gibbon therefore draws upon such figures as Hume's pessimistic and detached ironist, Fielding's benevolent judge, and Fielding's whimsical but controlling novel-ist-historian.[a]

In the *Decline and Fall* Gibbon expresses a new view of the past and history's relation to it: the past should be presented as history for its own sake rather than for its extractable precepts. Gibbon's characters and situations do not apply directly to our lives, as Bolingbroke would have liked them to. Although the past may be intimately related to the present, it must be understood on its own terms. The historian is the medium of that understanding. History for Gibbon is a chronological process that must be appre-hended and even rearranged intellectually. His work is a massive effort to shape a heterogeneous mass of material by the impress of his own understanding. In his *Essai sur l'Étude de la Littérature* Gibbon compares the order the historian brings to history with the way the Marquis de Dangeau gambled: "Il voyoit un système, des rapports, une suite, là, où les autres ne discernoient que les caprices de la fortune."[b] The coherence that Hume attempts through general tone Gibbon achieves by an increasing stress upon his own role as "the historian of the Roman empire." The choice of a controlling metaphor like "decline and fall" it-self emphasizes the intellectual order Gibbon first imposes upon his material, even though he later becomes uneasy with that particular trope.[c] The growth of the *Decline and*

a Frank E. Manuel remarks that the eighteenth-century philosophi-cal historians saw in history "a moral homily of a secular order, or an ugly spectacle of human vice and idiocy" primarily because "the sages had been the victims of history more often than its creators." See *The Eighteenth Century Confronts the Gods* (Cambridge, Massachusetts, 1959), p. 152. But Gibbon's "revenge" on the political types is more benevolent. See below, p. 263.

b *Miscellaneous Works of Edward Gibbon, Esquire*, 3 vols. (Dublin, 1796), III, p. 239. *Le Dictionnaire de Biographie Française* says of de Dangeau: "[Il] était beau, aimable, bon courtisan; il connaissait admirablement tous les jeux à la mode, était réfléchi, adroit, avait de la chance." Further references to the *Essai* will be included in the text.

c "So flexible is the title of my history that the final aera might be fixed at my own choice: and I long hesitated whether I should be con-

Fall could be seen, in one view, as Gibbon's effort to get away from his own metaphor and its implication of necessary corruption lest his inductively conceived history become stifled by deductive moralization. The *Decline and Fall* toys with limited and reductive interpretations like corruption, but ultimately discards them all. Like the novels of Fielding, it offers a method for understanding rather than a single thematic interpretation. It finds coherence through a total vision of the past rather than through a series of moral judgments.

Gibbon's style reflects his belief that any interpretation of the past is at best tentative. Hume attempted to express his balanced and measured view through the order of his periodic sentences. Fielding's typical sentence moves from certainty to contingency through a haze of qualifying clauses. Gibbon's method often seems similar to Fielding's. But his most typical device is a kind of epistemological doublet—"through sincerity or duplicity"—held in unresolved balance by the comprehension of his narrative voice.[1] Gibbon continually asserts in the *Essai* and the *Memoirs* that he believes history-writing necessitates a concern with probabilities rather than certainties. At best language is an inadequate tool for conveying the sense of probability and uncertainty:

> I owe it to myself, and to historic truth, to declare, that some *circumstances* in this paragraph are founded only on conjecture and analogy. The stubbornness of our language has sometimes forced me to deviate from the *conditional* into the *indicative* mood.[d]

Gibbon's ironic tensions do not exhaustively describe his world; they do imply its complexity. Although he speculates

---

tent with the three Volumes, the fall of the Western Empire, which fulfilled my first engagement with the public" (*Memoirs*, p. 164; Saunders, p. 187).

[d] *The History of the Decline and Fall of the Roman Empire*, ed. J. B. Bury, 7 vols. (London, 1909-14), III, xxxi, p. 373 n184. I shall give references in my text by volume, chapter, and page.

upon motivation, he is more directly interested in acts. Whereas Hume's early practice exhibits the deterministic implications of psychological atomism, Gibbon reflects Fielding's view of the variety of possibilities in the human personality, no one of which has any sufficient effect on action. Action must first be examined in its own context. The number of actions Gibbon explains or deduces from "the basic principles of human nature" is small compared to the number of motivations he speculates about after observing events. He constantly refers to the complex mixture of circumstance and motive in any action.[2]

Gibbon can hold disparate elements in balance because he stresses the power of his own mind, moving over the materials of history, to present a world that compels assent through its plausibility and its order. The great nineteenth-century appreciators of Gibbon like Guizot and Milman praised his style and form, while they deplored his hostility to Christianity. Yet it is altogether fitting that one of the first great masters of history for its own sake should have been the man whom Boswell could refer to as "I." for "infidel." In the eyes of the generations of ecclesiastical historians who had previously studied the Roman Empire, transcendental causes were primary and history was a working out of foreknown moral and theological truths. Gibbon cuts history away from the "primary" causes of Christianity and establishes the primacy of the human "secondary" causes, the causes of earth. He treats Christianity historically, ruling out any explanation that relies on the interventions of Providence. History is for Gibbon an order of continuous time, worldly causes, and no eternity. Perhaps more than his theological detractors Gibbon is aware that the greatness of Christianity as a human force rests firmly on the idea that the transcendent was made immanent in and subject to human history.[3] In a way the *Decline and Fall* may stand against the kind of history presented by Michael in Books Eleven and Twelve of *Paradise Lost*. Gibbon appreciates more fully the perspective of Adam. After the providential epic of *Paradise Lost*, the

Decline and Fall is the euhemerist epic.[4] Although Gibbon's narrative voice may seem finally detached from the past he contemplates, his human point of view frequently enters into it and finally encompasses it.

II. THE THEORETICAL PREPARATION

. . . I *know* by experience that from my early youth I aspired to the character of an historian.
  Memoirs of My Life

Although the abstract portions of the *Essai sur l'Étude de la Littérature* (published in 1761 when Gibbon was 24) are concerned primarily with the study of history, the figures to whom Gibbon most often refers are Homer, Virgil, and Shakespeare. His observations attempt to balance the special claims of historical and imaginative creation. He lays the groundwork for the interplay in the *Decline and Fall* between the demands of facts and the need for an imaginative order. Departing from the Aristotelian subordination of history to poetry, Gibbon criticizes poets who distort history unnecessarily. Ovid, he says, makes gross and unpardonable errors in chronology and geography, but Virgil puts his changes to good use: "Que des beautés l'histoire faisoit perdre au poëte!" (*Essai*, p. 230). Gibbon's ideal is a balance of the factual methods of history with the imaginative order of poetry. He dislikes Livy because Livy entertains at the expense of accuracy. But, like Bolingbroke, Gibbon would forgive anachronisms before dullness: "Que le poëte, je le répète encore, ose hazarder, pourvû que le lecteur retrouve toujours dans ses fictions, ce même degré de plaisir que la vérité et les convenances lui eussent offert" (*Essai*, p. 230).

Gibbon's continual emphasis in the *Essai* rests upon the inclusive vision of the world that he believes to be the peculiar province of the historian. What interests him in the great imaginative writers are their overall schemes. The historian who wishes to build a system that pretends to absolute truth often makes small alterations; Gibbon would rather make the whole an imaginative unity, which would allow the facts freer play. His comments on Virgil demonstrate his interest in the unity that underlies the diversity of a particular work. Like the pattern seen by the Marquis de Dangeau, this unity is appreciated, developed, even half-created by a single mind. Like Hume, Gibbon associates coherence in a historical work with coherence in a literary work. But Gibbon makes a fuller commitment to the need for some kind of literary form. From facts the historian constructs an imaginative pattern called history, which is altered or reinforced by new facts. But without the prior work of the imagination, flexible and provisional as it may be, the facts are useless, for there is no potentiality for their use; there is no matrix to test them against, and be tested by them. Gibbon would probably agree fully with E. H. Carr's modern formulation of the interplay between facts and the historian's pattern for them: "The historian without his facts is rootless and futile; the facts without their historian are dead and meaningless."[5]

Like Fielding, Gibbon also rules out deductive pattern even while he asserts the power of imaginative pattern. In the *Essai* Gibbon is not quite sure how his ideal may be achieved. He is more concerned with attack than formulation. Under his fire come both the imposers of grand designs and the chroniclers of petty facts; these positions lead philosophically to complete determinism on one hand, and capricious chance on the other. Both falsify the pluralistic nature of man. One extreme builds systems:

> On a vu du dessein dans les actions d'un grand homme; on a aperçu un ton dominant dans son caractère, et des spéculatifs de cabinet ont aussitôt voulu faire de tous les hommes, des êtres aussi· systematiques dans la pratique que dans la speculation. Ils ont trouvé de l'art dans leurs passions, de la politique dans leurs foiblesses, de la dissimulation dans leur inconstance; en un mot, à force de vouloir faire honneur à l'esprit humain, ils en ont souvent faire bien peu au coeur. (p. 242).

The other extreme surrenders all to whim:

> Ils ont banni l'art du monde moral pour y substituer le hazard. Selon eux les foibles mortels n'agissent que par caprice. La fureur du écervelé établit un empire: la foiblesse d'une femme le détruit (p. 242).

GIBBON'S SYMPATHIES seem much closer to the latter formulation, although he does not accept its pessimistic conclusion. Most of his attack is leveled against simple-minded systematizing. Reflecting Fielding's attack on hypostatized abstractions, Gibbon asserts that the inherent love of system leads to a love of general principles, which then shows itself in a disregard of the details that do not fit. The true speculators, he points out, were always interested in the most minute facts; Gibbon offers the example of Newton's interest in constructing a historical chronology. The brilliant system builder is like the despot who sacrifices variety for control and stability. The metaphor is not inappropriate, for Gibbon terms the suppression of facts by deductive design to be a loss of freedom: "Le génie brillant se laisse éblouïr par ses propres conjectures: il sacrifie la liberté aux hypothèses" (p. 242).[e]

In the polemical terms of the *Essai*, Gibbon defends those the French called *érudits*, the antiquarians who dealt in facts. Gibbon discerns three orders of facts: those which prove nothing, those from which one can form a partial conclusion, and those whose influence spreads through an entire work, these being *"fort rares"* (pp. 239–40). Rarer still, says Gibbon, is the genius who can discern them. He ridicules d'Alembert's suggestion that at the end of every

---

[e] Gibbon's use of *"hypothèses"* here seems to echo seventeenth-century controversies, including Newton's attack on hypothesis as a deductive and non-empirical structure of thought. See E. A. Burtt, *The Metaphysical Foundations of Modern Science* (New York, 1954), pp. 215–20. But Gibbon expands the meaning of *"hypothèse"* to make it a tool of understanding that, when used well, can respond to facts, rather than repress them. See below, p. 223. This epistemological point may be paralleled by his political preference for the Republic over the Empire.

century the important facts be collected and the rest burned. There is, says Gibbon, always the possibility that "Un Montesquieu démêlera dans les plus chétifs, des rapports inconnus au vulgaire" (p. 242). He would like instead to integrate antiquarian and *erudit* research with the bent for abstraction of the "philosophic historians," who too often disdained documentation for general sweep.[6] The "true" historian, according to Gibbon, balances the demands of factual accuracy and imaginative pattern; he discerns a possible relation between the facts instead of imposing one upon them: "Déférez plutôt aux faits qui viennent d'eux-mêmes vous former un système, qu'à ceux que vous découvrez après avoir conçu ce système" (p. 240).[f]

There are three kinds of critics who deal with history: *"critiques grammairiens," "critiques rheteurs"* and *"critiques historiens"* (p. 224). The last of these is the "true" historian who brings together authority and experience in his views of history: "Il pèse, il combine, il doute, il décide" (p. 225). Historical truth is a balance of probabilities, rather than an attempt to establish certainty: " . . . la critique balance les différens degrés de vraisemblance" (p. 225). Gibbon compares the logical structure of history favorably to the logical structure of geometry, which refers only to its first principles, while history implicates the multiplicity of the universe. Gibbon himself had an early love for mathematics, but he remarks in the *Memoirs* that he is glad he stopped mathematical study before his mind "was hardened by the habit of rigorous demonstration" (*Memoirs*, p. 78; Saunders, p. 102).

[f] Such discernment is rarely given to the contemporary, who can at best report accurately what he has seen. Unlike Clarendon, Bolingbroke, and Hume, Gibbon does not unduly trust the perception of the historian who is a contemporary of the events he describes: "There are few observers who possess a clear and comprehensive view of the revolutions of society; and who are capable of discovering the nice and secret springs of action, which impel, in the same uniform direction, the blind and capricious passions of a multitude of individuals" (III, xxvii, p. 196).

The work of history should be created by a mind that gives value to both the facts and the contexts in which they appear. No one factor is ever sufficient. An age should not be judged by the nature of a single individual, nor should a single event or action be similarly overvalued. Often the smallest facts are the most relevant: "Alexandre se dévoile mieux dans la tente de Darius que dans les champs de Guagmela" (p. 240). Yet such details are fully realized only in a continuous narrative bound together by the sensibility and discernment of the author: ". . . il ne s'agit de saisir la démonstration, mais de comparer les poids des vraisemblances opposées; et combien il faut se défier des systèmes les plus éblouissans, puisqui'il y en a si peu qui soutiennent l'épreuve d'un examen libre et attentif" (p. 228).

Gibbon believes that the urge of the mind to combine details may lead to general laws (pp. 249, 250). But is order finally in the facts or in the mind of the "true" critic? Does history have something specific to say, or is its truth only what we read into it? What happens when two "true" critics differ? Gibbon indicates, I think, two answers to these questions. The first reflects the idea that truth is whole and "out there," where the individual can with fortitude and understanding find it. Gibbon often observes in the *Essai* how the "philosophic spirit" finds "simple ideas" or "simple causes" or "first principles" in the mass of historical material.[7] But this search for abstractions is halfhearted. Gibbon's stronger belief, which becomes embodied in the *Decline and Fall*, is in historical relativism. The emphasis on probability in historical method reflects the contextual nature of historical facts themselves.

Gibbon formulated his *Essai* in an atmosphere of awakening historical relativism encouraged by the work of Warton, Hurd, and Percy.[8] He too believes that the past should be studied not because it is better than the present, but because it is different (p. 218). Again his ideal of knowledge is inclusive. An attention to facts and circumstances is a means of appreciating people different from ourselves, "*placés sous un autre ciel, nés dans un autre siècle*" (p. 218). Gibbon

develops Hume's idea of the merely psychological necessity
of causal connection by defining facts themselves in terms
of time and space:

> . . . chaque chose qui existe a son existence déterminée
> à un tems ou à un lieu; et c'est ce qui la distinque de toute
> autre chose. L'homme a du se conduire différemment
> à l'égard de ces deux manières d'exister, l'une sensible
> et devant ses yeux, l'autre passagère, metaphysique, et
> qui n'est peut-être que la succession des idées (p. 249).

But the amount of historical certainty we have varies from
century to century, and the use of probability in assessing
facts is the only way to determine what we know (p. 226n).
Gibbons shows, for example, how we can understand a Roman treaty by using other knowledge of the time. Relativism of viewpoint justifies probability as a mode of explanation. As Gibbon remarks in considering another historical
crux, "Voici une hypothèse qui explique ce phénomène
d'une manière raisonnable; c'est tout ce qu'on est en droit
d'exiger d'une hypothèse" (p. 228).

Against the absolute empiricist attack on hypothesis
exemplified in Newton, Gibbon evolves a meaning of hypothesis that emphasizes its provisional truth. The idea of
historical relativism naturally points to the figure of the
historian, who is aware of historical context even while he
shapes and selects facts to form a coherent whole. The
standard of probability gives equal weight to the factors
and the mind that assesses and relates them. This kind of
ability, says Gibbon, is *"don du ciel."* The study of literature may nurture the ability, but cannot create it. The genius of the historian necessarily partakes of the prejudices
and attitudes of the age in which he lives. This subjectivity
not only helps to coordinate the historian's materials, but
it is also constantly corrected by them. The historian, according to Gibbon, should exult in the multiplicity and "inconsistencies" of all historical periods, including his own. As
E. H. Carr remarks, " . . . I shall venture to believe that the
historian who is most conscious of his own situation is also

most capable of transcending it. . . ."[9] The observations and judgments of the historian may be superseded by time, but his particular point of view will interest later readers much as Gibbon himself enjoys observing the prejudices that imply the impress of a powerful mind: "J'aime à voir les jugemens des hommes prendre une teinture de leurs préventions, à les considérer qui n' osent pas tirer des principes qu'ils reconnoissent pour être justes, les conclusions qu'ils sentent être exacte" (p. 238).[g]

Gibbon believes that the writing of history should be the conscious creation of a literary object whose structure represents and illuminates a full world. Facts without a frame, as they are presented by an annalist or a chronologer, are only facts; they are not more precise or true because they are presented alone. Facts have no intrinsic order, but many possible orders, since they are apprehended by many possible minds.

But despite all the pregnant and suggestive passages in the *Essai*, Gibbon has not yet defined his own ideas about history and its creation. He presents a variety of uncoordinated and uncertain views in a style that he later calls an attempt to achieve "sentencious and oracular brevity" (*Memoirs*, p. 127). A full expansion and consideration of his ideas in practice and process appears in the development of his methods during the writing of the *Decline and Fall*. At the end of his life he writes of Shakespeare: "Our dramatic Poet is generally more attentive to character than to history. . . ." (*Memoirs*, p. 9; Saunders, p. 34). By then he no doubt felt that he had given both their proper weight in his own work. But at the time of the *Essai* such inclusiveness is only an ideal, and Gibbon writes in his *Journal* words that could appropriately stand beside Fielding's remarks about Homer in *The Journal of a Voyage to Lisbon*: " . . . he

---

[g] This exultation in the variety of points of view occurs frequently in the *Decline and Fall*. See, for example, the Byzantine descriptions of England, France, and Germany (VII, lxvi, p. 98) . It is ironic that Gibbon's emphasis on his own subjective viewpoint anticipates those critics who consider his writings valuable primarily for their picture of "the eighteenth-century mind."

was not only the Poet, but the Lawgiver, the Theologian, the Historian, and the Philosopher, of the Ancients. . . ."[h]

III. The *Decline and Fall,* VOLUMES I–III: EXPERIMENTS WITH ORDER

Oddly enough, even while Gibbon wrote of the need to understand history as a narrative whole and rebuked Voltaire for separating public affairs into "articles," he himself was contemplating the practice of history as a biographer (*Journal,* p. 129). Perhaps he was not yet prepared to imitate the historian he had sketched in the *Essai* and felt that the narrative coherence he desired would be more easily accomplished if facts and judgments could be related to a central figure. After considering several subjects, Gibbon finally chose Sir Walter Raleigh. But, after he read into the sources, Gibbon decided that both the man and the age had already been adequately, even brilliantly, treated: ". . . the reigns of Elizabeth and James i are the periods of English history which have been the most variously illustrated: and what new lights could I reflect on a subject which has exercised the accurate industry of *Birch,* the lively and curious acuteness of *Walpole,* the critical spirit of *Hurd,* the vigorous sense of *Mallet* and *Robertson,* and the impartial philosophy of *Hume"* (*Memoirs,* p. 121; Saunders, p. 140; *Journal,* p. 103). He then vacillated between beginning a history of Swiss liberty or a history of Florence under the Medici; ultimately they were to be companion pieces, one the rise, the other the fall of a free republic. Gibbon and his friend Deyverdun compiled material for this project, and by 1767 Gibbon had completed about forty-three pages. This section was read before a literary society of foreigners in London. The severe criticisms of this group and the lukewarm reception of Hume, to whom a copy was sent, persuaded Gibbon to drop the project.[i]

---

[h] *Gibbon's Journal to January 28, 1763. My Journal, I, II, III, and Ephemerides,* intro. D. M. Low (London, 1929), pp. 115–16. Future references will be included in the text.

[i] Gibbon remarks in his covering letter (4 October 1767) that if

Meanwhile, as his *Journal* indicates, his studies began to point more and more toward the writing of the *Decline and Fall*.

The *Decline and Fall* breaks quite clearly into two parts, separated at the end of the third volume by the "General Observations on the Fall of the Roman Empire in the West."[10] The first volume is the most famous because of the chapters on Christianity. But, with its two companion volumes, it exhibits conceptions of both the meaning of history and the historian's role more rudimentary than Gibbon will later accept. I shall here treat the first three volumes as a kind of prelude, the first statement of problems that receive fuller and more mature consideration in the last three volumes. This distinction in a way reflects Gibbon's own "design," as he defines it in his comments at the end of Chapter xxxviii.[11]

While Hume emerges at the end of his *History* with a conception of the role of historian, Gibbon is interested from the start in defining that role. In the first half of the *Decline and Fall* Gibbon attempts to find his own voice. In the second half, once that voice has been defined and achieved, Gibbon is more ready to deal with historical themes that he had before considered only sporadically. Once he has achieved a strong narrative voice, he can use it more effectively as an interpretive tool. He becomes characterized by his style and his point of view—the implied self of the historian. The early volumes show evidence of a preoccupation with style, but usually Gibbon's comments are directed against bad style, the style that obscures and distorts. His remarks at this point are reminiscent of Hume's

---

Hume would so ask, he would burn the work: ". . . I have perhaps vanity enough to make so unlimited a sacrifice to no man in Europe but to Mr. Hume" (*The Letters of Edward Gibbon*, ed. J. E. Norton, 3 vols. [New York, 1956], I, p. 219). Hume actually admired "the spirit and judgment" of the work and urged Gibbon to continue, although he also thought that the choice of French as the language of composition was ill-advised (Greig, *Letters*, II, p. 171). Gibbon rejoined by saying that he had no claim on posterity (Norton, *Letters*, I, pp. 222–23).

efforts to purify the *History of England* of an excessive attention to metaphor and "the style of dissertation." Gibbon says later that " . . . many experiments were made before I could hit the middle tone between a dull Chronicle and a Rhetorical declamation" (*Memoirs,* p. 155; Saunders, p. 173). He frequently criticizes the overpowering use of metaphor by earlier historians because such a technique obscures the facts. Even the favored Ammianus Marcellinus is rebuked for strained mythological parallels and metaphorical extravagancies: "Such is the bad taste of Ammianus . . . that it is not easy to distinguish his facts from his metaphors" (III, xxvi, p. 72 n1). Gibbon is capable of such distortions himself: " . . . and a thousand swords were plunged at once into the bosom of the unfortunate Probus" (I, xii, p. 363). The metaphors of decline, fall, and corruption overshadow the first volume. But usually he is more scrupulous. At one point he speaks of a battle on the "frozen Danube," then notes: "This is not a puerile figure of rhetoric, but an allusion to a real fact recorded by Dion l. lxxi, p. 1181. It probably happened more than once" (I, v, p. 124 n35). After he has established his authority as a historian, Gibbon can afford to be metaphoric because his readers know exactly what liberties he is taking. The contemporary observer, he says, should not let metaphors obscure his clear observation. The historian, however, can use metaphors to clarify the relevance of facts so long as we are aware of the relation between the factual and the creative elements. As his narrative control becomes surer, Gibbon more easily holds these elements together.

Gibbon's conclusion from the necessary relativity of one man's point of view is not darkly pessimistic. He does not assume that the past is a chaos of unconnected facts that everyone interprets according to his lights. His authoritative but personal narrative voice is instead the medium within which, in E. H. Carr's terms, the "dichotomy of fact and interpretation" is reconciled. His historical methods attempt to discern and reconcile the relation between the views of individual observers, the recorded facts, and his

own judgment. Gibbon insists that point of view is a necessary part of any explanation. He knows that his interpretation of the "causes" of the decline and fall or the "causes"
of the spread of Christianity is both retrospective and
partial. Like Hume, he is not interested in "total" explanation because he is well aware of the dissimilar effects that
can arise from similar causes. The reign of Septimius
Severus was peaceful, although it began in cruelty. His
subjects considered it a good reign, but "Posterity, who experienced the fatal effect of his maxims and example, justly
considered him as the principal author of the decline of the
Roman empire" (I, v, p. 137). Prophecies can be self-ful-
filling; people often do things because they are expected to:
"An imaginary cause is capable of producing the most
serious and mischievous effects" (II, xxv, p. 18). Throughout the *Decline and Fall* Gibbon's favorite adverb for the
growth of causes is "insensibly." Both accident and causes
unrecognized by the actors are a great part of the movement
of events. In the early years of Christianity, the stream of
its development flows on, but is " . . . sometimes checked,
and sometimes diverted, by the accidental circumstances of
the times, and by the prudence, or possibly by the caprice,
of the monarch" (II, xx, p. 308). Time insensibly moves
on, accumulating the various acts of individuals into general causes, into history. Even the most trivial incident
can be a prelude to something important. Gibbon speaks
of the contest between Caecilian and Donatus for the primacy of Africa: "But this incident, so inconsiderable that
it scarcely deserves a place in history, was productive of a
memorable schism, which afflicted the provinces of Africa
above three hundred years, and was extinguished only with
Christianity itself" (II, xxi, p. 354).

Such examples in the first three volumes of the *Decline
and Fall* are often countered by Gibbon's uneasy urge to
name "causes" and follow out the implications of the "decline and fall." Yet, even in these volumes, Gibbon carefully avoids any statement about the inherent truth of the
pattern he has discerned. It is plausible, relevant, and in-

teresting, rather than true. Of course Gibbon believes that his interpretation is correct. But he offers such a wealth of causes that he seems to imply clearly that other interpretations are possible. Montesquieu might make something else of the same facts. Gibbon understands that what in retrospect may seem certain and necessary in a "chain" of events was at the time it occurred actually an accident. The first volume of the *Decline and Fall* was published in the same year as *The Wealth of Nations,* and there is an interesting parallel between Smith's reconciling hand of God and Gibbon's feeling for the unspecifiable movement of events:

> . . . the popular resentment was insensibly molded into a regular conspiracy; their just reasons of complaint were heightened by passion, and their passions were inflamed by wine . . . (II, xxii, p. 424).

> In its origin it could be no more than an accidental camp, which, by the long and frequent residence of Attila, had insensibly swelled into a huge village, for the reception of his court, of the troops who followed his person, and of the various multitude of idle or industrious slaves and retainers (III, xxxiv, p. 462).

But God, for Gibbon, is not a relevant cause. History should show how the past has a special nature all its own. In both the move to proclaim Julian emperor and the growth of Priscus, the capital city of Attila, Gibbon concerns himself with the unwilled mixture of capricious, adventitious, and perhaps irrational causes that build what appears often to be a willed and regular plan. When his sources present some prodigy, he refuses to go into the "truth or propriety" of the events: " . . . man has much more to fear from the passions of his fellow-creatures than from the convulsions of the elements" (III, xxvi, p. 73). Gibbon's view is earthly and man centered, and he believes that man's dignity will be enhanced if man gives up his pretensions to the transcendental: "Our habits of thinking so fondly connect the order of the universe with the fate of man, that this gloomy period of history [the reigns of Valerian and Gallienus] has been decorated with inundations, earthquakes, uncommon meteors, preternatural darkness, and a crowd of prodigies fictitious or exaggerated" (I, x, p. 302).[j]

Providential explanation, which so irked Hume and concerned Fielding, Gibbon dismisses as either time-serving or irrelevant. He condemns it in Eusebius as a kind of epistemological laziness, not unlike Voltaire's reliance on chance; neither historian wishes to go into the complexities of more real, and less precise, causes. But the glory of the historian, implies Gibbon, is his commitment to contingency and possibility in place of an easy acceptance of transcendental explanation.

ALTHOUGH GIBBON is usually associated with Montesquieu and Voltaire as a proponent of the importance of impersonal causes, his "causes" always work through individuals. They are not movements that sweep up petty human characters in their path, nor do individuals mold them unopposed; they are instead the accumulation of an infinite number of human motives and actions. Like Hume, Gibbon begins to organize the *Decline and Fall* around specific characters; but he quickly moves away from an inquiry into character that is supposed to yield a precise list of motivations. His view of character becomes instead one that accepts a modicum of mystery about the actual operations of the mind. Gibbon weighs the events of history rather than the protestations, possibilities, and psyches. Great personalities, Gibbon decides, are finally "inconsistent" and unexplainable in terms of a single psychological pattern. Only less significant historical characters can be psychologically catalogued, perhaps because of their peripherality.

[j] In a more ironic mood, Gibbon tells the story that Constantine was led by a heavenly messenger when he laid out the boundaries of Constantinople: "Without presuming to investigate the nature or motives of this extraordinary conductor, we shall content ourselves with the more humble task of describing the extent and limits of Constantinople" (II, xvii, p. 158).

Neither character nor cause is a static conception; both can grow and change, revealing previously unsuspected aspects.

In his movement to this point of view about character, Gibbon first tends to treat the emperor as a symbol of his empire. The "primary cause," he says, of the corruption of Roman soldiery in the late second century is the profligacy of Alexander Severus (I, v, p. 134). Gibbon's practice here is reminiscent of Hume's observations on medieval English history. W. R. Keast states one part of the problem well: "[Gibbon's] emphasis on the exploits and influence of great men like Julian and Justinian arises not from a preference for the dramatic, but from the fact that the fortunes of a country which had lost its fixed constitution and its stable national character must necessarily depend in large measure on the personal characters of those in power."[12]

But Gibbon's practice does not coincide with this interpretation for long. No matter what he thinks about the operative power of his characters, they are always his to manipulate. The term "great man," as Fielding would apply it and as Hume attempts to use it in the Stuart volumes of his *History,* is rarely if ever used by Gibbon. Gibbon tries to sketch what we might call Humian "characters" of Carinus and Diocletian early in his first volume.[k] But the rhetorical balance and tense certainty of Hume are gone because Gibbon is basically sceptical about the historian's ability to express the precise relations of motives and actions. Circumstances always play an overpowering role in his descriptions of human actions. Characters, he says, re-

---

[k] Carinus: "He was soft, yet cruel; devoted to pleasure, but destitute of taste; and, though exquisitely susceptible of vanity, indifferent to the public esteem" (I, xii, p. 368). Diocletian: "His abilities were useful rather than splendid; a vigorous mind, improved by the experience and study of mankind, dexterity and application in business; a judicious mixture of liberality and economy, of mildness and rigour; profound dissimulation under the guise of military frankness; steadiness to pursue his ends; flexibility to vary his means; and above all the great art of submitting his own passions, as well as those of others, to the interest of his ambition, and of colouring his ambition with the most specious pretences of justice and public utility" (I, xiii, p. 378).

spond, each to "its present condition," that is, to the world around them (II, xv, p. 41). Events force actions that were never contemplated. Gibbon remarks, while speaking of the many emperors of the second century: "However virtuous was their character, however pure their intentions, they found themselves reduced to the hard necessity of supporting their usurpation by frequent acts of rapine and cruelty" (I, x, p. 299).

Gibbon's sense of the circumstantiality of history supports his emphasis upon the actions of characters rather than their psychological makeup. As he says of Constantius, "His genuine character, which was composed of pride and weakness, of superstition and cruelty, has been fully displayed in the preceding narrative of civil and ecclesiastical events" (II, xxii, pp. 439-40). When Gibbon must give an interpretation of a character, as an important figure comes into or leaves his purview, he recognizes both the necessity and the danger of centering his interpretation of the past on human character. He comes to praise figures in history most highly for their ability to learn from situations and take advantage of circumstances.

As Cromwell could be the key to understanding Hume's early view of character in history, so Julian the Apostate might be considered the center, for the first three volumes, of Gibbon's.[1] Gibbon spends three chapters on Julian (xxii–iv) and portrays him more fully than any other character in the first section of the *Decline and Fall*. In his pur-

[1] Fielding may share Gibbon's fascination with Julian. But it is difficult to say exactly why Julian is the central character in Fielding's tedious Lucianic piece, *A Journey from this World to the Next*. It is tempting to rescue Fielding by calling the work an exercise in the boredom, irrelevance, and venality of public history; but that is an explanation, not an excuse. Gibbon calls *A Journey* "the romance of a great master, which may be considered as the history of human nature" (III, xxxii, p. 384 n13). The great influence on Gibbon, the Abbé de la Bléterie's biography of Julian, is not in the catalogue of Fielding's library nor is Warburton's *Julian* (1750; 2nd ed. 1757), a work to which Gibbon is probably reacting. For a further account of the figure of Julian in England, see Edgar Wind, "Julian the Apostate at Hampton Court," *England and the Mediterranean Tradition* (Oxford, 1945), pp. 131–38.

suit of the character of Julian, Gibbon tries to explore fully the complexities of a historical figure and he completely lays to rest any pretenses to complete explanation. Gibbon discerns elements of Julian's nature, but he does not present them in balanced and abstract contrasts. Instead he shows the variety of Julian's motivations, while he emphasizes our inability to know the quantities of the mixture and thereby predict behavior:

> His lively and active mind was susceptible of the various impressions of hope and fear, of gratitude and revenge, of duty and of ambition, of the love of fame and of the fear of reproach. But it is impossible for us to calculate the respective weight and operation of these sentiments; or to ascertain the principles of action, which might escape the observation, while they guided or rather impelled the steps, of Julian himself (II, xxii, p. 426).

Gibbon continually indicts Julian's "fanatical" belief in paganism as well as his intellectual vanity; but he balances this condemnation by praising Julian's good work as emperor, especially his submission of himself to the laws and forms of the republic (II, xxii, pp. 445–446). Julian's main fault is that he did not know himself and his limitations. Gibbon may speculate about what might have happened if Julian had lived to continue his persecution of the Christians. But he refuses to base his speculation on psychological insight: "It is impossible to determine how far the zeal of Julian would have prevailed over his good sense and humanity . . . " (II, xxiii, p. 504). All Gibbon will say at this point is that, in light of the similar strength and spirit of Julian and his main Christian opponent, Athanasius, there would probably have been civil war.

Gibbon's liking for Julian is often explained by the assertion that the eighteenth-century deist saw an affinity between himself and the pagan reformer. Yet Gibbon blames Julian as much as he praises him. Gibbon is more intrigued by Julian's ability to assume the roles of both philosopher and emperor. Through this interest Gibbon moves toward a conception of the complex personality that he develops more fully in the latter half of the *Decline and Fall* and in his *Memoirs*. The fully-aware individual or the admirable historical character understands the necessity for different roles and has the ability to assume them when necessary. As Julian's strengths often lie in his ability to assume varied roles, so his weakness comes from his confusions about these roles: "In the cool moments of reflection, Julian preferred the useful and benevolent virtues of [Marcus Aurelius] Antoninus; but his ambitious spirit was inflamed by the glory of Alexander; and he solicited, with equal ardour, the esteem of the wise and the applause of the multitude" (II, xxiv, p. 506).

Gibbon finally, in fact, describes Julian's faults in terms of an inability to choose appropriate roles: "Alexander was transformed into Diogenes; the philosopher was degraded into a priest" (II, xxiv, p. 558). Gibbon's estimate of Julian's greatness is necessarily expressed in similar terms. He juxtaposes Libanius and Ammianus Marcellinus to present their claims to Julian's body:

> The philosopher expressed a very reasonable wish that the disciple of Plato might have reposed amidst the groves of the academy; while the soldier exclaimed in bolder accents that the ashes of Julian should have been mingled with those of Caesar, in the field of Mars and among the ancient monuments of Roman virtue. The history of princes does not very frequently renew the example of a similar competition (II, xxiv, p. 558).

This inclusive view of the character of a historical figure, in which Gibbon emphasizes richness rather than intelligibility, frees him to exult in the complexities and inconsistencies of character displayed in action. Only a few pages after Julian's death he is pleased to point out that Valentinian, who kept a bear named Innocence to execute rebels against his rule, also condemned by law the practice of exposing newborn infants. His character and actions reveal other anomalies: "The good sense of an illiterate soldier founded a useful and liberal institution for the education of youth, and the support of declining science" (III, xxv, p. 22). Reflecting the Humian idea that dissimilar effects can arise from similar impersonal causes, Gibbon later points out that both vice and virtue can follow from the same abstractly considered character traits. Characters act "anomalously" only when one has omitted the influence of circumstances. Like the point of view of the historian, the concept of character should structure but not restrict our understanding of an array of incidents. Gibbon mocks less expansive views of character when he fully treats another historical figure: "Within the space of three years, the inconsistent historian of Theodosius must relate the generous pardon of the citizens of Antioch and the inhuman massacre of the people of Thessalonica" (III, xxvii, p. 177). Complex character presupposes the ability to understand and change situations. It is not inappropriate that Gibbon characterizes both Julian and Theodosius as readers of history (II, xxiv, p. 530; III, xxvii, p. 177).

Situation must be included in the view of character, because a bare account of virtues and vices is static and non-historical. Gibbon's uneasiness with the theme of corruption becomes more apparent in the later parts of the first half of the *Decline and Fall*; except for sporadic reappearances, it later disappears as a mode of organization. He follows Montesquieu's idea of the decaying military structure of Rome as long as he can, until he finally runs into paradoxes fostered by his own ideas: " . . . the arts which adorn and improve the state of civil society, corrupt the habits of military life" (III, xxvi, p. 77). In the character of Julian he concentrates on his own synthesis of Julian's traits. Similarly he may rely on his own vision to structure his history, rather than use mechanically-applied metaphors of corruption that spring ultimately from a simple-minded view of the decline and fall.ᵐ He chooses to present character, like

ᵐ Gibbon's direct concern in the early chapters of the *Decline and Fall* with "effeminacy" and "corruption" may reflect the influence of John Brown's *Estimate of Manners and Principles* (1757) , although as other historical data, in terms of an intelligible literary structure. A preliminary estimate of character may be judiciously extracted from the biased accounts of contemporary historians by "an impartial historian, who is obliged to extract truth from satire, as well as from panegyric" (I, xiii, p. 415). But in its own way this method is falsifying and insufficient. The figure of Constantine evokes a theoretical statement:

> By the impartial union of those defects which are confessed by his warmest admirers and of those virtues which are acknowledged by his most implacable enemies, we might hope to delineate a just portrait of that extraordinary man, which the truth and candour of history should adopt without a blush. But it would soon appear, that the vain attempt to blend such discordant colours, and to reconcile such inconsistent qualities, must produce a figure monstrous rather than human, unless it is viewed in its proper and distinct lights by a careful separation of the different periods of the reign of Constantine (II, xviii, p. 214).

Gibbon develops and strengthens his narrative voice in order to achieve a control over just such materials, a control denied to those who seek impersonal judgments or undiscriminated facts. His sense of the uses and abuses of character and metaphor reflects his conviction that the historian must distinguish the literary pattern that falsifies from the literary pattern that illuminates.

JULIAN IS ALSO a key figure in the first half of the *Decline and Fall* because in his synthesis of roles he represents an appropriate and possible balancing of public and private

---

a theme in the history of Rome, it goes back at least to Leonardo Bruni. The contrast between the effeminate, supine Romans and the free, hardy Goths was a frequent seventeenth-century theme. See Kliger, *Goths in England*, pp. 2–3. Kliger calls Gibbon's account of Odin and the chastising of Rome by the North (I, x) a common "revenge-motif" (pp. 95–96). James Thomson's *Liberty* (1735–36) also argued along familiar lines that Rome fell through spiritual corruption rather than military reverses. Naturally, the Spirit of Liberty thereupon migrated to England.

virtue. This balance is parallel to Gibbon's own attempts to balance the historian's search for factual truth with his consciousness of the subjectivity of individual interpretation. In the history of the Roman Empire, Gibbon praises those emperors who possess both hereditary power and personal merit. Julian has " . . . the impatience of a philosopher, who considered every moment as lost that was not devoted to the advantage of the public or the improvement of his own mind" (II, xxii, p. 443). While emperor, he served as a judge in court, performing functions that are "sometimes incompatible with those of a prince" (II, xxii, 454). But Gibbon's praises are never unalloyed: Julian's personal virtues only "in some measure" justify the "accident" of his birth. Julian does bring his private virtues into the service of the public good, but he is not an exemplary figure who can be taken out of context as a general ideal: "A more accurate view of the character and conduct of Julian will remove this favourable prepossession for a prince who did not escape the general contagion of the times" (II, xxiii, p. 456).[n]

Julian's synthesis of philosopher and emperor is a possible ideal because both the Roman Empire and Christianity in different ways upset the balance of private virtue and public good. He is almost unique among Roman emperors because the imperial system could only emphasize "the instability of a happiness which depended on the character of a single man" (I, iii, p. 86).[o] Christianity, on the other hand, is so exclusively interested in the relation of the in-

[n] Julian's possession of both private and public sanctions should insure political stability. But Gibbon has no illusions about the frequency with which figures like Julian appear: "The generality of princes, if they were stripped of their purple and cast naked into the world, would immediately sink to the lowest rank of society without a hope of emerging from their obscurity" (II, xxii, pp. 454–55) .

[o] Even under the reign of the five "Good Emperors" the evils of the imperial system were still present, although in abeyance because of the virtue of the rulers. Gibbon's general argument on this point is very similar to Fielding's in his account of the gypsies in *Tom Jones*. Fielding remarks here that "the true era of the Golden Age, and the only Golden Age which ever had any existence" was in the time of these emperors (p. 571) . Bacon, in *The Advancement of Learning*, commends them specifically as "learned princes."

dividual and the transcendental that it dispenses with the earthly state completely. Gibbon highly praises Zoroastrianism for its mixture of private religion and social utility (I, viii, p. 217). But the institutions of both empire and Christianity hamper the exercise of individual virtue, the first by emphasizing the purely pragmatic ends of the state and the second the purely transcendental ends of religion. In practice these emphases often become public masks for private venality, when the emperor pretends that his personal good is the good of the state and the ecclesiastic pretends that his personal ambitions are countenanced and approved by God. Gibbon is frequently pessimistic about man's ability to act amid "the contagion of the times." Unlike Hume, he does not believe that law, the codification of individual insight and virtue, is the appropriate answer. For law to work, he says, it must be well-administered:

> But the operation of the wisest laws is imperfect and precarious. They seldom inspire virtue, they cannot always restrain vice. Their power is insufficient to prohibit all that they condemn, nor can they always punish the actions which they prohibit (II, xx, p. 312).

And surrounding this pre-Benthamite assertion are chapters filled with venal judges and logic-chopping lawyers, all twisting law to their private advantage.

The true interpreter and actor is a person who does not seek reflections of himself in either the state or the skies. Julian may be a first essay of the figure. But, as the *Decline and Fall* moves on, this personage appears anonymously as the "disinterested spectator," "the obscure citizen," "the observant traveller," who views the events of history with detached interest. Through this private observer Gibbon emphasizes the separation between public and private perspectives, while, like Fielding in *Amelia*, he points out that the latter can reinvigorate the former. The metaphor of corruption must drop away not only because it asserts an overly simple causality, but also because it is based upon a false analogy between the individual and the state.[13] The historian, too, must understand the relation between his own point of view and what he sees. The growing emphasis on the value of private virtue and the detached point of view is an essential part of the development of Gibbon's idea of the role of the historian. But detachment does not involve a Humian kind of depersonalization; it involves instead our sense of the capabilities of the person who is being subjective. In the first half of the *Decline and Fall* the reader finds the personal "I" appearing more and more in Gibbon's judgments: "I might wish to think . . . "; "Yet I shall not easily be persuaded . . . "; " . . . nor can I believe . . . "; " . . . and I wish to persuade myself. . . ." The "I" represents a continuous point of view that takes leave of the various historians who in their turn have been Gibbon's guide; it implies his own larger perspective. Gibbon here has attempted something similar in its way to Fielding's narrative stance in *Tom Jones*. A personalized narrator gives to the reader the benefit of his experience and learning. Gibbon emphasizes both the objective truth of his materials and the imaginative truth of his manipulation of them. The mere volume and verifiable minutiae of his references and footnotes convey the impression of authority. The rhythm of his sentences expresses the balance of his judgment. The personal quality of his narrative voice emphasizes that Gibbon will never mold his facts into absolute forms, but instead will be always ready to change, qualify, or contradict past interpretations on the basis of new data.

No simple interpretation must be allowed complete validity. The theme of corruption disappears because it has achieved too much of a life of its own beyond Gibbon's manipulation of it. Gibbon says that he will not go into the manners and luxury of the Rome of Alaric " . . . as such inquiries would divert me too long from the design of the present work" (III, xxxi, p. 31). Words like "design" and "purpose" appear more often, because Gibbon feels more confident of his own control. "I have purposely delayed the consideration of two religious events, interesting in the study of human nature, and important in the decline and fall of the Roman empire" (IV, xxxvii, p. 62). And the mood has begun in which he can call himself "the historian of the Empire" (IV, xxxvii, p. 104). The design of the *Decline and Fall* is specifically his own. He can even afford digressions: "I am impatient to pursue . . . " (IV, xxxviii, p. 121). In the last pages of the first half of the *Decline and Fall*, the implied narrator has begun to approximate Gibbon himself, the historian of Rome who is an eighteenth-century Englishman and wants to follow for a moment a particular interest: ". . . the historian of the empire may be tempted to pursue the revolutions of a Roman province, till it vanishes from his sight; and an Englishman may curiously trace the establishment of the Barbarians from whom he derives his name, his laws, and perhaps his origins" (IV, xxxviii, p. 156). In exploring the problem of historical character the historian has more fully defined his own nature. The achievements of his sureness and control, and the further development of his view of history, will be fully displayed in the fourth, fifth, and sixth volumes of the *Decline and Fall*.

IV. THE *Decline and Fall*, VOLUMES IV–VI: THE
HISTORIAN'S STANCE AND THE WHIRLIGIG OF TIME

We imperceptibly advance from youth to age, without observing the gradual, but incessant, change of human affairs, and, even in our larger experiences of history, the imagination is accustomed, by a perpetual series of causes and effects, to unite the most distant revolutions. But, if the interval between two memorable eras could be instantly annihilated; if it were possible, after a momentary slumber of two hundred years, to display the *new* world to the eyes of a spectator, who still retained a lively and recent impression of the *old*; his surprise and his reflections would furnish the pleasing subject of a philosophical romance (III, xxxiii, p. 439).

The movement of the *Decline and Fall* marks Gibbon's increasing awareness of the complex process of time, which accumulates and includes impersonal causes, complex events, and human characters. In response to its variety he more closely defines his own perspective. Hume had gradually discovered time to be the essential element in the historical process; he made his form display its irrational gatherings and juxtapositions. Gibbon emphasizes the control of time; he establishes the historian as the man best suited to understand and manipulate its processes. The first half of the *Decline and Fall* emphasizes the authority of the narrative voice, the second half its creativity. Like the prized rulers who can take advantage of situations, the historian controls time through both his empathy and his detachment. Gibbon's preoccupation with the historian's relation to time is foreshadowed in the first half of the *Decline and Fall* by his interest in the legend of the Seven Sleepers, illustrated in the above quotation. He asserts that it has a fascination for all of us. But it more clearly fascinates him, because the legend images the way the historian can achieve mastery of time. Gibbon emphasizes the literary consciousness that makes such connections. The purpose of juxtaposing eras is more than didactic; it is pleasing and enlightening in a much wider sense. It becomes the measure of a new kind of consciousness. Gibbon later expands the Seven Sleepers legend into a myth of the historian:

> A being of the nature of man, endowed with the same faculties, but with a longer measure of existence, would cast down a smile of pity and contempt on the crimes and follies of human ambition, so eager, in a narrow span, to grasp at a precarious and short-lived enjoyment. It is thus that the experience of history exalts and enlarges the horizon of our intellectual view. In a composition of some days, in a perusal of some hours, six hundred years [of Byzantine history] have rolled away, and the duration of a life or reign is contracted to a fleeting moment; the grave is ever beside the throne; the success of a criminal is almost instantly followed by the loss of his prize; and our immortal reason survives and disdains the phantoms

of kings, who have passed before our eyes and faintly dwell on our remembrance (V, xlviii, p. 258–59).

Gibbon here recognizes three processes in time: the action of the writer, the understanding of the reader, and the movement of history. In working with all three in the latter half of the *Decline and Fall*, Gibbon follows the stipulation of his *Essai* that historical perspective is similar in many ways to the shaping and creative vision of the novel writer or epic poet. In this latter half Gibbon also continues to develop his ideas about the uses of character in both history and history-writing and he further explores the relation of private to public life.

Early in the second half of the *Decline and Fall* Gibbon brushes aside the didactic assumptions of exemplary history:

> The experience of past faults, which may sometimes correct the mature age of an individual, is seldom profitable to the successive generations of mankind. The nations of antiquity, careless of each other's safety, were separately vanquished and enslaved by the Romans (IV, xli, 318-19).

Time does not teach. In the rush of time's multiplicity Gibbon stands by two constants: the firmness of his own point of view and an almost Virgilian sense of the existence of a geographic site through time. I have already sketched the developing strength of his narrative stance. Through the array of partially explained and haphazard causes that form the *Decline and Fall*, geography too is established as a touchstone in the midst of the flux of time. Gibbon may remark generally on the political, social, and economic structure of the empire, following Montesquieu's and Voltaire's themes of the corrupt populace and the mercenary army. But he contributes a new context to his judgments by his emphasis on the cities of Rome and Constantinople. This method develops possibilities that were present in the first half of the *Decline and Fall*. Gibbon glimpses Constantinople first as a physical setting: "After the defeat and abdication of Licinius, his victorious rival [Constantine] proceeded to lay the foundations of a city destined to reign in future times the mistress of the East, and to survive the empire and religion of Constantine" (II, xvii, p. 149).

The description that follows is itself timeless, not only in its concentration on the immutable features of sea and land, but also in the way Gibbon mingles observations of the landscape from different periods, fabulous and factual, conflating the observations of Strabo, Polybius, Tacitus, and Procopius with the acts of Ulysses, Leander, Constantine, and Justinian. Similarly interposed as islands of solidity amid the uncertainties of historical narrative are descriptions of Jerusalem (II, xxiii, pp. 479–80), Daphne (II, xxiii, pp. 491–93), and Assyria (II, xxiv, pp. 522–23). Gibbon admires the Greek rhetorician Chrysoloras's ability to confound "the past and the present, the times of prosperity and decay" in his picture of Constantinople (VII, lxvii, p. 140).ᵖ These descriptions are more than merely picturesque. They focus the dim rays of historic truth at a place for the most part unaffected by the passage of time, at a vantage point from which to contemplate the changing fortunes of man, much like the point of view of the timeless spectator. Man vanishes but geography remains through "the boundless annals of time" (VII, lxxi, p. 317).

The emphasis on physical situation also represents a psychological truth about man and his preoccupation with the visible. Gibbon concentrates upon the physical situations of Rome and Constantinople because they are what fire the imaginations of their inhabitants: " . . . when the Roman princes had lost sight of the senate and of their ancient capitol, they easily forgot the origin and nature of their legal power" (I, xiii, p. 410). Although Gibbon may focus his historical gaze on geography in general, he peers most steadily at Rome and Constantinople. They are the

---

ᵖ A similar comment is made about Florus, who wrote at the time of Hadrian: "The pride of his contemporaries was gratified by the contrast of past and present [in his description of the early wars of Latium]: they would have been humbled by the prospect of futurity . . ." (VII, lxix, p. 246) .

cities of history, the habitations of men, the staging ground and tiring houses for his secondary causes. In what may be a self-conscious answer to the Augustinian view of history, Gibbon concludes his sketch of the plan for the last two volumes by another example of his reliance on secondary and earthly causes: "I shall return from the captivity of the new, to the ruins of the ancient ROME; and the venerable name, and the interesting theme, will shed a ray of glory on the conclusion of my labours" (V, xlviii, p. 185).

Even without prince or people Constantinople is still great, " . . . and the genius of the place will ever triumph over the accidents of time and fortune" (VII, lxviii, p. 209). To concentrate on the cities as places reflects a belief about the nature of history and the historian's role: "As, in his daily prayers, the Musulman of Fez or Delhi still turns his face towards the temple of Mecca, the historian's eye shall always be fixed on the city of Constantinople" (V, xlviii, p. 182).

The specific link between the existences of the city at various points in its history is the mind of the historian. The emphasis on setting has become increasingly deliberate in the second half of the *Decline and Fall* because Gibbon himself has become more conscious of the way the imaginative pull of the city of Rome has directed his own efforts. It is doubtful that Gibbon in his *Memoirs* would have stressed so strongly the genesis of the *Decline and Fall* in the Forum, while he sat listening to vespers being sung in Sta. Maria in Ara Coeli, if he had not worked through the geographic theme in the writing of the *Decline and Fall*.[14] The themes of narrative control, time, and place come together when Gibbon returns to the Forum at the end of his history. The climate may no longer be the same at the beginning of the Renaissance as it was at the time of the Republic, but Rome still exists as an entity, in all of her variety, not only in the mind of Gibbon, but also in the minds of Petrarch and Cola di Rienzi: " . . . the venerable aspect of her ruins, and the memory of past greatness, rekindled a spark of the national character" (VII, lxix, p. 219). In the later chapters of

the *Decline and Fall* Gibbon continually refers to the cities
of Rome and Constantinople as the centers of his formal
design. And at the end of the history we return to the ruined
Forum, while Cola de Rienzi attempts to revive the classical
spirit by crowning Petrarch poet laureate in the Capitol,
and the narrator reviews for us the ruins and history of the
Coliseum.[15]

THE EMPHASIS ON PLACE reflects Gibbon's effort to move
away from overly determined systems of explanation. Often,
especially in the latter *Decline and Fall*, he reels off the
phrase "the causes of the decline and fall of the Roman empire" in an almost perfunctory manner. But he presents no
total pattern of explanation. Like Hume and Fielding,
Gibbon seems to extend his criticism of the self-serving nature of providential explanation to include all systematic
explanations. Gibbon's complaints about Procopius can
stand as a general indictment of the falsified causalities that
self-interest, either religious or political or personal in
origin, imposes upon history:

> Ambiguous actions are imputed to the worst motives;
> error is confounded with guilt, accidents with design, and
> laws with abuses; the partial injustice of a moment is
> dexterously applied as the general maxim of a reign of
> thirty-two years; the emperor alone is made responsible
> for the faults of his officers, the disorders of the times, and
> the corruption of his subjects; and even the calamities of
> nature, plagues, earthquakes, and inundations, are im-
> puted to the prince of demons, who had mischievously
> assumed the form of Justinian (IV, xl, p. 252).

The comment on Procopius indicates Gibbon's growing
discomfort with long-drawn causal lines.[16] As his narrative
voice becomes stronger, his arguments for relativity of vision become more frequent. His most famous judgments
are actually open ended, to allow for later facts, new ideas,
and different points of view. After hearing, for example,
the famous statement about barbarism and religion quoted

so damningly against Gibbon, one examines it and finds it clearly presented as an interpretation, appropriate for both the point in the narrative and the facts Gibbon knows: "In the preceding volumes of this History I have described the triumph of barbarism and religion; and I can only resume, in a few words, their real or imaginary connection with the ruins of ancient Rome" (VII, lxxi, pp. 320–21).[q]

The epistemological doublet used here, "real or imaginary," is an integral part of Gibbon's developing style and an index to the nature of his relative and pluralistic vision. It gives a sense of the possibilities of interpretation: "by art or by accident," "in truth, or in opinion," "genuine or fictitious," "chance or merit." The problem is not either-or. Gibbon does not wish to exhaust a world with his polarities. Instead he wishes to convey a sense of the multiplicity of causes that surround any event, some of which at least may be discerned and crudely ranked, without any final judgment. He exemplifies such methods throughout the *Decline and Fall.*

> The sincerity or the cunning of the Arian chiefs, the fear of the laws or of the people, their reverence for Christ, their hatred of Athanasius, all the causes, human and divine, that influence and disturb the counsels of a theological faction, introduced among the sectaries a spirit of discord and inconstancy, which, in the course of a few years, erected eighteen different models of religion, and avenged the violated dignity of the church (II, xxi, p. 370).

It might rightly be objected that Gibbon speaks here of theological affairs, which he always considered a mare's nest of confusion. But in later volumes he stresses this kind of causal complexity even more. On Tamerlane's victory over Bajazet:

> For this signal victory the Mogul emperor was indebted

[q] In subsequent remarks Gibbon concludes that, at least in this case, the connection is much more imaginary than real.

to himself, to the genius of the moment, and the discipline of thirty years (VII, lxv, p. 61).

Hope or fear, lassitude or remorse, the characters of men, and the circumstances of the times, might sometimes obtain an interval of peace and obedience. . . (VII, lxix, p. 227).

Gibbon thus continues the emphasis on relativism first voiced in the *Essai.* He does not seek detachment so much as he affirms the need to see differently according to context:

Our estimate of personal merit is relative to the common faculties of mankind. The aspiring efforts of genius or virtue, either in active or speculative life, are measured not so much by their real elevation as by the height to which they ascend above the level of their age or country; and the same stature, which in a people of giants would pass unnoticed, must appear conspicuous in a race of pygmies (IV, xlii, p. 364).

Phrases like "such a character, in such an age" or "at least to our eyes" display the rhetoric of relative judgment.[r] In this way Gibbon attempts, for example, to puncture the reputation of Charlemagne: "His *real* merit is doubtless enhanced by the barbarism of the nation and the times from which he emerged: but the *apparent* magnitude of an object is likewise enlarged by an unequal comparison; and the ruins of Palmyra derive a casual splendour from the nakedness of the surrounding desert" (V, xlix, p. 303).

Even Gibbon's most appreciative critics attack his "inability" to appreciate the religious mind. Perhaps the early ironies exhibited in chapters fifteen and sixteen merit such a judgment. But his growing use of a relative point of view yields passages which such "inability" could never attain,

[r] Gibbon notes the way in which Boccaccio, Chaucer, and Shakespeare make Theseus "duke" of Athens: "An ignorant age transfers its own language and manners to the most distant times" (V, lxii, p. 505 n69) .

like the sympathetic interpretation of the First Crusade and of the characters of St. Bernard and Peter the Hermit.

The increase in relative and contextual judgments is directly related to Gibbon's growing narrative power. In the course of the *Decline and Fall* he becomes more clearly aware of his own perspective in time and the new modes of narrative organization which that perspective demands. He says in speaking of Alaric: "At the distance of fourteen centuries we may be satisfied with relating the military exploits of the conquerors of Rome without presuming to investigate the motives of their political conduct" (III, xxxi, p. 330). The slow growth and proliferation of institutions and cities becomes an important theme, for Gibbon sees in this growth the haphazard interplay of plan and chance, man and time. The perspective of the Seven Sleepers can juxtapose personalities, events, and actions that time has otherwise separated. In other words, it supplies a perspective for interpretation. Metaphorically Gibbon makes great leaps, to display his own perspective mastering an incredible stretch of time: "Justinian, the Greek emperor of Constantinople and the East, was the legal successor of the Latin shepherd who had planted a colony on the banks of the Tiber" (IV, xliv, p. 541).

Gibbon appreciates at once his limited place in time as a man and his expanded vision of time as a historian. Although he thinks that the progress of law is irregular and obscure, he will make of it a narrative in time (IV, xliv, p. 541). As the processes of writing and living go on, Gibbon marks the points when he leaves his favorite past historians and commemorates the deaths of his favorite contemporary historians, like the geographer D'Anville and the military historian Guischardt. And his historian's vision can extend even into the remote future. He traces the later appearances of the comet that appeared in the reign of Justinian: "At the eighth period, in the year two thousand two hundred and fifty-five, their calculations may perhaps be verified by the astronomers of some future capital in the Siberian or American wilderness" (IV, xliii, p. 463).

Gibbon consolidates his role as the master of time in many comparisons that stress the inclusiveness of his view. "Since the days of Scipio and Hannibal . . . " no enterprise had been as bold as Heraclius' expeditions against the Persians (V, xlvi, p. 87).

> . . . the decay of genius may be measured by the distance between Horace and George of Pisidia . . . (V, xlvi, p. 103).

> If we annihilate the interval of time and space between Augustus and Charles [IV of Germany], strong and striking will be the contrast between the two Caesars . . . (V, xlix, p. 330).

Gibbon views with special irony and interest the repetition of similar actions at the same place: "In the revolution of human events, a new ambuscade was concealed in the Caudine Forks, the fields of Cannae were bedewed a second time with the blood of the Africans, and the sovereign of Rome again attacked or defended the walls of Capua or Tarentum" (VI, lvi, p. 175).

There is obviously a degeneration from Horace to George of Pisidia, but Gibbon's point is not meant to support the Ancients position. He can say that Robert Guiscard had a voice "like that of Achilles" and show Guiscard repeating the heroic adventures of the past: "After winning two battles against the emperor [Henry III], he descended into the plain of Thessaly, and besieged Larissa, the fabulous realm of Achilles, which contained the treasure and magazines of the Byzantine camp" (VI, lxi, p. 210). More historical exemplars are also cited. Gibbon describes Guiscard's strategy at the Battle of Durazzo: "His rear was covered by a small river; his right wing extended to the sea; his left to the hills; nor was he conscious, perhaps, that on the same ground Caesar and Pompey had formerly disputed the empire of the world" (VI, lxvi, p. 207).

The reader has already seen Caesar and Pompey earlier in the *Decline and Fall* performing these very actions. It is Gibbon himself, not the abstract spirit of history, who moves through time, making such connections. He establishes continuity in a past otherwise made of separate Humian moments: "After pursuing above six hundred years the fleeting Caesars of Constantinople and Germany, I now descend, in the reign of Heraclius, on the eastern borders of the Greek monarchy" (V, 1, p. 332). By exhibiting his ability to shift easily through time, Gibbon conveys an intellectual and artistic control over a basically irrational process. He refers from one part of his Roman world to another, binding it together through webs of reference. At one point Gibbon regards this internal unity of the *Decline and Fall* almost ruefully. He had earlier mentioned the "judicious contemporaries" who believed that Rome suffered more damge from the Gauls than from the Goths. "The experience of eleven centuries has enabled posterity to produce a much more singular parallel; and to affirm with confidence that the ravages of the Barbarians, whom Alaric led from the banks of the Danube, were less destructive than the hostilities exercised by the troops of Charles the Fifth, a Catholic prince, who styled himself Emperor of the Romans" (III, xxxi, p. 347).

By the time the last volume has come around, Charles V can make his appearance in person rather than in analogy. Gibbon exhibits here a keen awareness of the ironic collision of the narrative time of the *Decline and Fall* and the historical time to which it is an analogy. Within the bounds of Gibbon's narrative, historical time has in a way come full circle. Gibbon makes the analogy in his text: "The nice balance of the Vatican was often subverted by the soldiers of the North and West, who were united under the standard of Charles the Fifth; the feeble and fluctuating policy of Clement the Seventh exposed his person and dominions to the conqueror; and Rome was abandoned seven months to a lawless army, more cruel and rapacious than the Goths or Vandals" (VII, lxx, p. 308). The awareness appears in the footnote: "In the history of the Gothic siege, I have compared the Barbarians with the subjects of Charles V. (vol. iii, p. 347-8); an anticipation, which, like that of the Tar-

tar conquests, I indulged with the less scruple, as I could scarcely hope to reach the conclusion of my work" (VII, lxx, p. 308 n102).

Talk of time substitutes for talk of cause in the later *Decline and Fall.* Such causal doublets as "time and policy" or "time and accident" appear more frequently. Gibbon now defines "insensible" more precisely as "not accompanied with any memorial of time or place" (V, li, p. 519). He has even less desire than before to say what causes are embedded in the texture of history. Characters may work from design or accident, but Gibbon denies that either interpretation alone is necessary. He allows himself more freedom to make causes suggestive rather than exhaustive or rigorous. He more clearly implies that causes in history are usually sought only after effects are known.

The freedom the creative narrative voice gives to Gibbon finally allows him to speculate on the "might have been" of history without restricting himself to direct interpretation.[s] Gibbon justifies a seeming digression on revolts in the sixth century:

> This narrative of obscure and remote events is not foreign to the decline and fall of the Roman empire. If a Christian power had been maintained in Arabia, Mahomet must have been crushed in his cradle, and Abyssinia would have prevented a revolution which has changed the civil and religious state of the world (IV, xlii, p. 414).

Gibbon also introduces fanciful "literary" causes, which, much in the manner of Carlyle, emphasize that immediate

---

[s] Marc Bloch remarks that 'might have been' questions are "simple rhetorical devices intended to illuminate the role of contingency and the unforeseeable in the progress of mankind" (*The Historian's Craft,* p. 125). In the early chapters of the *Decline and Fall* Gibbon implies that people may be happier when they have no knowledge of other possibilities: "Chardin says that European travellers have diffused among the Persians some ideas of the freedom and mildness of our governments. They have done them a very ill office" (I, iii, p. 88 n63). Speculation on the 'might have been' therefore also represents an important change in Gibbon's approach. Its relation to Fielding's speculation about motive and circumstance in *Tom Jones* may be suggestive.

events are symbols of vaster and more obscure causal concatenations:

> Perhaps the Greeks would still be involved in the heresy of the Monophysites, if the emperor's horse had not fortunately stumbled; Theodosius expired; his orthodox sister, Pulcheria, with a nominal husband, succeeded to the throne; Chrysaphius was burnt, Dioscorus was disgraced, the exiles were recalled, and the *tome* of Leo was subscribed by the Oriental bishops (V, xlvii, pp. 131–32).

> In this eventful moment, the lance of an Arab might have changed the history of the world (V, l, p. 379).

> The immediate loss of Constantinople may be ascribed to the bullet, or arrow, which pierced the gauntlet of John Justiniani (VII, lxviii, p. 199).

Perhaps, like Keast, one could explain such remarks by invoking Gibbon's concentration on the central figure of the emperor. But Gibbon's practice appears closer to Hume's than Keast would allow. These "causes" imply a density of context rather than a pattern of history, or of history-writing. Gibbon emphasizes their concurrence rather than their linearity when, for example, he remarks on the failure of Bajazet to capture Constantinople:

> His progress was checked, not by the miraculous interposition of the apostle, not by a crusade of the Christian powers, but by a long and painful fit of the gout. The disorders of the moral, are sometimes corrected by those of the physical, world; and an acrimonious humour falling on a single fibre of one man may prevent or suspend the misery of nations (VII, lxiv, p. 37).

Such effects are only immediate. The long lines of causes are never certain. Gibbon is more comfortable than Hume with the idea that no one can deduce effect from cause in political life, that ill things can have beneficent effects, and vice versa. The search for cause becomes in the later chapters of the *Decline and Fall* an effort to understand rather than to codify; and understanding can remain various, eclectic, and undogmatic. As Gibbon remarks of the destruction of pagan monuments in Rome, "The change of religion was accomplished, not by a popular tumult, but by the decrees of the emperor, of the senate, and of time" (VII, lxxi, p. 322). Long-range causes are at once more important and more unspecifiable than the causes of the moment.

HISTORICAL CHARACTER, like cause in general, is a problem for understanding rather than for the testing of deductive categories. Without a commitment to a system of historical or psychological explanation, with a commitment only to his own narrative voice and the coherence it creates, Gibbon can afford to present character in the fullness of its "contradictions" and "inconsistencies." Like the later Hume, he can concentrate on character for its own sake, rather than as a precise key to the truth of public events. He can emphasize the intrinsic interest of personal details. It is in this light his famous salacious footnotes might be understood. For Gibbon the interest in others is directly related to an interest in self, and the sexual references display his own peculiar slant. They often seem purposefully chosen to be the most irrelevant details to give in a work that purports to present itself as an "explanation" of what happened in history. But they actually contribute to a rich and flexible view of human character. Gibbon has no explicit criteria for judging between characters. Depending on the person and situation, he may judge either way, or reserve judgment, while using the same descriptive terms. Theophano (the wife of Romanus II, a tenth-century Byzantine king) is described as "a woman of base origin, masculine spirit, and flagitious manners" (V, xlviii, p. 224), traits which are excused or at least ameliorated in the characters of Mohammed, Zenobia, and Theodora, respectively.

Discrete lists of vices and virtues appear in Gibbon only while he is most obviously transcribing his sources. He has become more fully aware of the ways in which patterns of mind can have disparate effects when expressed in action. Time itself interposes when one tries to recapture a personality in any degree of fullness. Gibbon speaks more personally of his difficulties in understanding character to the degree that he feels more strongly the special role of the historian:

> At the conclusion of the life of Mahomet, it may perhaps be expected, that I should balance his faults and virtues, that I should decide whether the title of enthusiast or imposter more properly belongs to that extraordinary man. Had I been intimately conversant with the son of Abdallah, the task would still be difficult, and the success uncertain: at the distance of twelve centuries, I darkly contemplate his shade through a cloud of religious incense; and could I truly delineate the portrait of an hour, the fleeting resemblance would not equally apply to the solitary of Mount Hera, to the preacher of Mecca, and to the conqueror of Arabia (V, l, p. 400).

The balancing of vices and virtues can create only monsters. Learning from the treatment of Julian, Gibbon has come to see his problem as an attempt to encompass the various roles which an individual may play in his life. In fact he often uses "character" in a way that might be interpreted as "role."[t] Gibbon proceeds to make some statements about Mohammed's life, but the disclaimer has taken effect and the reader is prepared for the exhibition of character qualified by specific time and place, rather than an abstract account of the contents of Mohammed's mind, however reconciled and assorted. On another occasion Gibbon shakes his head philosophically at the spectacle of Tamerlane, whose first wish was to conquer and rule the world, and whose second was "to live in the memory and esteem of fu-

---

[t] On Vataces: ". . . without deciding the precedency, he pronounced with truth, that a prince and a philosopher are the two most eminent characters of human society" (VI, lxii, p. 477). Gibbon's idea of role will be discussed more fully in the Appendix, which deals with the *Memoirs*.

ture ages." Tamerlane attempted to perpetuate his memory in extensive journals of civil and military life to be kept during his reign. As a result the reconstruction of his character and reign would seem to be a simple historical problem, with all the materials lying open before the historian. Yet actually, says Gibbon, Tamerlane's efforts were "ineffectual"; his true character is elusive; and we can know him only through his deeds (VII, lxv, pp. 44–45).

The human is the ground of the institutional, decides Gibbon, and large movements in history can and should be understood in terms of their human components. Chapter fifteen, for all its fame and importance, embodies only a first statement of Gibbon's final view. This early attitude toward Christianity results from the evaluation of an institution too exclusively on the basis of its individual members, the bad who make us condemn it and the good who make us accept it. Gibbon realizes gradually that the importance of "human causes" can be oversimplified, if only because people are not so easy to categorize. The metaphor of corruption becomes less operative because it is too simple and too reductive to express the multiplicity of causes and effects, motives and actions, which make up history. By concentrating on individual weakness, the metaphor obscures individual strength and understanding, even on a small scale. Gibbon, unlike Voltaire, does not believe that man is trapped in history. Man has instead the possibility, if not the certainty, of understanding and ordering his life.

The way to such understanding involves first an understanding of man's public and private roles. The first half of the *Decline and Fall* reflects Hume's ideas when it deals with the relation between private interest and public trust. In the second half, perhaps partly as a result of the period under consideration, perhaps under the influence of Fielding, Gibbon emphasizes the possibilities for individual virtue in a world of venal institutions and public chaos. He begins to show a greater appreciation for the man, like Mohammed or Tamerlane, who rises through merit from obscure beginnings.[u] He concentrates on individuals who embody and define rather than servilely illustrate the ages in which they live. The perceptive personality need not be overcome by circumstance. No generalization about personality is absolute, and Gibbon continually makes exceptions to his own earlier judgments: Froissart is a good "monkish historian"; Narses is a good eunuch; and St. Bernard can be regarded as a "spiritual hero." Gibbon concentrates on the private acts that give life to the narrative of public events, and his anecdotes bespeak a new interest in the common actions of men.

Gibbon's central concern has become the relation of the individual to both the immediacy and the process of time. A figure like Mohammed stands for a combination of individual humanism and a social virtue that goes beyond the immediate (V, 1, p. 421). Gibbon praises the Arabs in general for being able to see beyond the momentary concerns of public history. Almost every major Arab figure who appears in the *Decline and Fall* has a highly developed and poetic sense of what Gibbon usually calls "the vicissitudes of fortune." The Arabs' awareness of the vanity of human wishes is in fact a reflection of the historian's view of the rapid passage of time. Gibbon's "digression" on the Courtenay family makes a similar point. It is ostensibly presented as a means of binding together the histories of several nations (VI, lxi, pp. 466–74). Gibbon is primarily interested in the survival of the Courtenays through time; the issue of hereditary power never arises. The Courtenays are an interesting and irrational growth, like the many metaphoric trees that appear in these later chapters. Their continuity is causal only by the loosest definition. Gibbon uses them as still another example of the vagaries of the process of time, like Horace and George of Pisidia:

[u] In earlier chapters the man who rose through merit was often found to be stained with ambition. See, for example, III, xxvi, p. 127. Perhaps the new factor is Gibbon's appreciation for the renewing vigor of the barbarians.

. . . the descendants of Hugh Capet could no longer be visible in the rural lords of Tanlay and Champignelles (VI, lxi, p. 470).

. . . in the lapse of six generations, the English Courtenays had learned to despise the nation and country from which they derived their origin (VI, lxi, p. 473).

The Courtenays are an image of the individual caught in the irrational multiplicity of history; the narrative hand of Gibbon is the image of an individual consciousness triumphing over that multiplicity by including and ordering it.[v]

THE TRUE VOICE of control, the true organizer, the force that shapes and gives meaning to history is, as I have asserted all along, Gibbon's own narrative voice. Now that I have attempted to examine its judgments, it is time to look at its nature in more detail. Gibbon's narrative voice, like Fielding's, gradually develops a method that stresses full awareness rather than rigid interpretation. His personal tone implies that any manipulation of the material is obviously his own. The palpable presence of Gibbon's narrator announces a freedom from the temptations to seek inherent patterns, a freedom to give all truths full play.

Gibbon differs from Fielding in that he must make his audience believe in his control over the factual material, while Fielding can demonstrate his sensitivity to human nature without drawing upon an array of evidence. Gibbon accomplishes the assertion of authority in the first half of the *Decline and Fall* by his voluminous documentation, itself a great departure from, for example, the practice of Vol-

---

[v] Gibbon also considers the family to be an institution that can possibly have more coherence and relevance than the public ones he has watched rise and fall in his long journey through time. He points out that, although the citizens of the early Empire gave their political power to Augustus ". . . they defended the freedom of domestic life" (IV, xliv, p. 477). Compare Fielding's similar sentiments in *Amelia*, above, pp. 200–01, and the concluding section of Pope's *Epistle to Dr. Arbuthnot*.

taire. Here are the factual resources of the *érudit* mustered with appropriate and graceful scholarship and not a little of the pure exuberance in fact that informs the great collections of Hume's "transactions." The vast flow of factual reference continues through the history, but Gibbon's rhetorical point has largely been made: his scholarly authority is to be respected. Now he can build upon his authority as a historian to demonstrate what he believes should be the historian's proper role.[17]

Gibbon experiments with his narrative in many different ways. To show his freedom from the time that binds his characters, he often leaves chronological order behind. As Gibbon continues his story, the dates have been relegated to the table of contents; they rarely appear in the text. Early in the *Decline and Fall* Gibbon offers an elaborate justification for following the fates of the separate barbaric nations, rather than using a straightforward time sequence. The growing confidence in his own voice and its "design" prepares the way for him to follow later themes athwart the flow of time. Whereas in the earlier chapters he often justified a treatment of subjects by saying that they were "naturally divided" into several headings, he now considers "I shall treat" to be a sufficient preamble.

The increase in the use of "I" in the second half of the *Decline and Fall* is enormous. Gibbon less frequently refers to himself in the third person as the "philosophic observer" and more frequently employs direct statement. He would rather, for example, that the art of printing had been imported from China than the art of making silk, although "I am not insensible to the benefits of elegant luxury . . . " (IV, xl, p. 250). He speculates genially on the minds of his characters: "I desire to believe, but I dare not affirm, that Belisarius sincerely rejoiced in the triumph of Narses" (IV, xliii, p. 454). He mocks the passionate distortions of those who have written before him: "Attached to no party, interested only for the truth and candour of history, and directed by the most temperate and skilful guides, I enter with just diffidence on the subject of civil law, which has exhausted so many learned lives and clothed the walls of such spacious libraries" (IV, xliv, p. 471).

He throws off modesty: ". . . perhaps the Arabs might not find in a single historian so clear and comprehensive a narrative of their own exploits, as that which will be deduced in the ensuing sheets" (V, li, p. 429). He treats the past with the methods he thinks most appropriate, even if they are not the "normal" interests of history: "I should not be apprehensive of deviating from my subject if it were in my power to delineate the private life of the conquerors of Italy, and I shall relate with pleasure the adventurous gallantry of Autharis, which breathes the true spirit of chivalry and romance" (V, xlv, p. 29).

Gibbon can include such incidents because his definition of history is expansive, limited only by his power to make it into a whole. He ennobles by notice: the vale of Damascus "has hitherto escaped the notice of the historian of the Roman empire . . . " (V, xlvi, p. 75). He looks "on the throne, in the camp, in the schools" for historical characters to rescue from undeserved oblivion (V, xlviii, pp. 181–82). He decides what is relevant and what is not: "From the antiquities of, I. *Bulgarians,* II. *Hungarians,* and III. *Russians,* I shall content myself with selecting such facts as yet deserve to be remembered" (VI, lv, p. 136). Such statements are justified by a narrative presence built up through hundreds of pages. Gibbon's own view is superior because it includes the insights of past historians, as well as his own interpretation. His sense of facts, human nature, and the awesome stretches of the past is the appropriate corrective for earlier bias. He is "the calm historian of the present hour," who can without compunction assert his own ability to select and form (VI, lii, p. 1). Gibbon is really creating history, giving the past the form the mind requires to seize it. The work of writing the *Decline and Fall* is consciously a process of creation by a specific person: "If I may speak of myself, (the only person of whom I can speak with certainty), *my* happy hours have far exceeded, and far exceed, the scanty numbers of the caliph of Spain [fourteen days]; and I shall not scruple to add, that many of them are due to the pleasing labour of the present composition" (VI, lii, p. 27 n60).

Gibbon stresses the self-contained unity of the *Decline and Fall* through a device like the circular comparison of Charles V and the Goths. He also can refer freely to his earlier self, correcting past statements. He notes, for example, that the city of Azimuntium was the only one to withstand Attila: "On the evidence of this fact, which had not occurred to my memory, the candid reader will correct and excuse a note in the iiird volume of this history, p. 456, which hastens the decay of Asimus, or Azimuntium: another century of patriotism and valour is cheaply purchased by such a confession" (V, xlvi, p. 62 n46). The mind of Gibbon shapes and gives meaning to the otherwise inanimate artifacts and crumbled manuscripts that constitute his material. The *Decline and Fall* even becomes a source for itself, as Gibbon suggests possible new methods of organization, when, for example, he comes to give an account of the progress of the Moguls: "The reader is invited to review the chapters of the third and fourth volumes; the manners of the pastoral nations, the conquests of Attila and the Huns, which were composed at a time when I entertained the wish, rather than the hope, of concluding my history" (VII, lxiv, p. 1 n1). When explanations falter Gibbon can ruefully adduce his own work as an appropriate test of alternate possibilities. He uses an Indian source for remarks about the equipages of Persian armies: "From these Indian stories the reader may correct a note in my first volumes (p. 226); or from that note he may correct these stories" (VI, lvii, p. 238 n11).

Gibbon is aware of the time elapsed in the creation of his work; he is also aware of the time spent by the reader, who has traveled with him for these hundreds of pages and years. Fieldingesque injunctions to the reader are liberally scattered in the text and footnotes. Gibbon demands that the reader participate in his own process of understanding:

Read and feel the xxiiid book of the Iliad, a living picture of manners, passions, and the whole form and spirit of the chariot race (IV, xl, p. 233 n41).

The reader starts; and before he is recovered from his surprise, I shall add . . . (VI, lviii, p. 303).

Read, if you can, the Life and Miracles of St. Louis, by the confessor of Queen Margaret . . . (VI, lix, p. 374 n104).

The sense of his work as a process of understanding intimately related to his own life permeates the later chapters of the history and is reminiscent of Johnson's remarks in the Preface to his *Dictionary.* Gibbon says: "In the long career of the decline and fall of the Roman empire, I have reached at length . . . " (VII, lxvii, p. 161). But Gibbon is more sanguine than Johnson about the possibilities of ultimate understanding, perhaps because his inclusive and eclectic view of historical process affirms the power of the controlling mind to make sense of what it apprehends. The convergence of historical time, narrative time, and reading time begins as Gibbon returns to his center at Rome, after sojourns among the barbarians. The shape of history is almost complete; Gibbon's task nears its end; and "The reader has been so long absent from Rome, that I would advise him to recollect or review the 49th chapter, in the 5th volume of this history" (VII, lxix, p. 219 n3).

THE PECULIAR CENTRALITY of the theme of the public and private man in the works of Fielding and Gibbon is an image of their concern with the relation between the author and his materials. The narrative "I" fashions from fifteen hundred years of history something called *The History of the Decline and Fall of the Roman Empire.* Like the narrative voice in *Tom Jones,* the "I" of the *Decline and Fall* makes inseparable claims of public authority and private point of view. The kind of objective public orientation assumed by Clarendon, postulated by Bolingbroke, and reflected in the early chapters of Hume's *History* implies a public historian speaking to public men about public events. In Fielding and Gibbon the distinction between public and private is not so certain. Gibbon continually distinguishes in his judgments between the public and the private man, and "public or private" is a frequently used doublet. In accord with such distinctions Gibbon finally evolves a new definition of the historian's role.

Gibbon's view of the historian develops through three figures: the philosopher, the judge, and the man of literature. The philosopher appears as the philosophic historian, who makes detached observations and balanced generalizations. Like Hume and Fielding, Gibbon also believes that the role of the judge approximates his own need to balance the claims of truth in the midst of multiplicity (IV, xliv, p. 534). But these two figures are only preliminary sketches; each is deficient. The philosophic historian frequently ignores relevant facts. Gibbon also does not fully trust judges perhaps for reasons that seem to presage Bentham. He speaks at the end of his chapter on Roman law about the greater advantage of a rich plaintiff in a court of law:

> The experience of an abuse from which our own age and country are not perfectly exempt may sometimes provoke a generous indignation, and extort the hasty wish of exchanging our elaborate jurisprudence for the simple and summary decrees of a Turkish cadhi. Our calmer reflection will suggest that such forms and delays are necessary to guard the person and property of the citizen, that the discretion of a judge is the first engine of tyranny, and that the laws of a free people should foresee and determine every question that may probably arise in the exercise of power and the transactions of industry (IV, xliv, p. 542).

The figure who becomes the exemplary consciousness, the proper analogy to the historian, is the literary man who must act publicly. In the course of the *Decline and Fall* Gibbon generally turns aside from his narrative to note the presence of a literary figure. The presence of Longinus in the court of Zenobia, although perhaps not a historical fact, piques his curiosity: "The fame of Longinus, who was included among the numerous and perhaps innocent victims of her fear, will survive that of the queen who betrayed or the tyrant [Aurelian] who condemned him" (I, xi, p. 332). Similarly, Gibbon distinguishes Claudian in the court of Stilicho, while the western Empire disintegrates under the attacks of Alaric: "Among the train of dependents whose wealth and dignity attracted the notice of their own times, *our* curiosity is excited by the celebrated name of the poet Claudian" (III, xxx, pp. 297–98). The prefect Hadrian, whom Claudian satirized, may have brought about Claudian's death, " . . . but the name of Hadrian is almost sunk in oblivion, while Claudian is read with pleasure in every country which has retained, or acquired, the knowledge of the Latin language" (III, xxx, p. 299). Two separate urges may be distinguished here: the responsibility to the public facts of the time and the acknowledgement of the judgment of posterity, which values a man for his creative power. But in a footnote to his account of Claudian, Gibbon turns about to mourn the loss of some books of antiquarian interest composed by the poet: "It is more easy to supply the loss of good poetry than of authentic history" (III, xxx, p. 300 n121).

Gibbon attempts to reconcile these two urges by finding figures who can combine them more fully. Boethius, for example, is an attractive figure for the historian who seeks to relate political and literary ability; and Gibbon views him in this light. He praises Boethius as a classicist, philosopher, and beyond: "From these abstruse speculations, Boethius stooped, or, to speak more truly, he rose to the social duties of public and private life: the indigent were relieved by his liberality; and his eloquence, which flattery might compare to the voice of Demosthenes or Cicero, was uniformly exerted in the cause of innocence and humanity" (IV, xxxix, p. 213).

Gibbon says that the example of Boethius shows the need for private goodness to be applied to public office. He distinguishes between Boethius' point of view and that of a Cato, who believes his contribution to public life is his inflexible moral standard, while actually, says Gibbon, he often confounds "private enmities with public justice" (IV, xxxix, p. 214). Boethius' contribution to public life results from his position as a private man with literary ability and a literary viewpoint. After this exploration of the importance of Boethius, Gibbon moves naturally to say of Samosata, for example, that it is "more famous for the birth of Lucian than for the title of a Syrian kingdom" (VI, liv, p. 117). However true this may be, the fact that Gibbon needs to make such an assertion implies his newly defined standard of value. Where previous comparisons to the heroic political events of the past might seem warranted, Gibbon can now make comparisons of another kind: "The revolution of human affairs had produced in Apulia and Calabria a melancholy contrast between the age of Pythagoras and the tenth century of the Christian era" (VI, lvi, p. 178).

The culmination of such comparisons occurs in the final chapters, with the contrast between Cola di Rienzi and Petrarch, and the final figure of Poggius, the Renaissance humanist, author of an "elegant dialogue on the vicissitudes of fortune" (VII, lxv, p. 65), sitting, like Gibbon, on the Capitoline Hill and viewing the ruins of Rome. Rienzi and Petrarch attempt to revive classical Rome, in politics and literature. Both have an acute sense of the past, and both eagerly take part in the coronation of Petrarch as poet laureate amid the ruins of the Forum: "In the act or diploma which was presented to Petrarch, the title and prerogatives of poet-laureate are revived in the Capitol, after the lapse of thirteen hundred years . . ." (VII, lxx, p. 268). Like Gibbon, they appreciate both the heritage of the past and the need to use the past to renovate the present. Rienzi exclaims, "Where are now these Romans? their virtue, their justice, their power? why was I not born in those happy times?" (VII, lxx, p. 270). He further attracts Gibbon's attention because he is plebeian in origin and an example therefore of the energy with which the barbarians might have restored the Empire: "Never, perhaps, has the energy and effect of a single mind been more remarkably felt than in the sudden, though transient, reformation of Rome by the Tribune Rienzi" (VII, lxx, p. 275).ʷ

But despite his own sympathy for the efforts of Petrarch and Rienzi, Gibbon never relinquishes the historical perspective that qualified his praise of Julian. Rienzi is deficient by real Roman standards, as Gibbon applies them (VII, lxx, p. 282). By his participation in public affairs his ideals are compromised; and when he cuts himself off from the vital spirit that nourished him, his power gradually becomes frenzy. Rienzi assumes all the flummery of public life, and Gibbon chronicles his decline through the metaphor of a flashing meteor and the descriptions of his elaborate public costumes: " . . . without acquiring the majesty, Rienzi degenerated into the vices, of a king" (VII, lxx, p. 282).

Petrarch himself was not unscathed by the experience. After the death of Rienzi, he attempted to restore Rome by having Charles IV, the Holy Roman Emperor, rule the city. But this method was doomed to failure. Like Rienzi, Petrarch did not fully understand the progress of time and the elements of the past that were irredeemably past: "A false application of the names and maxims of antiquity was the source of the hopes and disappointments of Petrarch; yet he could not overlook the difference of time and characters; the immeasurable distance between the first Caesars and a Bohemian prince, who by the favour of the clergy had been elected the titular head of the German aristocracy" (VII, lxx, p. 291).

w Interestingly enough, Gibbon compares Rienzi's ability to assume command to Cromwell's: "It was thus that Oliver Cromwell's old acquaintance, who remembered his vulgar and ungracious entrance into the House of Commons, were astonished at the ease and majesty of the Protector on the throne. . . . The consciousness of merit and power will sometimes elevate the manners to the station" (VII, lxx, pp. 277–78 n32).

Petrarch next tried to restore the pope from Avignon to Rome and at least preserve the Roman administrative model. Then, as far as the *Decline and Fall* is concerned, the stream of Petrarch's personal history is lost in the sands of the Babylonian captivity. Gibbon points out that Petrarch's understanding was not clear enough to encompass both the change from the old to the new Rome, and the similarities between them. But the inadequacies of Petrarch's understanding do provide a backdrop for Gibbon's final attempt to distinguish the genius and special nature of the "true" historian. Tradition and the wisdom of the ancients can be as binding as they can be liberating. The scattered allusions in the *Decline and Fall* to the creative literary genius finally focus on his ability to integrate ancient and modern wisdom, much the same synthesis in practice that Gibbon developed theoretically in the *Essai*.[x] The individual lives within time, and understands its force, through the power of his own mind. Man actually engages in and creates history, in the past, present, and future. The training of the historian is not specialized, but can stand for the growth in perception of any single person or nation: "Genius may anticipate the season of maturity; but in the education of a people, as in that of an individual, memory must be exercised, before the powers of reason and fancy can be expanded: nor may the artist hope to equal or surpass, till he had learned to imitate, the works of his predecessors" (VII, lxvi, p. 137).

"The sportive play of fancy and learning" Gibbon calls the process by which the factual and the creative spirits are combined. At his first introduction Petrarch is a great lit-

---

[x] This interesting change from the 1776 to the 1782 quarto edition, quoted by Bury (I, p. 508), might be apposite: 1st ed. ". . . but if we except the inimitable Lucian, *an* age of indolence passed away without *producing* a single writer of genius, *who deserved the attention of posterity*"; 2d ed. ". . . but if we except the inimitable Lucian, *this* age of indolence passed away without *having produced* a single writer of *original* genius, *or who excelled in the arts of elegant composition*" (Bury's italics). This contrast between creative and rhetorical abilities marks a change from earlier statements. Gibbon might have taken with poor grace our lavish praise of his style.

erary figure who exemplifies the classical revival in the Renaissance. As he enters more and more into political life, so he increasingly compromises his talents. It is finally not Petrarch but the historian himself who emerges as the figure who can combine political acumen with literary ability. This conclusion is not an abrupt insult to Petrarch, but a subtly prepared argument. In the first lines about Petrarch, Gibbon personally disclaims the Italian veneration for Petrarch's works: "Whatever may be the private taste of a stranger, his slight and superficial knowledge should humbly acquiesce in the judgment of a learned nation; yet I may hope or presume that the Italians do not compare the tedious uniformity of sonnets and elegies with the sublime compositions of their epic muse, the original wildness of Dante, the regular beauties of Tasso, and the boundless variety of the incomparable Ariosto" (VII, lxx, p. 265).

The appropriate epic sweep is, of course, to be found in the *Decline and Fall*. And the new epic hero is the human consciousness that can organize and control the disparate and often chaotic elements that form the onrushing flow of time. Gibbon's praise of literary men strengthens his own positions as the literary historian, the "stranger" with "private taste." His remarks on Spenser and Fielding in the *Memoirs* bear out this identification: "The nobility of the Spencers has been illustrated and enriched by the trophies of Marlborough; but I exhort them to consider *The Faery Queen* as the most precious jewel of their coronet. . . ."[y] The literary consciousness is superior not only to the momentary grandeur of public exploits, but also to one of the most longlived of European institutions. Gibbon relates the (actually fallacious) genealogy that made Fielding a relation of the Habsburgs and then concludes: "The successors of Charles the fifth may disdain their brethren of England, but the Romance of Tom Jones, that exquisite picture of human manners will outlive the palace

[y] Compare Bolingbroke's view that Marlborough was the prime, perhaps the only, example of a private man who selflessly contributed to the public good. See above, pp. 23–24.

of the Escurial and the Imperial Eagle of the house of Austria" (*Memoirs*, p. 5; Saunders, pp. 29–30).

The final impression the reader keeps of the *Decline and Fall* is of the mind which created it, which has worked on it for twenty years, and which now delivers it "to the curiosity and candour of the public" (VII, lxxi, p. 388). History is what this mind has made of the past. Gibbon's true optimism in the *Decline and Fall* rests not in any case he makes for "progress," but in his belief and demonstration that the human mind is capable of imposing order on the flux and arbitrary movement of time. For Marvell's static sundial of flowers, Gibbon substitutes a moving and shaping force that liberates as well as designs. In the midst of a Heraclitean world, he can appreciate and even exult in the world's variety and multiplicity. It is no wonder that in his concluding pages Gibbon can review the work of man for fifteen hundred years and conclude that "the noblest and most important victory which man has obtained over the licentiousness of nature" has been "the servitude of rivers" (VII, lxxi, p. 320).

Appendix

MEMOIRS OF MY LIFE:
THE SHAPE OF THE IMMEDIATE

IN THE *Decline and Fall* Gibbon works out problems of presentation and explanation in ways that reflect literary methods as often as they embody historiological assumptions. In the *Memoirs* certain important ideas about history as the continuing process of human life receive a greater emphasis, which can throw into relief some of the themes discussed above. These themes, principally, are Gibbon's ideas of chance and character.

The whole of the *Memoirs* is imbued with a radical sense of contingency in human affairs and the workings of time, especially in terms of individual fate: "My lot might have been that of a slave, a savage or a peasant; nor can I reflect without pleasure on the bounty of Nature, which cast my birth in a free and civilized country, in an age of science and Philosophy, in a family of honourable rank and decently endowed with the gifts of fortune" (p. 24 n; Saunders, p. 49).

Passages like this one are often adduced as support for an estimate of Gibbon's optimistic, if not fatuous, pleasure in the accomplishments of the eighteenth century. But such passages also link with many similar ones that stress the operations of chance instead of its consequences. Introductory phrases like "If not for . . . " and "I might have . . ." appear often in the work. Gibbon's preoccupation in the *Decline and Fall* with the arbitrary workings of time and circumstance make him more appreciative of beneficial effects in a world that is too immediate for complete literary control. It strengthens the feeling that the *Decline and Fall* is conceived as a retrospective order which does not imply anything about man's ability to control or order the present.[1] Gibbon remarks on his meeting and subsequent friendship with Sheffield: "Our lives are in the power of chance, and a slight variation, on either side, in time or place might have deprived me of a friend, whose activity in the ardour of youth was always prompted by a benevolent heart, and directed by a strong understanding" (p. 131; Saunders, p. 149).

At the end of the *Memoirs* Gibbon again sounds this theme by concluding that he has "drawn high prize in the lottery of life" and proceeds to demonstrate his good fortune statistically.[a] The retrospective time of the *Decline and Fall* can be manipulated with more success than can the immediacies of human life. But even though life may be largely a matter of chance, it is also an opportunity to exercise human intelligence and perception. When we contemplate the massive and ordered bulk of the *Decline and Fall*, we should be able to see it as the work of a man who could write not long after its completion:

> The present is a fleeting moment; the past is no more; and our prospect of futurity is dark and doubtful. This day may *possibly* be my last: but the laws of probability, so true in general, so fallacious in particular, still allow me about fifteen years . . . (p. 188; Saunders, pp. 206–07).

The way out of this dilemma is the same in the *Memoirs* as it appears to be in the *Decline and Fall*. The historian can understand the past by bringing a variety of methodological and theoretical approaches to his material. Man can work well in time by being able to assume various roles that are especially suited to different situations. Through the idea of role, Gibbon tries to relate individuals and the historical times to which they belong. He attributes a capacity for creative artifice to his characters at least equal to that which he supposes for himself, as man and historian. Gibbon uses the idea of roles where a later historian might adduce the various capacities of original genius. Consider the

---

[a] Compare Fielding's remarks on "the grand lottery of time" and his own role as one of the "registers of the lottery" (*Tom Jones*, II, i, p. 65).

difference between Gibbon's and Carlyle's estimates of Guischardt, the author of *Mémoires Militaires*:

> *Gibbon*: "the only writer who has united the merits of a professor and a veteran."
> *Carlyle*: "The first man who ever understood both war and Greek."[2]

Gibbon foreshadows this formulation of character when he says in the *Essai* that original genius is developed through the reading of literature: "*cette habitude de devenir, tour-à-tour, Grec, Romain, disciple de Zénon ou d'Épicure*" (p. 237). The construction of life can be accomplished by the same tools of understanding used in the construction of history. But it will not be equally successful. The true mark of a complete consciousness, in the knowledge of self and the knowledge of others, is the ability to distinguish the appropriate roles for the time, and to form them into an integrated rather than a fragmented personality. Gibbon's remark that a psychologically atomistic account is unable to do justice "to the solitary of Mount Hera, to the preacher of Mecca, and to the conqueror of Arabia" has many echoes in the *Decline and Fall*. It also has stylistic echoes when the doublet that pairs possibilities turns into a parallel ordering that stresses the discernment, but not the reduction, of multiple motivation. Here is Gibbon's estimate of Louis IX: "The voice of history renders a more honourable testimony [than his sainthood], that he united the virtues of a king, an hero, and a man; that his martial spirit was tempered by the love of private and public justice; and that Louis was the father of his people, the friend of his neighbours, and the terror of the infidels" (VI, lix, p. 374).

Such estimates give new relevance and context to the famous moment in the *Memoirs* when Gibbon describes his response to his father's desire that he terminate his relation with Suzanne Curchod: "I sighed as a lover; I obeyed as a son." His full consciousness of his own situation is expressed in the claims of the different roles.

ℕotes

ONE. Introduction

¹ These issues and others are perceptively explored by Robert W. Hanning in *The Vision of History in Early Britain* (New York, 1966). For the problem of history versus fiction, see especially the chapter on Geoffrey of Monmouth. A provocative discussion of similar problems is contained in William Brandt, *The Shape of Medieval History* (New Haven, 1966).

² Felix Gilbert makes a distinction between the use of documentary sources as a mere convenience and as a methodological innovation (*Machiavelli and Guicciardini* [Princeton, 1965], p. 224). In writing a classically sanctioned history of a city-state, the early humanists, says Gilbert, turned naturally to readily accessible chancery material. Factual accuracy as a standard was first asserted by Guicciardini (pp. 231, 246). Eugenio Garin in *Italian Humanism*, tr. Peter Munz (New York, 1965), cites Speron Speroni's *Dialogo delle lingue* (1552): "He reduced history to a description of the particular and described the particular as *truth*, reported by the historian with the help of rhetorical artistry" (p. 183). In addition to these books, I have found particularly helpful in understanding the humanist attitude toward history two essays by Myron P. Gilmore: "The Renaissance Conception of the Lessons of History" and "Individualism in Renaissance Historians," both contained in *Humanists and Jurists* (Harvard, 1963); the first is also in *Facets of the Renaissance*, ed. W. K Werkmeister (New York, 1959). The classic work is of course Theodor E. Mommsen, "Petrarch's Conception of the Dark Ages," *Speculum, 17* (1942), pp. 226–42. B. L. Ullman calls Bruni "the first modern historian" in "Leonardo Bruni and Humanistic Historiography," *Studies in the Italian Renaissance* (Roma, 1955), pp. 321–44, for his critical use of source material. But Ullman glosses over any distinction between accurate recovery of ancient texts, use of documentary sources, and theoretical commitment to factual accuracy: ". . . the humanist's curiosity led him to search far and wide for correct historical data as he did for correct textual readings" (p. 322). For the background of antiquarianism in England see *English Historical Scholarship in the Sixteenth and Seventeenth Centuries*, ed. Levi Fox (London, 1956) and David Douglas, *English Scholars, 1660-1730* (London, 1939). A recent survey that concentrates on historiography in the English Renaissance is Herschel Baker, *The Race of Time* (Toronto, 1967). For the eighteenth-century background see especially R. N. Stromberg, "History in the Eighteenth Century,"

JHI, *12* (1951), pp. 295-304 and H. R. Trevor-Roper, "The Historical Philosophy of the Enlightenment," *Studies on Voltaire and the Eighteenth Century*, 27 (1963), pp. 1667-87.

3 For the claims of factual truth and moral relevance in the theory of the novel see Joseph P. Heidler, *The History, from 1700 to 1800, of English Criticism of Prose Fiction, Illinois Studies in Language and Literature*, *13* (1928), chs. I-III. Samuel Kliger deals with eighteenth-century theories of the common origin of fiction and romance in the Orient. See *The Goths in England* (Cambridge, Massachusetts, 1952), pp. 210–40.

4 For Gibbon's place in the history of source criticism, see Arnaldo Momigliano, "Gibbon's Contribution to Historical Method," *Studies in Historiography* (New York, 1966), pp. 40-55.

5 Carl Becker, *The Heavenly City of the Eighteenth-Century Philosophers* (New Haven, 1932).

6 J. B. Black, *The Art of History* (London, 1926). Becker's thesis has, of course, been chipped away by many studies. Black's analysis of Voltaire, Hume, Robertson, and Gibbon has fewer competitors.

7 For a wide-ranging account of the background of historical theory in England and on the Continent and its influence on eighteenth-century English thought, see J. W. Johnson, *The Formation of English Neo-Classical Thought* (Princeton, 1967).

8 *Ductor Historicus: or, A Short System of Universal History, and An Introduction to the Study of it*, second edition, 2 vols. (London, 1705), I, p. 113. Further references will be included in the text.

9 J.G.A. Pocock in *The Ancient Constitution and the Feudal Law* (Cambridge, England, 1957; new edition, New York, 1967) examines the idea of the "immemorial" common law and the way it affected the English sense of the past. An interesting discussion of providential interpretations of history in the seventeenth century is contained in Herschel Baker, *The Wars of Truth* (Cambridge, Massachusetts, 1952). A fuller account is given in C. A. Patrides, *The Phoenix and the Ladder: The Rise and Decline of the Christian View of History* (Berkeley and Los Angeles, 1964); an abridged version of these remarks also appears in Patrides's *Milton and the Christian Tradition* (Oxford, 1966), chapter 8.

10 The prevalence of these commonplaces is discussed by Herschel Baker in *The Race of Time* and by David Douglas in *English Scholars*.

TWO. *Clarendon and Bolingbroke*

1 For the biographical background of *The History of the Rebellion*, see C. H. Firth, *Essays Historical and Literary* (Oxford, 1938), B.H.G. Wormald, *Clarendon* (Cambridge, England, 1951), and H. R. Trevor-

Roper, "Clarendon and the Practice of History," in *Milton and Clarendon* by French Fogle and H. R. Trevor-Roper (Los Angeles, 1965).

2 Trevor-Roper makes this point in a different fashion: "Clarendon accepted the form of society and government that he had inherited, valued it as the vehicle of culture and tradition, and refused to believe that, simply because it was the illogical creature of time and custom, it was therefore incapable of absorbing social strains, or expanding to embrace new developments" ("Clarendon," p. 42).

3 Wormald argues that Clarendon's view of history contains an idea of process and change because he saw historical events through the developing perspective of his own point of view: "The Remonstrance was a turning-point in events largely because it was a turning-point for Hyde himself. . . . The setback to the cause of peace was less decisive than the setback to himself" (*Clarendon*, p. 31). But this view allows too little weight to the possibility that Clarendon was quite conscious of what he was doing and the connections he was making.

4 Trevor-Roper suggests that Clarendon may even have been deluded by the "historical" look of his documents: ". . . he comments [on] the documents (which are documents of propaganda) instead of [on] the facts which they conceal" ("Clarendon," p. 29).

5 The remark is Bacon's, in *The Advancement of Learning*. See also Herbert Davis, "The Augustan Conception of History," in J. A. Mazzeo, ed., *Reason and the Imagination* (New York, 1962), p. 214.

6 J.Y.T. Greig, ed., *The Letters of David Hume*, 2 vols. (Oxford, 1932), I, p. 170.

7 This and much other information about the historiography of the period is contained in Dorothy A. Koch, "English Theories Concerning the Nature and Uses of History, 1735-1791," Yale Ph.D. diss., 1946. See also Johnson, *English Neo-Classical Thought* and Douglas, *English Scholars*.

8 Smollett's *History* treated the period from Julius Caesar to the treaty of Aix-la-Chapelle (1748). From 1760 to 1765 he published a five-volume history of England from the Glorious Revolution to the death of George II. Designed to be a continuation of Hume's *History*, this later work was usually bound with Hume's in a single volume. After Smollett's death, anonymous writers would periodically increase its chronological scope.

9 Koch, p. 73.

10 Although Hume disliked Bolingbroke, he knew his works. Most of the references to Bolingbroke in Hume's letters are slights. See especially a letter of 24 October 1754 to the Abbé Le Blanc (Greig, *Letters*, I, p. 208). Fielding owned a copy of Bolingbroke's *Letters on History* (listed as item 503 in the sale catalogue of his library), as well as a volume listed as "Bolingbroke's Letters on Patriotism, 1749"

(item 243), probably the edition that includes "On the Idea of a Patriot King" and "On the State of Parties at the Accession of George the First." Fielding comments somewhat ambiguously on Bolingbroke's recently published *Works* in an incomplete piece that is probably his last writing ("A Fragment of a Comment on L. Bolingbroke's Essays"). Austin Dobson has taken this essay to be an attack on Bolingbroke, an interpretation that seems strained at best. The essay is a complicated, inflated, almost self-consciously silly work that seems like an overlong joke, perhaps first conceived as a stylistic parody. See Henry Fielding, *Journal of a Voyage to Lisbon*, ed. and intro. Austin Dobson (Oxford, 1907). Dobson's view is supported by Wilbur Cross and F. Homes Dudden, who generally follow Arthur Murphy's account of Fielding's indignant attack against Bolingbroke's "impiety." See Murphy's life of Fielding prefaced to many collected editions; Wilbur L. Cross, *The History of Henry Fielding*, 3 vols. (New Haven, 1918); F. Homes Dudden, *Henry Fielding, His Life, Works, and Times*, 2 vols. (Oxford, 1952).

The possibility exists that through the agency of George, Lord Lyttelton, a mutual friend, both Hume and Fielding may have seen the 1738 edition of the *Letters on History*, privately printed by Alexander Pope. For Lyttelton's possession of an original copy, see George H. Nadel, "New Light on Bolingbroke's 'Letters on History,' " *JHI, 23* (1962), pp. 550-57. For Hume's associations with Lyttelton, see the many references in his letters: Greig, *Letters*; Raymond Klibansky and Ernest C. Mossner, eds., *New Letters of David Hume* (Oxford, 1954). *Tom Jones* is, of course, dedicated to Lyttelton. For Fielding's earlier associations with him since they were at Eton together, see Cross and Dudden.

11 For an important statement of this idea that Bolingbroke may have been familiar with, see John Locke, *Some Thoughts Concerning Education* (London, 1705), pp. 331-35. An informative account of the history of this attitude after Locke appears in Dorothy Koch's third chapter, "History as the Proper Study for the Gentleman," pp. 151-227.

12 *The Life of Reason: Hobbes, Locke, Bolingbroke* (London, 1949), p. 200. James generally follows Douglas, *English Scholars*, pp. 273-74, 277, in his charge.

13 *The Works of Lord Bolingbroke*, 4 vols. (Philadelphia, 1841), III, p. 17. Bolingbroke seems to imply a distinction between the contemporary and the retrospective historian. Compare, for example, Swift's presentation of his credentials as an unbiased and "constant witness and observer" in *The History of the Four Last Years of the Queen*, vol. 7, *The Prose Works of Jonathan Swift*, ed. Herbert Davis (Oxford, 1951). Swift mentions his use of documents and other original sources. But he does not therefore say that his work pretends to ab-

solute truth. It is still "my own opinion." Bolingbroke and Hume tend to believe the contemporary observer without noticeable qualification or criticism, once corroboration of a sort has been made. Gibbon is not so trusting; see below, page 221, note f.

14 D. G. James does not believe that Bolingbroke's treatment of history gives it any preference over poetry (*The Life of Reason*, p. 199).

15 For a brilliant exposition of similar ideas in another context, see the suggestive essay by William L. Hedges, "Knickerbocker, Bolingbroke, and the Fiction of History," *JHI, 20* (1959), pp. 317–28. Hedges argues that Washington Irving set out to write in *Knickerbocker* a history that emphasized the underlying chaos rather than the imposed pattern. He cites as evidence the presence of large transcribed sections of the *Letters on History* in Irving's commonplace book.

16 Another possibility, perhaps complementary to this one, is that, because of his personal involvement in the Treaty of Utrecht (which concludes his sketch), Bolingbroke wishes to emphasize the objective validity of what he did. See Jeffrey Hart, *Viscount Bolingbroke* (London, 1965), pp. 37–38.

THREE. Hume: The Structure of the Past

1 See "My Own Life," the short autobiography prefixed to most editions of the *History* and often reprinted, most recently by Ralph Cohen in *Essential Works of David Hume* (New York, 1956), pp. 2–9.

2 Greig, *Letters*, I, p. 179.

3 *Essays and Treatises on Several Subjects*, a new ed. (London, 1758), p. 297. I have also used this volume as the source for Hume's essays.

4 *Essays*, p. 294.

5 *The Art of History*, pp. 98–99. Compare J. R. Hale, *The Evolution of British Historiography* (New York, 1964), p. 21: "By the time of Hume the 'character' had degenerated into a mechanical balancing of virtues against vices. . . ."

6 *The Idea of History* (New York, 1956), pp. 75–76. For attempts to qualify or refute this argument see Ernest C. Mossner, "An Apology for David Hume, Historian," *PMLA, 56* (1941), pp. 657–90; P. H. Meyer, "Voltaire and Hume as Historians: A Comparative Study of *Essai sur les Moeurs* and the *History of England*," *PMLA, 73* (1958), pp. 51–68. Although Meyer asserts Hume's complete awareness of psychological complexity in his characters, he seems uncertain in judging specific cases. He says, for example, that Hume ". . . is content to let the different facts of [Elizabeth's] personality stand side by side." In the character of Mary, however, Hume is so conscious of contradictory evidence about her conduct ". . . that he somewhat unsuccessfully attempts to include and reconcile all points of view in his judgment"

(p. 55). Meyer then proceeds to accept partially some of Black's strictures.

7 *Letters on History*, pp. 137–38.

8 *Essays*, p. 85.

9 See, for example, Greig, *Letters*, I, p. 379.

10 Ms. note on the first volume of Gibbon's *Decline and Fall*. Quoted by E. C. Mossner, "Was Hume a Tory Historian? Facts and Reconsiderations," *JHI*, 2 (1941), p. 230. Compare D. M. Low, *Edward Gibbon, 1737–1794* (London, 1937), p. 201.

11 *The Whig Interpretation of History* (London, 1931), pp. 11, 39, 49–50, 64–65.

12 For a comparison of Hume's *History* with Voltaire's *Siècle de Louis XIV*, see E. C. Mossner, "An Apology for David Hume." P. H. Meyer in his intelligent and discerning article, "Voltaire and Hume as Historians," believes that *Essai sur les Moeurs* is a more apt comparison. Koch, "English Theories of History," tries to make a case for a slim sense of historical relativism in Bolingbroke, although she confines it primarily to his appreciation of the customs and superstitions of other ages and lands.

13 See Shirley Letwin, *The Pursuit of Certainty* (Cambridge, England, 1965), p. 76. Compare E. C. Mossner, "An Apology for Hume": ". . . the chief defect in Hume as historiographer, in contradistinction to Voltaire, is that he nowhere once and for all sets down together all his attitudes judiciously systematized" (p. 660).

14 *Essays*, p. 70.

15 See Benjamin Boyce, *The Theophrastan Character in England to 1642* (Cambridge, Massachusetts, 1947).

16 See his introductory essay to *Characters from the Histories and Memoirs of the Seventeenth Century* (Oxford, 1918). Boyce mentions that John Earle was a member of the Great Tew group at Falkland's estate, as was Clarendon *(Theophrastan Character*, p. 236).

17 See, for example, Nichol Smith, *Characters of the Seventeenth Century*, xvi-xvii. Compare Hume, V, lxii, p. 532: "He is less partial in his relation of facts, than in his account of characters: he was too honest a man to falsify the former; his affections were easily capable, unknown to himself, of disguising the latter."

18 Greig, *Letters*, I, p. 216.

19 See Ernst Kantorowitz, *The King's Two Bodies* (Princeton, 1957). For a discussion of this theory as it affects seventeenth-century poetry and politics, see the 1965 Yale Ph.D. dissertation by Peter M. Hughes, "'The Monarch's and the Muse's Seats': Stuart Kingship and Poetry of the Royal Estate."

20 "Voltaire's chapters on *moeurs* are among his most brilliant; Hume's register his most signal failure" (J. B. Black, *Art of History*, p. 115).

21 Greig, *Letters*, I, p. 237; dated "1756."

22 He makes the same distinction in "Of the Parties of Great Britain," *Essays*, pp. 41–47.

23 Addison Ward characterizes this interpretation: "Caesar's whole career is read in the light of his usurpation as a fully formulated campaign toward the kingship." See "The Tory View of Roman History," *SEL*, *4* (1964), p. 430.

24 Greig, *Letters*, I, p. 193. Compare Hume's remarks about the partisan treatment of the character of Walpole, *Essays*, p. 17.

25 *Essays*, pp. 324–25.

26 *Essays*, p. 329.

27 *Essays*, p. 17.

28 Greig, *Letters*, I, p. 139.

29 "That Politics May Be Reduced to a Science," *Essays*, p. 12.

30 J. B. Black asserts that the portrait of Luther concentrates on temperament to the exclusion of beliefs and merely enumerates vices and virtues. Like all of Hume's "characters," Luther is "not a real person, but a dexterously poised, mechanically sustained assemblage of divergent, disconnected, or conflicting qualities" (*Art of History*, p. 99).

31 In *The Hero in History* (New York, 1943) Hook distinguishes between "eventful" and "event-making" men. The former, of whom Napoleon is an example, step into, focus, and command an existing situation; the latter, exemplified by Lenin, actually change history by their actions.

32 See, for example, IV, xlii, pp. 229, 237.

33 See, for example, III, xxvii, p. 99. Compare Hume's belief in the philosophical truth to be found in detachment in *The Natural History of Religion*, ed. H. E. Root (Stanford, California, 1957): "Every bystander will easily judge (but unfortunately the bystanders are few) . . ." (p. 57).

34 Spelman's biography of Alfred, first published in 1709 by Hearne, popularized the notion of Alfred as both great warrior and great scholar, perhaps making him the ideal man for the philosopher-historian perplexed by the relation of contemplation and action. Hume's admiration for Alfred may be then a strong qualification of the value of the philosophical retreat from life counselled by Hume at the end of *The Natural History of Religion* (1757).

35 See letter of 29 January 1748; Greig, *Letters*, I, p. 109.

36 This belief occurs early in his life. See E. C. Mossner on a school exercise by Hume: "David Hume's 'An Historical Essay on Chivalry and Modern Honour,'" *MP*, *45* (1947), pp. 54–60. Hume could praise chivalry, however, when he believed that it had helped to foster amiable character traits, as in the Black Prince (II, xvi, p. 246).

[37] J. B. Black does not think that Hume ever departs very much from the political and military narrative (*Art of History*, p. 86).

[38] *Oeuvres Complètes de Voltaire*, 52 vols. (Paris, 1877–85), XXV, p. 173. Compare Joseph de Maistre: "Son venim glacé est bien plus dangereux que la rage écumante de Voltaire. . . ." Quoted in an anonymous review of *David Hume: Prophet of the Counter-Revolution* by Laurence L. Bongie in *TLS* (7 July 1966), p. 593.

[39] *The Spectator*, ed. Donald F. Bond, 5 vols. (Oxford, 1965), #170, II, p. 171.

[40] Compare on this point the observation of Shirley Letwin that Hume's generalizations are couched in terms of probability, not necessity, and are presented as maxims, not laws (*Quest for Certainty*, p. 91).

[41] See, for example, I, vi, pp. 254–55.

[42] It would be interesting to study how the effects of factional violence are reflected in Hume's attitudes. His letters and essays are filled with general assumptions that seem to result directly, and even exclusively, from his observations of his own times. In "Whether the British Government inclines more to Absolute Monarchy, or to a Republic," for example, he argues that if parliament would dissolve itself for regular elections, there would be a civil war each time (*Essays*, p. 35).

[43] *Essays*, p. 57.

[44] Greig, *Letters*, II, p. 310.

FOUR. Fielding: Public History and Individual Perception

[1] The sale catalogue was first discovered by Austin Dobson. A copy of it appears in the appendix to Ethel M. Thornbury's *Henry Fielding's Theory of the Comic Prose Epic, University of Wisconsin Studies, 30* (1931). There is an alphabetic arrangement done by Frederick S. Dickson in the Beinecke Library at Yale. For an account of the libraries of Congreve, Addison, Swift, Garrick, and Johnson, see J. W. Johnson, *English Neo-Classical Thought*, p. 271 n14.

[2] Robert M. Wallace, in his 1945 unpublished University of North Carolina Ph.D. dissertation, "Henry Fielding's Narrative Method: Its Historical and Biographical Origins," includes an extensive list of all references in the novels and periodical writings to historians and biographers.

[3] The anonymous author of *An Essay on the New Species of Writing Founded by Mr. Fielding* supports this view: "As this sort of Writing was intended as a Contrast to those in which the Reader was even to suppose all the Characters ideal, and every Circumstance quite imaginary, 'twas thought necessary to give it a greater Air of Truth, to entitle it *an History* . . ." (ed. Alan D. McKillop, *Augustan Reprint*

Society, *95* [1962], p. 18). Wilbur Cross thinks that the author is Francis Coventry, but McKillop disagrees.

4 Wilbur Cross, for example, asserts that Fielding called *Tom Jones* a "history" because "many of its characters were drawn from real men and women [and] many of its incidents had come within his observation" (*History of Henry Fielding*, II, p. 161). Ethel M. Thornbury supports the other interpretation: "Time and again Fielding insists that he is the historian. He did not mean, of course, that he was writing a history of his own times in terms of battles or political struggles. But he obviously meant, among other things, that he was the historian of modern manners in contrast to the manners of former days" (*Fielding's Theory of the Comic Prose Epic*, p. 13). Ronald Paulson, in his recent *Satire and the Novel in Eighteenth-Century England* (New Haven, 1967), says that "history" in *Tom Jones* implies "detachment and larger perspective" (p. 154). On this basis he asserts the similarity of Hume and Fielding.

5 Robert M. Wallace concentrates so much on "history" defined as factual accuracy that Fielding emerges as a misguided biographer or historian rather than a novelist: "Specifically he was moving toward the style of those who depended on first-hand knowledge. . . . Though neither they nor he overlooked available written sources, all relied chiefly on information gathered by word of mouth, by observation, and by personal correspondence." Wallace considers Fielding's narrative voice to be an authority by which Fielding vouches for the truth of his sources and observations: "Fielding's shift to the entirely respectable personal standard of accuracy was accompanied by an inconsistent admission that, after all, his stories were fiction. . . . Theoretically, the conflict in attitude is irreconcilable" ("Henry Fielding's Narrative Method," pp. 402, 494–95).

6 Philip Stevick, in "Fielding and the Meaning of History," *PMLA*, *79* (1964), pp. 561–68, believes that Fielding's idea of history is exuberantly eclectic and committed primarily to the concept of historical progress. He broadly assumes that Fielding had the "whig interpretation of history," an assertion readily contradicted by Fielding's many remarks on party history. Stevick finally subsumes Fielding's view of history into a concept of comedy much like Northrop Frye's. He thereby concludes that there is no important or extensive satire in Fielding's novels. The presence of satire would make a "generic distortion" of *Tom Jones* (p. 566). The exuberance of comedy must, for Stevick, be related to a belief in progress. But his invocation of genres finally becomes too confusing, and Stevick never differentiates between a progress toward individual human perfection like that Fielding mentions in *Covent-Garden Journal* #29 and a generally teleological view of history.

7 This view is exemplified in Martin Battestin's *The Moral Basis of*

Fielding's Art: A Study of "Joseph Andrews" (Middletown, Connecticut, 1959).

8 *The Journal of a Voyage to Lisbon*, intro. A. R. Humphreys (London, 1964), pp. 185–86. The *Journal* is bound with *Jonathan Wild* in this edition. Ronald Paulson says that this passage "could be an echo of Hume" (*Satire and the Novel*, p. 154).

9 Fielding's objections to *Pamela* often seem to involve questions of form rather than matter. William Coley and Martin C. Battestin have recently criticized the belief that *Joseph Andrews* was originally an attack against the morality of *Pamela* and only later struck off on its own. See "The Background of Fielding's Laughter," *ELH, 26* (1959), pp. 229–52; "Fielding's Revisions of *Joseph Andrews*," *Studies in Bibliography, 16* (1963), pp. 81–117. In a quite recent full-scale treatment of Fielding, Andrew Wright says that *Joseph Andrews* is "its own novel from the beginning . . . [and] the coherent expressions of an experienced author's intention." See *Henry Fielding, Mask and Feast* (London, 1965), p. 58. Ian Watt is a prominent supporter of the "reaction" theory of the writing of *Joseph Andrews*, perhaps in order to support his own idea that Richardson is artistically and theoretically superior. See *The Rise of the Novel* (Berkeley and Los Angeles, 1957), pp. 239–59.

10 A full account of the opinion that Fielding is the novelistic Hogarth may be found in Robert E. Moore, *Hogarth's Literary Relationships* (Minneapolis, 1948), pp. 77–161.

11 *The Covent-Garden Journal*, ed. Gerald E. Jensen, 2 vols. (New Haven, 1915), II, p. 50. Fielding's library contained nine separate editions of Lucian, which attest to his plans for a new translation proposed in this issue of the *Covent-Garden Journal*. Billy Booth gives such an edition a plug in *Amelia*, VIII, v, p. 75. Booth also here echoes Fielding's remark that Swift was the "English Lucian." For the translation plans and Fielding's relation with the Reverend William Young, who was his collaborator and general classical amanuensis, see Wilbur Cross, II, pp. 374, 434. Robert Levi Lind, in "Lucian and Fielding," *Classical Weekly, 29* (1936), pp. 84–86, discusses stylistic similarities and the common use of such satiric forms as the journey to Hell. Henry Knight Miller, in *Essays on Fielding's Miscellanies: A Commentary on Volume One* (Princeton, 1961), notes that both writers use techniques like the pose of naivete or mock innocence, the solemn detail in the midst of a fantastic narrative, and the scholarly treatment of dubious material. Most of Miller's remarks, however, remain on the level of style: ". . . the parenthesis and the afterthought or extension and the qualifying phrase are highly typical of [Fielding's] serious style and the source as well of some of his most delectable humor" (p. 381).

12 Henry Knight Miller refers to an analogy between "the controls that [Fielding and Lucian] used to maintain an ironic tie between the

worlds of historic truth and of fantasy" (*Fielding's Miscellanies*, p. 373).

[13] "How to Write History," p. 61.

[14] "How to Write History," p. 63.

[15] Aristotle comments on the difference between poetry and history in *Poetics*, ix and on the impersonality of the poet in *Poetics*, xxiv.

[16] For an earlier satire of antiquaries along similar lines, see *The Champion* for 8 December 1739 in *The Champion*, 2 vols. (London, 1741), I, pp. 69–73.

[17] Compare Andrew Wright, *Henry Fielding*, p. 122: "Fielding's admiration for Hogarth, his experience as a playwright, his knowledge of stagecraft . . . made possible the making of something new in fiction: novels which are a series of speaking pictures. . . ." Wright likes the prison scenes in *Amelia* best of the whole novel because they are Hogarthian. See below, p. 192. It is tempting to consider *Shamela* transitional in Fielding's practice; it translates stage methods of expressing hypocrisy into novel form. But by the time of *Joseph Andrews* hypocrisy is already presented as a more internalized force.

[18] *The Complete Works of Henry Fielding, Esq.*, ed. W. E. Henley, 16 vols. (New York, 1902), XIV, p. 289. The date is the speculation of Henry Knight Miller in *Fielding's Miscellanies*, p. 189. Miller believes that Fielding's acceptance of physiognomics vacillates until the *Journal to Lisbon* and compares his ideas to Addison's in *Spectator* #86 (*Fielding's Miscellanies*, p. 193 n67). Fielding's argument in this essay has many similarities with Pope's in *Moral Essay I*, published in 1734.

[19] William Gaunt gives a similar estimate of Hogarth in *A Concise History of English Painting* (New York, 1965), p. 57: "It was his achievement to give a comprehensive view of social life within the framework of moralistic and dramatic narrative, this creation of a world being far more important than the system of ethics or the tale involved."

[20] Ronald Paulson awards Adams the palm in this debate because, if we draw on their satiric exemplars, Adams is the impractical Quixote faced by the excessively practical innkeeper (*Satire and the Novel*, p. 119). But in terms of understanding and dealing with the world, the innkeeper is both as benevolent as Adams and yet more perceptive. Fielding constantly makes us aware of the need for practical knowledge as well as ideals.

[21] In the next scene Adams hears at an inn three opinions of the same man. He thinks three different men are being referred to. Because he cannot accept that each opinion may have some truth in it, he concludes that all three men are maliciously lying, either gratuitously or through personal interest. Because his view of the world is so extreme, it can easily turn into Wilson's. This incident may remind us of the historians with different views of human nature satirized by Fielding in III, i.

22 Critics often insist that Adams is a virtually unqualified positive character. Martin Battestin calls him the "incarnation" of the novel's theme of charity; Mark Spilka says that he is the "touchstone" of all its moral truth. See the Introduction to *Joseph Andrews* and *Shamela*; "Comic Resolution in Fielding's *Joseph Andrews,*" *Fielding,* ed. Ronald Paulson (Englewood Cliffs, New Jersey, 1962), pp. 59-68.

23 In the final scenes at Booby Hall, Adams appears "naked" himself, and becomes the test for Joseph, making the circle complete. Ronald Paulson calls such scenes "the touchstone structure" of *Joseph Andrews (Satire and the Novel)*; Spilka ("Comic Resolution in *Joseph Andrews*") uses the same term.

24 Spilka has an interesting discussion of this point in "Comic Resolution," p. 66. Martin Battestin reflects the estimate of many critics when he depicts Lady Booby as primarily an embodiment of ungoverned lust (Introduction to *Joseph Andrews* and *Shamela*, p. xxvii).

25 Andrew Wright is one of many critics who emphasize the picaresque structure of *Joseph Andrews*: "Unity is achieved in the fact of the journey itself" *(Henry Fielding,* p. 62). But even the character of Lazarillo de Tormes changes in the course of his travels.

26 Compare Thomas Gray's remark about *Joseph Andrews* in a letter to Richard West: "The incidents are ill-laid and without invention; but the characters have a great deal of nature, which always blesses even in her lowest shapes." See *The Correspondence of Thomas Gray,* ed. Paget Toynbee and Leonard Whibley, 3 vols. (Oxford, 1935), I, p. 191 (letter dated 8 April 1742). Although Gray is certainly wrong about the "invention" of the incidents, such a statement perfectly illustrates the relative value Fielding assigned to character and incident in *Joseph Andrews.*

27 The dates of the composition of *Joseph Andrews* and *Jonathan Wild* have usually posed a problem to both Fielding's biographers and critics. See, for example, Wilbur Cross, I, pp. 409–12 and William Robert Irwin, *The Making of Jonathan Wild* (New York, 1941). The *TLS* for 14 August 1943 contains a largely suppositious argument for dating *Jonathan Wild* earlier, based primarily on considerations of style: "On the whole, the work suffers from prolixity, and shows other signs of immaturity." In view of the counterpart relation that I argue exists between the two novels, I opportunistically seize upon this bibliographical uncertainty to support my point.

28 Irwin, in *The Making of Jonathan Wild,* assimilates it to Fielding's other novels and calls it "a popular allegorical presentation of a fundamentally moral problem" (p. 79) that follows Fielding's usual practice of transforming moral precept into example (p. 70). Irwin says that the novel is basically "an imperfect version of the comic epic in prose" (p. 95).

29 In order to extract a coherent moral structure from *Jonathan*

Wild, critics have often set up Wild and Heartfree as moral polarities, while they parenthetically admit that Heartfree's character is a little thin. Irwin, for example, would justify this insubstantiality by a theory of passive goodness, making Heartfree resemble Desdemona or some other Christ-like character (*The Making of Jonathan Wild,* p. 75).

30 Irwin says that Fielding's sense of truth was outraged by the historians who heroicized Great Men (*The Making of Jonathan Wild,* p. 66) and this accounts for his interest in that question throughout the novel.

31 *The Champion,* I, p. 64.

32 William Coley believes that there is a great contrast between these two passages and calls the change "the defeat of jesting Fortune by Prudence" ("Fielding's Laughter," p. 251).

33 For a consideration of Hume according to these terms from Sidney Hook's *The Hero in History,* see above, p. 70.

34 *The Champion,* I, p. 66.

35 *The Champion,* I, pp. 67, 67–68. Robert M. Wallace believes that Fielding's estimate of Cromwell follows Abraham Cowley in ascribing the passage of events to Cromwell's planning from the start ("Fielding's Narrative Method," p. 68). For the traditional nature of this interpretation, see above, pp. 52–53.

36 William Coley calls this a typical Augustan technique: ". . . to beat dulness at its own game [was] to put on more leads and outsink it, to formalize its imperfection" ("Fielding's Laughter," p. 244).

37 *Fielding's Works,* ed. Browne, XI, pp. 90–91.

38 4 March 1739, I, p. 330.

39 *Fielding's Works,* ed. Browne, XI, p. 91.

40 Ian Watt complains that the many coincidences in *Tom Jones,* although "they make it possible to weave the whole narrative into a very neat and entertaining formal structure," in the end "compromise verisimilitude" (*The Rise of the Novel,* p. 253). To assume that the causal patterns of *Tom Jones* are a transcript of the causal patterns of actuality can lead to an overestimation of Fielding's belief in the complete and ultimate intelligibility of the world. See, for example, Dorothy Van Ghent, *The English Novel, Form and Function* (New York, 1953), pp. 66, 80.

41 Martin C. Battestin, among others, believes that the plot of *Tom Jones* completely mirrors, in some Stendhalian way, Fielding's idea of the pattern of the real world. See "Osborne's *Tom Jones*: Adapting a Classic," *Man and the Movies,* ed. W. R. Robinson (Baton Rouge, 1967), pp. 31–45.

42 Wayne C. Booth mentions the relation between the narrator and the reader in *Tom Jones,* but does not pursue the subject very far: "In *Tom Jones,* the 'plot' of our relationship with Fielding-as-narrator has no similarity to the story of Tom. There is no complication, not

even any sequence except for the gradually increasing familiarity and intimacy leading to farewell. And much of what we admire or enjoy in the narrator is in most respects quite different from what we like or enjoy in his hero." See *The Rhetoric of Fiction* (Chicago, 1961), pp. 216–17.

43 Sheldon Sacks and Ronald Paulson, among others, stress Fielding's desire to seek an explanation, that is, an ending. They believe he is interested in the need to ascertain motivation, rather than to develop a method of understanding. Sacks argues, in *Fiction and the Shape of Belief* (Berkeley, 1964), p. 229, that "Fielding's notions about whether actions were good or bad depended heavily on his attitude toward the motive which led to the action being evaluated." Compare Paulson, *Satire and the Novel*, p. 147: "As Fielding learns how misleading not only words but even actions and consequences can be, he finds it increasingly difficult to judge actions except in terms of motives." This strangely Aquinian concept of explanation yields a static Fielding, who in Sacks deals in moral absolutes and in Paulson manipulates timeless genres.

44 Philip Stevick neglects the difference between immediate and retrospective experience when he considers such passages: "The very amplitude of *Tom Jones* testifies to Fielding's pleasure in seeing causal patterns and complex chains of events in terms of their unity and coherence . . . " ("Fielding and the Meaning of History," p. 561).

45 "Fielding and the Meaning of History," p. 564.

46 See W. B. Gallie's discussion of contingency in literature and life in *Philosophy and the Historical Understanding*, p. 29: "In all good stories the factor of contingency matches that which we feel to be part and parcel of daily life." Compare Paulson, *Satire and the Novel*, p. 156: "In *Tom Jones* . . . everything is tied together tightly by causation, and Fielding always wants to know what the causes of a given 'accident' were."

47 *The Philosophy of the Enlightenment*, trans. Fritz C. A. Koelln and James P. Pettegrove (Princeton, 1951), p. 80.

48 Dorothy Van Ghent contrasts *Tom Jones* as chance with *Clarissa* as fatality, but does not explore the relation further (*Form and Function*, p. 78).

49 In *Joseph Andrews* (III, i) Fielding uses the Horatian excuse that he shows a species, not an individual. But, by *Tom Jones*, such a distinction is too limiting. It surely goes against Fielding's expansive view of character to interpret, say, Partridge as the artful realization of a stock type, with a "long romance-ancestry." Kermode also makes a similar remark about Squire Western: ". . . realized with wonderful freshness, [he] is a development of a type already presented by Fielding in the theater" (p. 860). I would argue that Fielding's novelistic presentation criticizes the theatrical presentation of character.

[50] Kermode, Afterword to *Tom Jones*, p. 861. In this piece Kermode makes the peculiar error of calling Jenny Jones Partridge's wife (p. 857).

[51] Wilbur Cross says that Fielding considered it necessary in his "disguise as historian . . . to state not only *where* but also *when* the events of his novel occurred" (II, pp. 188–189). Cross follows Frederick S. Dickson in allocating the days in *Tom Jones* to specific dates in the eighteenth century. When something does not fit, like the date of the Garrick *Hamlet*, he says that Fielding has made a "mistake" or perpetrated an "anachronism." The discovery that all the Sundays must be dropped to make a one-to-one correlation disturbs Cross only for a moment: "The truth is, of course, that Fielding, if he considered the Sunday and Christmas question at all, decided to disregard it in the interest of an uninterrupted narrative" (II, pp. 192–93). Oliver W. Ferguson believes that the actor Fielding alludes to in the role of Claudius is Billy Mills, who generally took the part, although he did not appear in Garrick's *Hamlet*. Ferguson thinks that the reference might be a "wilful anachronism," although he does not say to what purpose ("Partridge's Vile Encomium: Fielding and Honest Billy Mills," *PQ, 43* [1964], p. 74).

[52] R. S. Crane interprets them this way in "The Plot of *Tom Jones*," *Essays on the Eighteenth-Century Novel*, ed. Robert Donald Spector (Bloomington, 1965), p. 105.

[53] The partial withdrawal of the narrative presence in *Amelia* has been enough to discomfit those critics who are looking for the hearty and jovial Harry Fielding of *Joseph Andrews* and *Tom Jones*. Andrew Wright complains that *Amelia* is "a domestic novel written by a man whose taste and talents are for panorama" (*Henry Fielding: Mask and Feast*, p. 53). Later Wright denies the novel even this precarious status: ". . . Fielding's failure ot illustrate the domestic life of the Booths weakens very considerably the force of this book" (p. 112).

[54] John S. Coolidge, in his generally perceptive "Fielding and 'Conservation of Character,'" *Fielding*, ed. Paulson, makes *Amelia* too great a departure from the earlier novels: ". . . *Tom Jones* may be called a deductive presentation of reality; *Amelia* sets out to follow a process of observation and discovery" (p. 165). But the change is more one of emphasis than method.

[55] Martin Battestin examines this "ambiguous parable of government" in "Tom Jones and 'His *Egyptian* Majesty': Fielding's Parable of Government," *PMLA, 82* (1967), pp. 68–77.

[56] Sheridan Baker, in an interesting examination of Fielding's use of romance conventions in *Amelia*, believes that the romantic ending is to be taken without qualifications. See "Fielding's *Amelia* and the Materials of Romance," *PQ, 61* (1962), pp. 437–49.

[57] Martin Price associates Adams, Allworthy, and Harrison as char-

acters for whom there is no difference between appearance and reality (*To the Palace of Wisdom* [New York, 1964], p. 304). However relevant these terms may be for *Joseph Andrews*, by the time of *Tom Jones* and especially *Amelia*, they no longer seem to be Fielding's main concern.

58 "Fielding and 'Conservation of Character,'" p. 166.

59 Quoted by Frederic T. Blanchard, *Fielding the Novelist* (New Haven, 1926), p. 102.

60 Ronald Paulson asserts that this dinner is "a parody *komos*" (*Satire and the Novel*, p. 164). "The public and the private themes fail to mesh. . . . The society remains as corrupt at the end as at the beginning" (p. 163). This view substantially follows that of George Sherburn in "Fielding's *Amelia*: An Interpretation," *ELH*, *3* (1936), pp. 1–14, and in "Fielding's Social Outlook," *PQ*, *35* (1956), pp. 1–23.

61 George Rogers Swann, in *Philosophical Parallelism in Six English Novelists* (Philadelphia, 1929), juxtaposes Hume and Fielding for their common interest in empirical detail.

FIVE. *Gibbon: Public History and the Shaping Self*

1 William Empson and Martin Price have commented on the similarities between the prose styles of Fielding and Gibbon: "Tom Jones" in *Fielding*, ed. Ronald Paulson (Englewood Cliffs, New Jersey, 1962), p. 125; Introduction to *English Prose and Poetry, 1660-1800, A Selection*, ed. Frank Brady and Martin Price (New York, 1961), xxix-xxx. For an interesting description of the balanced elements in Gibbon's style, see Harold Bond, *The Literary Art of Edward Gibbon* (Oxford, 1960), pp. 136–58.

2 For another point of view, see G. R. Cragg, *Reason and Authority in the Eighteenth Century* (Cambridge, England, 1964), p. 149: "He did not enter into the hearts of his characters. He could interpret their thoughts; he could not appreciate their emotions or their convictions." For an example of Gibbon's sympathy with the religious mind, see below, pp. 247-48.

3 Marc Bloch believes that Christianity is pre-eminently the religion of historians (*The Historian's Craft* [New York, 1953], p. 4). Yet even after Gibbon, or perhaps because of him, many historians perceived some incommensurability between Christianity and chronological history. Lord Acton tells the story of a "strenuous divine" who had written on the Reformation and therefore greeted Ranke as a comrade. But Ranke "repelled his advances. . . . 'You . . . are in the first place a Christian: I am in the first place a historian. There is a gulf between us.'" Quoted in "Inaugural Lecture on the Study of History," *Essays*

on Freedom and Power, intro. Gertrude Himmelfarb, pref. Herman Finer (Glencoe, Illinois, 1949), p. 20.

4 For an account of euhemerist strains in eighteenth-century thought, see Manuel, *Eighteenth Century Confronts the Gods*, pp. 85–125. Gibbon is certainly also interested in the relations of gods, heroes, and men. See below, p. 249.

5 *What is History?* (New York, 1962), p. 35.

6 Arnaldo Momigliano makes this point in "Gibbon's Contribution to Historical Method," pp. 40–55. But Momigliano denies that Gibbon ever "went beyond a superficial impression of the comparative value of his sources," although he was often very shrewd. Yet Gibbon's awareness of the prejudices of contemporary historians and his interest in the special quality of their points of view might imply a more critical attitude. This problem might be explored through Nicolas Fréret's essay on discerning truth in mythological and legendary stories, *Réflexions générales sur l'étude de l'ancienne histoire et sur le degré de certitude des différentes preuves historiques*. Frank E. Manuel says that Fréret's essay is "a brilliant examination of the problems of historical method and historical scepticism, and the validity of using mythology as a source" (*Eighteenth Century Confronts the Gods*, pp. 92–93). Manuel further remarks that Fréret's essay was "buried in the *Memoires* of the Academy [of Inscriptions and Belles-Lettres] and rarely noticed." For someone interested in Gibbon's relation to French source criticism, this passage in the *Memoirs of My Life* might be relevant: ". . . I cannot forget the joy with which I exchanged a bank-note of twenty pounds for the twenty volumes of the Memoirs of the Academy of Inscriptions; nor would it have been easy by any other expenditure of the same sum to have procured so large and lasting a fund of rational amusement" (p. 97; Saunders, p. 121).

7 See, for example, *Essai*, p. 216.

8 See Wellek, *Rise of English Literary History*.

9 *What is History?*, p. 53.

10 J. B. Bury notes this division but treats it as an inequity in Gibbon's method and view of Byzantine history (I, p. xvi). The *Decline and Fall* was conceived and published in three sections: the first volume (chapters i–xvi, 1767–76); the second and third volumes (chapters xvii–xxxviii, 1776–80); and the last three volumes (chapters xxxix–lxxi, 1780–8).

11 Few critics have treated the *Decline and Fall* as a developing work. Lewis P. Curtis, in "Gibbon's Paradise Lost," *The Age of Johnson*, ed. F. W. Hilles (New Haven, 1949), pp. 73–90, considers it in terms of a Bolingbrokian handbook for training in political power. W. R. Keast, in "The Element of Art in Gibbon's *History*," *ELH*, *23* (1956), pp. 153–62, applies Northrop Frye's distinction between literature as process and literature as product to it, but confines himself to a dem-

onstration of Gibbon's artistic form, which he believes to be completely independent of chronology. J. W. Swain's "Edward Gibbon and the Fall of Rome," *South Atlantic Quarterly, 39* (1940), pp. 77–93, relates Gibbon's political judgments in the *Decline and Fall* to his political career, thus arguing a development of a sort. He expands (and in the process thins out) his ideas in *Edward Gibbon the Historian* (London, 1966). In the most extensive consideration of the literary aspects of the *Decline and Fall*, Harold Bond's *Literary Art of Edward Gibbon*, the history's "epic structure" is mentioned, but there is no consideration of any development. Of course, the belletristic view of Gibbon has always emphasized the author, but again in an unchanging stance.

12 "The Element of Art in Gibbon's *History*," p. 158.

13 J. J. Saunders remarks: "I believe it was the Roman epitomist Florus who started the practice of comparing the rise and fall of states and kingdoms with the youth, maturity, decreptitude and death of men; may he be forgiven!" See "The Debate on the History of Rome," *History, 48* (1963), p. 11, and also J. W. Johnson, *Neo-Classical Thought*, pp. 57–58.

14 This beginning seems after all to have been more symbolic than actual. The evidence of the *Journal* supports the idea that preliminary readings had begun much earlier. Trevor-Roper makes a similar point in "Edward Gibbon After 200 Years," *The Listener, 72* (1964), p. 618.

15 Humanist historians had followed classical models when they organized their histories as the life of a city-state. See, for example, Hans Baron, *The Crisis of the Early Italian Renaissance*, revised ed. (Princeton, 1966), pp. 47–78, 94–120, 167–88.

16 Gibbon has often been criticized because his causes are not strict enough. For an excellent statement of this view, see Christopher Dawson, *The Dynamics of World History*, ed. John J. Mulloy (New York, 1956), pp. 319–45. Compare the discussion of provisional causes, above, pp. 227–28.

17 See *A Vindication of some Passages in the Fifteenth and Sixteenth Chapters of the History of the Decline and Fall of the Roman Empire, Miscellaneous Works of Gibbon*, III, pp. 313–91.

APPENDIX: Memoirs of My Life: *The Shape of the Immediate*

1 John N. Morris in *Versions of the Self* (New York, 1966) believes that Gibbon's frequent references to chance in the *Memoirs* are evidences of both his humility (p. 78) and his historical principles: "It

is a principle in harmony with the historian's professional assumption that the true nature of events can only be understood in retrospect" (p. 85) .

2 Low, *Journal*, xcvi; quoted by Geoffrey Keynes, intro., *The Library of Edward Gibbon* (London, 1950) , pp. 17–18.

BIBLIOGRAPHY OF WORKS CITED AND
WORKS OF INTEREST

IN THE FOLLOWING BIBLIOGRAPHY I have included a section on works that were generally useful, as well as sections on primary and secondary sources for each of the major authors.

I. GENERAL

Few works consider the relation of fiction and history beyond the use of literature as a source for historical background. The question of narrative form in history-writing is discussed by W. B. Gallie, *Philosophy and the Historical Understanding* (London, 1964); Arthur C. Danto, *Analytical Philosophy of History* (Cambridge, England, 1965); Morton White, *Foundations of Historical Knowledge* (New York, 1965); Maurice Mandelbaum, "A Note on History as Narrative," *History and Theory, 6* (1967), pp. 413–19; William H. Dray, Richard G. Ely, and Rolf Gruner, "Mandelbaum on History as Narrative: A Discussion," *History and Theory 8* (1969), pp. 275–94. Other works I have found useful for their theoretical approaches:

Auerbach, Erich. *Mimesis*, trans. Willard Trask. Princeton, 1953.

Bloch, Marc. *The Historian's Craft.* New York, 1953.

Burtt, E. A. *The Metaphysical Foundations of Modern Science.* New York, 1954.

Butterfield, Herbert. *The Whig Interpretation of History.* London, 1931.

Carr, E. H. *What is History?* New York, 1961.

Collingwood, R. G. *The Idea of History.* New York, 1956.

Hook, Sidney. *The Hero in History.* New York, 1943.

Kantorowitz, Ernst. *The King's Two Bodies.* Princeton, 1957.

Kitson Clark, George. *The Critical Historian.* New York, 1967.

Knowles, David. *The Historian and Character and Other Essays.* Cambridge, England, 1967.

Lukács, Georg. *The Historical Novel*, trans. Hannah and Stanley Mitchell. New York, 1963.

Mandelbaum, Maurice. "The History of Ideas, Intellectual History, and the History of Philosophy." *History and Theory*, Beihelft 5 (1965), pp. 33-66.

Manuel, Frank E. *Shapes of Philosophical History*. Stanford, 1965.

Neff, Emery. *The Poetry of History*. New York, 1947.

Scholes, Robert and Kellogg, Robert. *The Nature of Narrative*. New York, 1966.

Starnes, D. T. "Purpose in the Writing of History." *MP, 20* (1923), pp. 281-300.

Wimsatt, W. K., and Brooks, Cleanth. *A Short History of Literary Criticism*. New York, 1957.

History and Theory has also published two works entitled *A Bibliography of Works in the Philosophy of History, 1945–57* compiled by J. C. Rule (Middletown, 1960), 1958–61 by M. Nowicki (1962), 1962–65 by Lewis D. Wurgaft (1967).

An interesting book that in some ways replaces the survey histories of historiography by Harry Elmer Barnes, James T. Shotwell, and James Westfall Thompson is *The Discovery of Time* by Stephen Toulmin and June Goodfriend (New York, 1965).

English historiography in the seventeenth and eighteenth centuries in some interesting ways recapitulates Italian historiography in the fifteenth and sixteenth centuries. Works that I have found useful in understanding Renaissance Italian historiography are:

Baron, Hans. *The Crisis of the Early Italian Renaissance*, 2 vols. Princeton, 1955; single volume edition with epilogue, 1966.

Chabod, Federico. *Machiavelli and the Renaissance*. Cambridge, Massachusetts, 1958.

Ferguson, W. P. *The Renaissance in Historical Thought*. Cambridge, Massachusetts, 1948.

Garin, Eugenio. *Italian Humanism*, trans. Peter Munz. New York, 1965.

Gilbert, Felix. *Machiavelli and Guicciardini: Politics and History in Sixteenth-Century Florence*. Princeton, 1965.

Gilmore, Myron. *Humanists and Jurists*. Cambridge, Massachusetts, 1963: contains especially "Individualism in Renaissance Historians" and "The Renaissance Conception of the Lessons of History." The latter essay is also readily available in *Facets of the Renaissance*, ed. W. K. Werkmeister (New York, 1959).

———. *The World of Humanism*. New York, 1952.

Ullman, B. L. "Leonardo Bruni and the humanistic historiography." *Medievalia et Humanistica*, 1946, pp. 45–61; also in *Studies in the Italian Renaissance*. Roma, 1955, pp. 321–44.

Further comments on some of these works can be found in Part One, footnote 2.

The background of English historiography before the eighteenth century is treated in the following works:

Baker, Herschel. *The Race of Time*. Toronto, 1967.
———. *The Wars of Truth*. Cambridge, Massachusetts, 1952.
Boyce, Benjamin. *The Theophrastan Character in England to 1642*. Cambridge, Massachusetts, 1947.
Brandt, William. *The Shape of Medieval History*. New Haven, 1967.
Douglas, David C. *English Scholars, 1660–1730*. London, 1939; 2d revised ed., 1951.
Firth, C. H. *Essays Historical and Literary*. Oxford, 1938.
Fox, Levi, ed. *English Historical Scholarship in the Sixteenth and Seventeenth Centuries*. London, 1956.
Fussner, F. Smith. *The Historical Revolution: English Historical Writing and Thought, 1580–1640*. London, 1962.
Greenleaf, W. H. *Order, Empiricism and Politics: Two Traditions of English Political Thought, 1500–1700*. Oxford, 1964.
Hale, J. R. *The Evolution of British Historiography*. New York, 1964.
Hanning, Robert W. *The Vision of History in Early Britain*. New York, 1966.
Hexter, J. H. "The Education of the Aristocracy in the Renaissance." In *Reappraisals in History*. Chicago, 1961; New York, 1963, pp. 45–70.
Hill, Christopher. *Puritanism and Revolution*, new edition. New York, 1964.
Hughes, Peter M. " 'The Monarch's and the Muse's Seats': Stuart Kingship and Poetry of the Royal Estate." Yale Ph.D. dissertation, 1965.
Kliger, Samuel. *The Goths in England*. Cambridge, Massachusetts, 1952.
Nearing, Jr., Homer. *English Historical Poetry, 1599–1641*. Philadelphia, 1945.
Nevo, Ruth. *The Dial of Virtue*. Princeton, 1963.

Nichol Smith, David. *Characters from the Histories and Memoirs of the Seventeenth Century.* Oxford, 1918.

Patrides, C. A. *The Phoenix and the Ladder: The Rise and Decline of the Christian View of History.* Berkeley, 1964; abridged as chapter 8 in *Milton and the Christian Tradition.* Oxford, 1966.

Pocock, J.G.A. *The Ancient Constitution and the Feudal Law,* new edition. New York, 1967.

Wormald, B.H.G. *Clarendon: Politics, History & Religion, 1640–1660.* Cambridge, England, 1951.

Works that deal with the eighteenth century itself are:

Becker, Carl E. *The Heavenly City of the Eighteenth-Century Philosophers.* New Haven, 1932.

Cassirer, Ernst. *The Philosophy of the Enlightenment,* trans. Fritz C. A. Koelln and James P. Pettegrove. Princeton, 1951.

Davis, Herbert. "The Augustan Conception of History." In *Reason and the Imagination,* ed. J. A. Mazzeo. New York, 1962, pp. 213–60.

Firth, C. H. *Modern Languages at Oxford, 1724–1929.* London, 1929.

Johnson, James W. *The Formation of English Neo-Classical Thought.* Princeton, 1967.

Koch, Dorothy A. "English Theories Concerning the Nature and Uses of History, 1735–1791." Yale Ph.D. dissertation, 1946.

Manuel, Frank E. *The Eighteenth Century Confronts the Gods.* Cambridge, Massachusetts, 1959.

Parker, Irene. *Dissenting Academies in England.* Cambridge, Massachusetts, 1914. [An interesting account of the introduction of history into the curriculum.]

Peardon, Thomas P. *The Transition in English Historical Writing, 1760–1830.* New York, 1933.

Stromberg, R. N. "History in the Eighteenth Century." *JHI, 12* (1951), pp. 295–304.

Thomson, M. A. *Some Developments in English Historiography during the Eighteenth Century.* London, 1957.

Trevor-Roper, Hugh. "The Historical Philosophy of the Enlightenment." *Studies on Voltaire and the Eighteenth Century, 27* (1963), pp. 1667–87.

Ward, Addison. "The Tory View of Roman History." *SEL, 4* (1964), pp. 413-56.

Winstanley, D. A. *Unreformed Cambridge.* Cambridge, England, 1935.

Wellek, René. *The Rise of English Literary History.* Chapel Hill, 1941.

For citations of works by other literary figures, the following editions were used:

Addison, Joseph, and Steele, Richard. *The Spectator,* 5 vols., ed. Donald F. Bond. Oxford, 1965.

Gray, Thomas. *The Letters of Thomas Gray,* 3 vols., ed. Paget Toynbee and Leonard Whibley. Oxford, 1935.

Halifax, George Savile, Marquess of. *Complete Works,* ed. Walter Raleigh. Oxford, 1912.

Johnson, Samuel. *Works,* 12 vols., ed. Arthur Murphy. London, 1792.

Lucian. *Works,* 8 vols., trans. A. M. Harmon and others. London, 1913.

Milton, John. *Complete Poems and Major Prose,* ed. Merritt Y. Hughes. New York, 1957.

Pope, Alexander. *Poems,* ed. John Butt. London, 1963.

Shaftesbury, Anthony Cooper, Earl of. *Characteristics,* 2 vols., ed. John M. Robertson. London, 1900.

Swift, Jonathan. *The History of the Four Last Years of the Queen,* intro. Harold Williams. In *The Prose Works of Jonathan Swift,* vol. 7, ed. Herbert Davis. Oxford, 1951.

II. Clarendon and Bolingbroke

For my Clarendon text I have used the laboriously collated edition by W. Dunn Macray, 6 vols. (Oxford, 1888), supplemented by Bulkeley Bandinell's 1826 edition. Although Macray is much more definitive in his reconstruction of Clarendon's final text, Bandinell includes much of the providential language and abrupt causal connectives present in the earlier, less polished form. Secondary sources that raise and discuss some important issues for the study of Clarendon are:

Coltman, Irene. *Private Men and Public Causes.* London, 1962.

Firth, C. H. *Essays Historical and Literary.* Oxford, 1938.

Trevor-Roper, H. R. "Clarendon and the Practice of History." In *Milton and Clarendon*. French Fogle and H. R. Trevor-Roper. Los Angeles, 1965.

Wormald, B.H.G. *Clarendon*. Cambridge, England, 1965.

The main text I used for Bolingbroke is *Letters on the Study and Use of History*, A New Edition Corrected (London, 1770). For Bolingbroke's general works the most easily accessible edition is *The Works of Lord Bolingbroke*, 4 vols. (Philadelphia, 1841). John Locke's *Some Thoughts Concerning Education*, Fifth Edition Enlarged (London, 1705), may be one direct influence on Bolinbroke's ideas. Other useful works include:

Hart, Jeffry. *Viscount Bolingbroke, Tory Humanist*. London, 1965.

Hedges, William L. "Knickerbocker, Bolingbroke, and the Fiction of History." *JHI*, 20 (1959), pp. 317–28.

Jackman, Sidney Wayne. *Man of Mercury*. London, 1965.

James, D. G. *The Life of Reason: Hobbes, Locke, Bolingbroke*. London, 1949.

Mansfield, Jr., Harvey C. *Statesmanship and Party Government*. Chicago, 1965.

Nadel, George H. "New Light on Bolingbroke's 'Letters on History.' " *JHI*, 23 (1962), pp. 550-57.

Voltaire, François Marie Arouet de. *A Defense of the late Lord Bollingbroke's* [sic] *Letters on the Study and Use of History*. London, 1753.

III. HUME

The *History of England* was reprinted innumerable times until the later nineteenth century. I used *The History of England from the Invasion of Julius Caesar to the Abdication of James the Second, 1688*, 6 vols. (Boston, 1856). For Hume's other works, an early and a more recent edition: *Essays and Treatises on Several Subjects*, A New Edition (London, 1758); *Essential Works of David Hume*, ed. Ralph Cohen (New York, 1965). John Hill Burton's *Life and Correspondence of David Hume*, 2 vols. (Edinburgh, 1846), is the ground for later work; it is well supplemented by Ernest C. Mossner's *The Life of David Hume* (Austin, 1954). The basic editions of Hume's correspondence are *The Letters of David Hume*, 2 vols., ed. J.Y.T. Greig (Oxford, 1932) and *New Letters of*

David Hume, ed. Raymond Klibansky and Ernest C. Mossner (Oxford, 1954). Other works I have found helpful are:

Abbott, Wilbur C. *Adventures in Reputation.* Cambridge, Massachusetts, 1935.

Bates, Blanchard W. *Literary Portraiture in the Historical Narrative of the French Renaissance.* New York, 1945.

Bisset, Andrew. *Essays on Historical Truth.* London, 1871.

Black, J. B. *The Art of History.* London, 1926. [Voltaire, Hume, Robertson, Gibbon.]

Cranston, Maurice. "Rousseau's Visit to England, 1766–67." *Essays by Divers Hands,* n.s. 31 (1962), pp. 16–34.

Davies, Godfrey. "Hume's History of the Reign of James I." In *Elizabethan and Jacobean Studies presented to Frank Percy Wilson.* Oxford, 1959, pp. 231–49.

Fink, Zera S. *The Classical Republicans.* Evanston, 1945.

Giarrizzo, G. *David Hume politico e storico.* Turin, 1962.

Grene, Marjorie. "Hume: Sceptic and Tory?" *JHI,* 4, (1943), pp. 333–48.

Hunt, William. "Hume and Modern Historians." *CBEL,* X, pp. 316–35.

Letwin, Shirley. *The Pursuit of Certainty.* Cambridge, England, 1965. [Hume, Bentham, J. S. Mill, Beatrice Webb.]

Meyer, P. H. "Voltaire and Hume as Historians: A Comparative Study of *Essai sur les Moeurs* and the *History of England.*" *PMLA, 73* (1958), pp. 51–68.

Mossner, Ernest C. "An Apology for David Hume, Historian." *PMLA, 56* (1941), pp. 657–90.

———. "David Hume's 'An Historical Essay on Chivalry and Modern Honour.' " *MP, 45* (1947), pp. 54–60.

———. "Hume and the Ancient-Modern Controversy, 1725–52." *UTSE, 28* (1949), pp. 139–53.

———. "Philosophy and Biography: the Case of Hume." *Phil R, 59* (1950), pp. 184–201.

———. "Was Hume a Tory Historian? Facts and Reconsiderations." *JHI, 2* (1941), pp. 225–35.

———, and Ransom, H. "The Publication of Hume's History of England." *UTSE, 29* (1950), pp. 162–82.

Noyes, Charles E. "Hume's 'Umbrage to the Godly' in the *History of England.*" *UMSE, 1* (1960), pp. 86–96.

————. "Samuel Johnson: Student of Hume." *UMSE, 3* (1962), pp. 91–94.

Palgrave, Francis. "Hume and his Influence upon History." *Quarterly Review, 73* (1843–44), pp. 536–92.

Price, John V. *The Ironic Hume.* Austin, 1965.

Review of *David Hume: Prophet of the Counter-Revolution* by Laurence L. Bongie. *TLS* (7 July 1966), p. 593.

Sabine, George A. "Hume's Contribution to the Historical Method." *Phil R, 15* (1906), pp. 17–38.

Strachey, Lytton. *Portraits in Miniature and other Essays.* New York, 1962.

Torrey, Norman L., and Havens, George R. "Voltaire's Books." *MP, 27* (1929), pp. 1–22.

Trevor-Roper, Hugh. "David Hume as a Historian." *Listener* (28 December 1961), pp. 1103–04; 1119.

Tsugawa, Albert. "David Hume and Lord Kames on Personal Identity." *JHI, 22* (1961), pp. 398–403.

Underdown, David. *Royalist Conspiracy in England, 1649–1660.* New Haven, 1960.

Voltaire, François Marie Arouet de. Review of the 1764 French edition of Hume's *History of England. Œuvres Complètes de Voltaire,* 52 vols., Paris, 1877–85, XXV, pp. 169–73.

Weston, Jr., J. C. "A Fragment of a New Letter by David Hume in Defense of his 'History of England.'" *NQ, 203* (1958), pp. 476–77.

Winks, Robin W. "Hume and Gibbon: A View from a Vantage." *Dalhousie R, 41* (1961), pp. 496–504.

IV. FIELDING

The most generally cited edition of Fielding's works is *The Complete Works of Henry Fielding, Esq.,* 16 vols., ed. W. E. Henley (New York, 1902). *The Works of Henry Fielding, Esq.,* 11 vols., ed. James P. Browne (London, 1903), contains a few items that Henley omits. The periodical writings have been sporadically edited. The basic text for Fielding's earliest periodical writings is still *The Champion,* 2 vols. (London, 1741), although recent attempts have been made to discern other hands. *The Covent-Garden Journal* has been edited by Gerald E. Jensen in two volumes (New Haven, 1915). The first elaborate edition of *The True Patriot: and The History of Our Own Times* has been done by Miriam Austin Locke (University of Alabama Press, 1964). Since Henley's text is

less than definitive, I have felt free to substitute either more definitive or more readily accessible texts of the novels. *Joseph Andrews*
and *Shamela*, ed. Martin C. Battestin (Boston, 1961), contains a
text similar to that Battestin has done of *Joseph Andrews* for the
first volume of the Wesleyan Fielding. *Jonathan Wild* and *The
Journal of a Voyage to Lisbon*, intro. A. R. Humphreys (London,
1964), handily brings together the two works, although both re-
quire more textual attention. Austin Dobson's edition of the
Voyage to Lisbon (Oxford, 1907) also includes "A Fragment of a
Comment on L. Bolingbroke's Essays." *Tom Jones*, afterword by
Frank Kermode (New York, 1963), introduces a few important
variants. *Amelia*, 2 vols., intro. A. R. Humphreys (London, 1962),
is the only easily available edition, although textual work is also
ultimately necessary for a definitive text of this novel. The
Wesleyan edition should solve the problem.

A more fugitive, but still interesting, piece of Fielding's writings
may be found in his preface to his sister Sarah's novel *The Adventures of David Simple*, 2 vols. (London, 1744). *A Catalogue of
the Entire and Valuable Library of Books of the Late Henry
Fielding, Esq.* was first brought to light by Austin Dobson. It is
bound into the early Sotheby catalogues in Sterling Memorial
Library at Yale; the Beinecke Library at Yale contains an alpha-
betized version by Frederick S. Dickson. For further comments,
see Part Four, footnote 1. The basic biography of Fielding is
still Wilbur L. Cross, *The History of Henry Fielding*, 3 vols. (New
Haven, 1918). F. Homes Dudden has built on Cross to some effect
in *Henry Fielding, His Life, Works, and Times*, 2 vols. (Oxford,
1952).

Other primary and secondary works that have helped me in the
study of Fielding are:

Baker, Sheridan. "Fielding's *Amelia* and the Materials of Ro-
mance." *PQ, 61* (1962), pp. 437–49.
Battestin, Martin C. "Fielding's Changing Politics and *Joseph
Andrews*." *PQ, 59* (1960), pp. 39–55.
———. "Fielding's Revisions of *Joseph Andrews*." *Studies in
Bibliography, 16* (1963), pp. 81–117.
———. *The Moral Basis of Fielding's Art: A Study of "Joseph
Andrews*." Middletown, Connecticut, 1959.

————. "Osborne's *Tom Jones*: Adapting a Classic." In *Man and the Movies*, ed. W. R. Robinson. Baton Rouge, 1967, pp. 31–45.

————. "Tom Jones and 'His *Egyptian* Majesty': Fielding's Parable of Government." *PMLA, 82* (1967), pp. 68–77.

Blanchard, Frederic T. *Fielding the Novelist*. New Haven, 1926.

Booth, Wayne C. *The Rhetoric of Fiction*. Chicago, 1961.

————. "The Self-Conscious Narrator before Tristram Shandy." *PMLA, 67* (1952), pp. 163–85.

Butt, John. *Henry Fielding*. London, 1959.

Coley, William B. "The Background of Fielding's Laughter." *ELH, 26* (1959), pp. 229–52.

Coolidge, John S. "Fielding and 'Conservation of Character.'" In *Fielding*, ed. Ronald Paulson. Englewood Cliffs, New Jersey, 1962, pp. 158–76.

Crane, Ronald S. "The Plot of *Tom Jones*." In *Essays on the Eighteenth-Century Novel*, ed. Robert Donald Spector. Bloomington, 1965, pp. 92–130.

Digeon, Aurelian. "*Jonathan Wild*." In *Fielding*, ed. Paulson, pp. 69–80.

Dobson, Austin. "Fielding and Andrew Millar." *The Library*, 3rd ser., 7 (1916), pp. 177–90.

Empson, William. "*Tom Jones*." In *Fielding*, ed. Paulson, pp. 123–45.

Ferguson, Oliver W. "Partridge's Vile Encomium: Fielding and Honest Billy Mills." *PQ, 43* (1964), pp. 73–78.

Gaunt, William. *A Concise History of English Painting*. New York, 1964.

Gide, André. "Notes for a Preface to Fielding's *Tom Jones*." In *Fielding*, ed. Paulson, pp. 81–83.

Heidler, Joseph Bunn. *The History, from 1700 to 1800, of English Criticism of Prose Fiction. Illinois Studies in Language and Literature, 13* (1928).

Humphreys, A. R. "Fielding's Irony: Its Method and Effects." In *Fielding*, ed. Paulson, pp. 12–24.

Irwin, William Robert. *The Making of Jonathan Wild*. New York, 1941.

Johnson, Maurice. *Fielding's Art of Fiction*. Philadelphia, 1965.

Jones, Claude E., ed. *Prefaces to Three Eighteenth-Century Novels. Augustan Reprint Society, 64* (1957).

Kettle, Arnold. *An Introduction to the English Novel*, 2 vols., New York, 1960.

Lind, Robert Levi. "Lucian and Fielding." *Classical Weekly, 29* (1936), pp. 84–86.

Mack, Maynard. "*Joseph Andrews* and *Pamela*." In *Fielding*, ed. Paulson, pp. 52–58.

McKillop, Alan D., ed. *An Essay on the New Species of Writing Founded by Mr. Fielding, 1751. Augustan Reprint Society, 95* (1962).

————. *Samuel Richardson, Printer and Novelist.* Chapel Hill, 1936.

————. "Some Recent Views of *Tom Jones*." *College English, 21* (1959), pp. 17–22.

————. *The Early Masters of English Fiction.* Lawrence, Kansas, 1956.

Miller, Henry Knight. *Essays on Fielding's Miscellanies: A Commentary on Volume One.* Princeton, 1961.

Moore, Robert E. *Hogarth's Literary Relationship.* Minneapolis, 1948.

Murry, John Middleton. "Fielding's 'Sexual Ethic' in *Tom Jones*." In *Fielding*, ed. Paulson, pp. 89–97.

Nathan, Sabine. "The Anticipation of Nineteenth-Century Ideological Trends in Fielding's *Amelia*." *Zeitschrift für Anglistik und Amerikanistik, 6* (1958), pp. 382–409.

Parry, Adam. "The Two Voices of Virgil's *Aeneid*." *Arion, 2* (1963), pp. 66–80.

Paulson, Ronald, ed. *Fielding.* Englewood Cliffs, New Jersey, 1962.

————. *Satire and the Novel in Eighteenth-Century England.* New Haven, 1967.

Powers, Lyall H. "The Influence of the *Aeneid* on Fielding's *Amelia*." *MLN, 71* (1956), pp. 330–36.

Price, Martin. *Swift's Rhetorical Art.* New Haven, 1953.

————. *To the Palace of Wisdom.* New York, 1964.

Review of *Jonathan Wild. TLS* (14 August 1943), p. 396.

Richardson, Samuel. *Clarissa: Preface, Hints of a Preface, and Postscripts*, intro. R. F. Brissenden. *Augustan Reprint Society, 103* (1964).

————. *Introduction to Pamela*, ed. and intro. Sheridan Baker. *Augustan Reprint Society, 48* (1954).

Sacks, Sheldon. *Fiction and the Shape of Belief.* Berkeley, 1964.

Seymour, Mabel. "Fielding's History of the '45." *PQ, 14* (1935), pp. 105–25.

Shea, Bernard. "Machiavelli and *Jonathan Wild.*" *PMLA, 62* (1957), pp. 55–73.

Sherburn, George. "Fielding's *Amelia*: An Interpretation." In *Fielding,* ed. Paulson, pp. 146–57.

———. "Fielding's Social Outlook." In *Eighteenth-Century English Literature,* ed. James L. Clifford. New York, 1959, pp. 251–73.

Sherwood, Irma Z. "The Novelists as Commentators." In *The Age of Johnson,* ed. F. W. Hilles. New Haven, 1949, pp. 113–26.

Spector, Robert Donald, ed. *Essays on the Eighteenth-Century Novel.* Bloomington, 1965.

Spilka, Mark. "Comic Resolution in Fielding's *Joseph Andrews.*" In *Fielding,* ed. Paulson, pp. 59–68.

Stevick, Philip. "Fielding and the Meaning of History." *PMLA, 79* (1964), pp. 561–68.

———. "The Augustan Nose." *UTQ, 34* (1965), pp. 110–17.

Swann, George Rogers. *Philosophical Parallelism in Six English Novelists; the Conception of Good, Evil and Human Nature.* Philadelphia, 1929.

Thornbury, Ethel M. *Henry Fielding's Theory of the Comic Prose Epic. University of Wisconsin Studies, 30* (Madison, 1931).

Van Ghent, Dorothy. *The English Novel: Form and Function.* New York, 1953.

Wallace, Robert M. "Henry Fielding's Narrative Method: Its Historical and Biographical Origins." University of North Carolina Ph.D. dissertation, 1945.

———. "Fielding's Knowledge of History and Biography." *SP, 44* (1947), pp. 89–107.

Watt, Ian. *The Rise of the Novel.* Berkeley, 1957.

Wells, J. E. "Fielding's Political Purpose in *Jonathan Wild.*" *PMLA, 28* (1913), pp. 1–55.

West, Rebecca. *The Court and the Castle.* New Haven, 1957.

Woods, Charles B. "Fielding and the Authorship of *Shamela.*" *PQ, 25* (1946), pp. 256–72.

Work, James A. "Henry Fielding, Christian Censor." In *The Age of Johnson,* ed. Hilles, pp. 139–48.

Wright, Andrew. *Henry Fielding: Mask and Feast.* London, 1965.

V. GIBBON

I have used the most definitive edition to date of the *Decline and Fall,* J. B. Bury's second edition, *The History of the Decline and Fall of the Roman Empire*, 7 vols. (London, 1909–14). Bury has thoroughly annotated the text, but a closer analysis and comparison of readings seems necessary. Frank Brady does such work for chapter fifteen in *English Prose and Poetry, 1660–1800, A Selection*, ed. Frank Brady and Martin Price (New York, 1961). Gibbon's *Memoirs of My Life*, usually called the *Autobiography*, has been minutely edited by Georges A. Bonnard (London, 1966). A more readily accessible reader's edition, which is well annotated and takes textual problems into account, is *The Autobiography of Edward Gibbon*, ed. Dero A. Saunders (New York, 1961). I include page references to both Bonnard and Saunders in my text. Sheffield's edition is interestingly presented by J. B. Bury in *The Autobiography of Edward Gibbon as Originally Edited by Lord Sheffield* (London, 1907). The original French of *Essai sur l'Étude de la Littérature* is contained in *Miscellaneous Works of Edward Gibbon, Esquire*, 3 vols., ed. John Lord Sheffield (Dublin, 1796). The *Vindication* and Gibbon's other works are also contained in this edition. The contemporary translation of the *Essai* is *An Essay on the Study of Literature, written originally in French, by Edward Gibbon, Jun. Esq.* (London, 1764); it includes many errors, including the famous translation of "Buffon" as "buffoon."

Gibbon's journals are available in *Gibbon's Journal to January 28, 1763. My Journal, I, II, III, and Ephemerides*, ed. D. M. Low (London, 1929) and *Le Journal de Gibbon à Lausanne 17 Août 1763–19 Avril 1764*, ed. Georges A. Bonnard (Lausanne, 1945). Low has also written the modern biography, *Edward Gibbon, 1737–1794* (London, 1937). Gibbon's letters have been edited in three volumes by J. E. Norton (New York, 1956). An invaluable reference source is *The Library of Edward Gibbon*, intro. Geoffrey Keynes (London, 1950).

Secondary works that have helped me to formulate my ideas about Gibbon are:

Africa, Thomas W. "Gibbon and the Golden Age." *Centennial R*, 7 (1963), pp. 273–81.
Black, J. B. [See above under "Hume."]
Bond, Harold. *The Literary Art of Edward Gibbon*. Oxford, 1960.
Bonnard, Georges A. "Gibbon's *Essai sur l'Étude de la Littérature* as judged by contemporary reviewers and by Gibbon himself." *ES, 32* (1951), pp. 145–53.

Cochrane, C. N. "The Mind of Edward Gibbon." *UTQ, 12* (1942), 1–17; *13* (1943), pp. 146–66.

Cragg, G. R. *Reason and Authority in the Eighteenth Century.* Cambridge, England, 1964.

Curtis, Lewis P. "Gibbon's Paradise Lost." In *The Age of Johnson,* ed. Hilles, pp. 73–90.

Dawson, Christopher. *The Dynamics of World History,* ed. John J. Mulloy. New York, 1956.

Fuglum, Per. *Edward Gibbon.* Oslo, 1953.

Giarrizzo. G. *Edward Gibbon e la cultura europea del settecento.* Napoli, 1954.

Gruman, Gerald J. " 'Balance' and 'Excess' as Gibbon's Explanation of the Decline and Fall." *History and Theory, 1* (1960), pp. 75–85.

Jordan, David P. "Enlightenment and Erudition in Gibbon's *Decline and Fall.*" Yale Ph.D. dissertation, 1966.

Katz, Solomon. *The Decline of Rome and the Rise of Medieval Europe.* Ithaca, 1955.

Keast, W. R. "The Element of Art in Gibbon's *History.*" *ELH,* *23* (1956), pp. 153–62.

MacRobert, T. M. "Gibbon's *Autobiography.*" *REL, 5* (1964), pp. 78–83.

Momigliano, Arnaldo. *Studies in Historiography.* London, 1966.

Morris, John N. *Versions of the Self.* New York, 1966.

Sarton, George. "The Missing Factor in Gibbon's Concept of History." *Harvard Library Bulletin, 11* (1957) , pp. 277–95.

Saunders, J. J. "Gibbon and *The Decline and Fall.*" *History, 23* (1939), pp. 346–55.

———. "The Debate on the Fall of Rome." *History, 48* (1963), pp. 1–17.

Strachey, Lytton. [See above under "Hume."]

Swain, Joseph Ward. "Edward Gibbon and the Fall of Rome." *South Atlantic Quarterly, 39* (1940), pp. 77–93.

———. *Edward Gibbon the Historian.* London, 1966.

Thomson, David. "Edward Gibbon: the master builder." *Contemporary R, 151* (1937), pp. 583–91.

Tillyard, E.M.W. *The English Epic and Its Background.* Oxford, 1954.

Trevor-Roper, Hugh. "Edward Gibbon after 200 Years." *The Listener, 72* (1964), pp. 617–19, 657–59.

Wedgwood, C. V. *Edward Gibbon.* London, 1955.

Wind, Edgar. "Julian the Apostate at Hampton Court." In *England and the Mediterranean Tradition*. Oxford, 1945, pp. 131–38.
Winks, Robin W. [See above under "Hume."]
Young, G. M. *Gibbon*. London, 1932.

Index